Building Urban Resilience through Change of Use

Series advisors

Clare Eriksson, Royal Institution of Chartered Surveyors
Carolyn Hayles, University of Bath
Richard Kirkham, University of Manchester
Andrew Knight, Nottingham Trent University
Stephen Pryke, University College London
Steve Rowlinson, University of Hong Kong
Derek Thomson, Loughborough University
Sara Wilkinson, University of Technology, Sydney

Innovation in the Built Environment (IBE) is a book series for the construction industry published jointly by the Royal Institution of Chartered Surveyors and Wiley-Blackwell. Books in the series address issues of current research and practitioner relevance and take an international perspective, drawing from research applications and case studies worldwide.
Innovation in the Built Environment:

- presents the latest thinking on the processes that influence the design, construction and management of the built environment based on strong theoretical concepts and draws on both established techniques for analysing the processes that shape the built environment – and on those from other disciplines

- embraces a comparative approach, allowing best practice to be put forward

- demonstrates the contribution that effective management of built environment processes can make

Books in the IBE series

Akintoye & Beck: *Policy, Finance & Management for Public-Private Partnerships*
Booth, *et al.*: *Solutions for Climate Change Challenges in the Built Environment*
Boussabaine: *Risk Pricing Strategies for Public-Private Partnerships*
Kirkham: *Whole Life-Cycle Costing*
London, *et al.*: *Construction Internationalisation*
Lu & Sexton: *Innovation in Small Professional Practices in the Built Environment*
Pryke: *Construction Supply Chain Management: Concepts and Case Studies*
Orstavik, *et al.*: *Construction Innovation*
Roper & Borello: *International Facility Management*
Senaratne & Sexton: *Managing Change in Construction Projects: a Knowledge-Based Approach*
Wilkinson, *et al.*: *Sustainable Building Adaptation*

We welcome proposals for new, high quality, research-based books which ARE Academically rigorous and informed by the latest thinking; please contact:

Viktoria Hartl-Vida
Senior Editorial Assistant
John Wiley & Sons Ltd
vhartlvida@wiley.com.

Building Urban Resilience through Change of Use

Edited by

Sara J. Wilkinson
University of Technology, Sydney, Australia

Hilde Remøy
Delft University of Technology, Netherlands

WILEY Blackwell

This edition first published 2018
© 2018 John Wiley & Sons Ltd

The right of Sara J. Wilkinson and Hilde Remøy to be identified as the authors of the editorial material in this work has been asserted in accordance with law.

Registered Offices
John Wiley & Sons, Inc., 111 River Street, Hoboken, NJ 07030, USA
John Wiley & Sons Ltd, The Atrium, Southern Gate, Chichester, West Sussex, PO19 8SQ, UK

Editorial Office
9600 Garsington Road, Oxford, OX4 2DQ, UK

For details of our global editorial offices, customer services, and more information about Wiley products visit us at www.wiley.com.

Wiley also publishes its books in a variety of electronic formats and by print-on-demand. Some content that appears in standard print versions of this book may not be available in other formats.

Library of Congress Cataloging-in-Publication data applied for

ISBN: 9781119231424

Cover Design: Wiley
Cover Images: (Top and background) © mustafa deliormanli/Gettyimages;
(Inset) Courtesy of Sara Wilkinson

Set in 10/12pt Sabon by SPi Global, Pondicherry, India
Printed and bound in Singapore by Markono Print Media Pte Ltd

10 9 8 7 6 5 4 3 2 1

Contents

About the Editors

Sara J. Wilkinson
Sara J. Wilkinson is an Associate Professor and at the University of Technology Sydney. She works at the intersections of sustainability, resilience, building adaptation and transformation. Her research aims to improve local, national and international outcomes of urban development in built environments in respect of the most pressing challenges of our time: climate change, energy and water use, and a growing, increasingly urbanised global population. Sara engages in trans-disciplinary research with colleagues from science, health, business and technology as well as built environment disciplines. She is well published, with over 290 outputs. including books, research reports, and journal and conference papers. She contributes to the surveying profession through various national and international committees, accreditation and APC assessment.

Hilde Remøy
Hilde Remøy is Associate Professor in Real Estate Management at the Faculty of Architecture and the Built Environment in the Department of Management in the Built Environment of Delft University of Technology. She followed an international educational and professional path in Norway, Italy, and the Netherlands, and obtained her PhD in Real Estate Management at Delft University of Technology. After her PhD on the theme of office vacancy and residential conversion as a means of coping, she is now teaching, researching and publishing on office market developments, and obsolescence, adaptation and conversion of offices and historic buildings in the Dutch and international contexts. Hilde is involved in research ranging from large-scale European-funded projects to contract research for Dutch practice, working with researchers and professionals of various disciplines and backgrounds.

Contributor Biographies

Hannah Baker
Hannah Baker is a PhD student at the University of Cambridge, UK, and part of the Future Infrastructure and Built Environment Centre for Doctoral Training, which is based in the Engineering department. Previously, she obtained degrees in architecture at the University of Cambridge and in Town Planning at the University of the West of England. She then worked for a research consultancy in Cambridge exploring risks associated with the built environment. Hannah's PhD is funded by the Engineering and Physical Sciences Research Council (EPSRC) and she is using her multi-disciplinary background to investigate the decision to demolish or adapt existing buildings on masterplan regeneration sites.

Rob Geraedts
Rob Geraedts is Associate Professor in Design and Construction Management in the Faculty of Architecture and the Built Environment, Department of Management in the Built Environment, at Delft University of Technology. His present research focuses on the flexibility and adaptability of buildings, the flexibility of the design and construction process, the reuse and adaptation of vacant buildings into new functions, and 'open building' to meet the continuously and rapidly changing market and individual user demands. Since 1996 he has been an active member and scientific reviewer of CIB W104, Open Building Implementation.

Fred Hobma
Fred Hobma is associate professor of planning and development law at Delft University of Technology, the Netherlands. He studied law (private and public) at Groningen State University and obtained his PhD from Delft University of Technology. Currently he is a staff member of the Department of Management in the Built Environment in the Faculty of Architecture and the Built Environment. Dr Hobma teaches planning law and real estate law in undergraduate, graduate and postgraduate programs. He has written extensively on these topics. He has performed research for governments, advisory bodies, businesses and parliament.

Erwin Heurkens
Erwin Heurkens is Assistant Professor in Urban Development Management in the Faculty of Architecture and the Built Environment, Department of Management in the Built Environment, Delft University of Technology. His

focus is on the management of public–private partnerships, state–market relations, and sustainability in urban (re)development projects. Since his PhD on 'Private sector-led urban development projects' (2012) a comparative international perspective has been key in his research. Erwin has co-edited the books *International Approaches to Real Estate Development* (2015) and *Routledge Companion to Real Estate Development* (2018). He has published numerous scientific and professional journal articles focused on conceptualising and drawing lessons from urban development practices.

Gordon Holden

Gordon Holden is an architectural and urban design education leader, having initiated, structured and directed several programs across four universities in three countries. He is the initiator of Australia's first Master's program in urban design. He is the foundation head of architecture at Griffith University, Queensland and he is the 2010 recipient of the Australian Institute of Architects Award the 'Neville Quarry Architectural Education Prize' for outstanding leadership in architectural education. He researches, publishes and teaches in architectural and urban design history, theory and practice and he has a long-standing interest in urban resilience.

Craig Langston

Craig Langston is rofessor of Construction and Facilities Management at Bond University. He has a combination of industry and academic experience spanning over 40 years. His research interests include measurement of sustainable development, adaptive reuse, life-cycle costing and productivity. Professor Langston has held four Australian Research Council Linkage Project grants, amounting to nearly AUD$1 million in external competitive funding. He was also the recipient of the Vice Chancellor's Quality Award (Research Excellence) at Bond University in 2010. He is an international author and has won a number of awards for his research including from Queensland, Australia and Asia-Pacific Research Award in the project management discipline in 2016.

Alice Moncaster

Alice Moncaster is a senior lecturer at the Open University, UK, where she focuses on reducing the environmental impact of construction, working closely with industry to create real change. A first degree in engineering from the University of Cambridge and three years of earthquake engineering research at the University of Bristol were followed by ten years in industry as a civil and building structures engineer. She returned to academia in 2008 for an interdisciplinary PhD at the University of East Anglia, then built up a research group at the University of Cambridge where she became a lecturer in 2014.

Chris Riedy

Chris Riedy is Professor of Sustainability Governance at the Institute for Sustainable Futures, University of Technology, Sydney. He is a transdisciplinary academic with a career focus on governance for sustainable futures. Chris draws on sociological and political theory, futures thinking and transformative science to design, facilitate and evaluate practical experiments in transformative change towards sustainable futures. Chris is a Senior Research Fellow of the Earth System Governance project, and on the editorial boards of *Futures* and the *Journal of Futures Studies*. He has published two books, 38 peer-reviewed articles or chapters, 56 research reports and hundreds of web articles.

Theo J.M. van der Voordt

Theo J.M. van der Voordt is Emeritus Associate Professor in Corporate and Public Real Estate Management at the Department of Management in the Built Environment, Faculty of Architecture and the Built Environment, Delft University of Technology. His research includes new ways of working, performance measurement, transformation and adaptive reuse as a means to cope with structurally vacant office buildings, and adding value by corporate real estate, facilities and services. His research aims to develop and test theories on successful real estate strategies and tools to support decision-making processes in practice.

Laura Wynne

Laura Wynne is a Senior Research Consultant with the Institute for Sustainable Futures at the University of Technology, Sydney. She conducts research projects in housing, urban sustainability, resilience and social change. Laura is an urban planner, and is interested in research that contributes to improving the health, resilience and sustainability of urban environvments. She has conducted research modelling peri-urban food futures, understanding the impacts of urban renewal on low-income communities, sustainable and regenerative models for development and on community engagement around sustainability.

Acknowledgements

Sara would like to thank Lindsay, Ted and Ruskin for their patience and support. She would like to thank her students and colleagues, who engage in dialogue, debate and action around the issues covered in this book, and of course, Chris, Laura, Hannah, Alice, Craig and Gordon for their contributions to this book.

Hilde would like to thank colleagues and students for input, especially all thesis students on topics related to adaptive reuse, and Erwin, Fred, Rob and Theo, who collaborated on this book. Thanks also to Jelle, for thoughtful advice and so much more.

Foreword: Resilience as a 'Lens' for Driving the Adaptive Capacity of Cities

Even though we are familiar with these mega trends, many of the chapters in this book startle with the magnitude and pace of urbanisation at the global scale. Progressing to the examination of the particular opportunities and pressures experienced by individual cities; some in decline, some subject to restructuring in a static or slow economy, some with rapid population and economic growth, it is made clear that there cannot be a simplistic template to address these challenges. How frustrating for universalists!

Perhaps more that anything, this variation reveals yet again how flawed the very notion of a singular 'world's best practice' is, once the inherent contradiction of best practice being dependent on particular and unique responses to local conditions is recognised. How then are we to share experience and develop knowledge globally in the face of this paradox?

In contrast to the normalising pressures of globalisation, the emerging framework of 'resilience' provides a way of approaching the challenges faced by cities in a way that places human values front and centre, while still allowing commonalities and differences to be perceived and mapped. In this way it can be seen at least as an alternative, if not a counter and resistance to globalising forces that work to deny and erase these differences.

Despite the disparate origins of the idea of resilience – in engineering, material science, infrastructure, psychology and ecology – there is an emerging coherent conception that draws on all of these to identify a number of common characteristics of resilient systems. Rather than attempting to create a single definition, the formulation, definition and application of ideas of resilience can itself be seen as a complex emergent system: open ended, resulting from discussions with multifarious starting points, but grounded in disaster and emergency.

Haven't we been here before? Critics of sustainability often dismissed it on the basis of being a 'contested' notion where there was not a universally agreed definition or a simple 'sustainability for dummies' manual to implement it, in every place, in every situation. The absence of a single definition, let alone a universal methodology, provided a basis for 'sustainability' to be dismissed by those in whose interest it has been to continue (unsustainable) business as usual.

As the effects of the continuation of unsustainable practice become more apparent and less contested, so the idea of 'resilience' has found a firm footing in the shared and acute appreciation the public has of both natural and human disasters. The clear and present danger of the effects of climate change are not as easily dismissed as the unfair characterisation of 'sustainability' being a nebulous, and therefore dispensable concept. The 'inconvenient truths' of climate change – extreme weather, increasing inequality, the spectre of health and infrastructure collapse – serve as sturdier fulcrums for leveraging broader discussions about 'resilience' than was available to 'sustainability'. These are unavoidable discussions that people want to have.

However, the conception of resilience by a wide range of theorists and organisations goes well beyond instrumental disaster preparedness and emergency management. In many of the chapters, there is also a hint that resilience cannot be easily or satisfactorily reduced to a 'risk' that actuaries can monetize and financialise. It delves deeper into social relations and authenticity, memories and collaboration; values that are not easily tractable to monetisation. In other words, the city seen through the lens of resilience sees a degree of loose-fit, redundancy, indeterminacy as a virtue, not a vice or weakness. This is entirely consistent with our understanding of the necessary characteristics of adaptive systems, and quite different the brittleness of a city that is 'fined-tuned' to eke out the vestigial capacity in every urban system – land, transport, utilities – in the name of 'efficiency'. The point is that in many developed cities, we can afford to have a degree of looseness, not every space has to be filled, not every system has to be operating at 99%.

From this perspective also, the idea of 'long life, loose fit low energy' can be extended from the individual building to the entire city. The whole city, as well as individual precincts and buildings, can be seen as an artifact that has the potential to be re-inhabited, re-used, re-purposed in different ways. From this perspective the entire material form of the city, both the public and private domain, can be seen as legacy 'infrastructure' that questions ownership and control (by who, for whom) and the need for reform or alternative approaches to regulatory, institutional and financial arrangements, as is identified in a number of the chapters.

Stepping aside from the purely 'functionalist' view of the city that such reform would involve, means that the city can be seen not simply in a material sense but also as the concretisation of innumerable collaborative and entrepreneurial efforts. The revealing of these values, obscured and ignored by functionalism, invites new modes of sharing and the development of new systems and arrangement enabled by information technology. In other words, considering the adaptation of the existing through the lens of resilience, is in essence writing an alternative 'functional brief' for information technology.

Perhaps most tellingly, and dauntingly for design and planning, seeing the city as an adaptive system, investigated and understood through the process of examining its resilience, is the question of whether we can consciously design and plan for increased adaptive capacity as the primary objective in city making.

We have moved from the 'desirability' of sustainability to the 'necessity' of resilience.

Roderick Simpson
Registered Architect 5868
AIA MPIA AILA
Environment Commissioner
Greater Sydney Commission

The Context for Building Resilience through Sustainable Change of Use Adaptation

Sara Wilkinson
University of Technology Sydney

1.1 Introduction

As the 21st century progresses, we are evolving our collective thinking and responses to the challenges of living with a changing climate, increasing global population and changing demographics, mass urbanisation, issues of inequality and instability, issues of food security and increasing scarcity of resources, as well as an increased need for sustainability in the built environment to name but a few (UN 2015; RICS, 2015). Climate change is held to be one of the greatest challenges of our time. The World Bank Group Report (2015) 'Building Regulation for Resilience: Managing Risks for Safer Cities' noted that in the last two decades natural disasters have claimed 1,300,000 lives, have affected 4.4 billion people – that is over half the global population, and have resulted in US$2 trillion of economic losses. They noted that high-income countries with advanced building-code systems experienced 47% of disasters but only 7% of the fatalities and therefore a *prima facie* case exists for rigorous regulation (The World Bank Group, 2015). Significantly, it also called for a shift from managing disasters to reducing the underlying risks. Increases in global temperature, sea level rise, ocean acidification and other climate change impacts are seriously affecting coastal areas and low-lying coastal countries. These are examples of chronic stresses and are defined in this chapter. In summary, the survival of many societies, and of the planet's biological support systems, are at risk. As a response, in December 2015, the UN published the report, 'Transforming Our World: The 2030 Agenda for Sustainable Development' stating that:

> The 17 Sustainable Development Goals and 169 targets demonstrate the scale and ambition of this new universal Agenda. They seek to

Building Urban Resilience through Change of Use, First Edition.
Edited by Sara J. Wilkinson and Hilde Remøy.
© 2018 John Wiley & Sons Ltd. Published 2018 by John Wiley & Sons Ltd.

build on the Millennium Development Goals and complete what they did not achieve. The Sustainable Development Goals are integrated and indivisible and balance the three dimensions of sustainable development: the economic, social and environmental. The Goals and targets will stimulate action over the next 15 years in areas of critical importance for humanity and the planet (UN, 2015: 1).

The 17 UN Sustainable Development Goals are shown in Box 1.1. Examining the goals, those that relate most directly to the built environment are;

- Goal 6. 'Ensure availability and sustainable management of water and sanitation for all',
- Goal 7. 'Ensure access to affordable, reliable, sustainable and modern energy for all'
- Goal 11. 'Make cities and human settlements inclusive, safe, resilient and sustainable' (UN, 2015).

However, it is also clear that 'inclusive, safe, resilient and sustainable,' urban settlements and cities provide the setting for the delivery of many of the other sustainable development goals too. For example, Goal 3 'Ensure healthy lives and promote wellbeing for all at all ages' is clearly related in part to the quality of the buildings in which people live and work. Our role as built environment stakeholders is therefore pivotal and cannot be underestimated.

Set against this background, the principal focus for this book is the role of sustainable change of use projects in buildings – or 'conversion' or 'adaptive reuse', as the approach is known in some countries – to assist in meeting these sustainable development goals. The concept of resilience is defined and explained and then related to change of use adaptation. The chapter also explains what is meant by 'sustainable change of use adaptation' and sets this in the context of related terminology such as adaptive reuse, conversion, refurbishment and renovation. Key terms are defined, such as decision-making for sustainable change of use adaptation: 'how we identify, model, evaluate and prioritise potential retrofit/reuse, including risk assessment, sustainability and latent conditions'. The costs and benefits of sustainable change of use adaptation are examined alongside a discussion of the property valuation impacts. Social issues covered include housing affordability and quality, changing cities and adaptation. This book covers all commercial land uses (including office, retail, industrial) and includes exemplars from three continents and several global regions.

Within this chapter, a model is presented to show the multiple benefits that can be derived from sustainable change of use adaptation. These accrue to multiple stakeholders on multiple levels (from city scale to building scale). In this book, sustainable change of use adaptation is focused on environmental, social and economic factors. Within these areas, the chapters are presented so that city-scale solutions and research are covered first, followed by building-scale solutions.

Box 1.1   UN sustainable development goals.

Goal 1   *Zero poverty:* End poverty in all its forms everywhere.
Goal 2   *Zero hunger:* End hunger, achieve food security and improved nutrition and promote sustainable agriculture.
Goal 3   *Good health and wellbeing:* Ensure healthy lives and promote well-being for all at all ages.
Goal 4   *Quality education:* Ensure inclusive and equitable quality education and promote lifelong learning opportunities for all.
Goal 5   *Gender equality:* Achieve gender equality and empower all women and girls
Goal 6   *Clean water and sanitation:* Ensure availability and sustainable management of water and sanitation for all.
Goal 7   *Affordable clean energy:* Ensure access to affordable, reliable, sustainable and modern energy for all.
Goal 8   *Decent work and economic growth:* Promote sustained, inclusive and sustainable economic growth, full and productive employment and decent work for all.
Goal 9   *Industry, innovation and infrastructure:* Build resilient infrastructure, promote inclusive and Sustainable industrialisation and foster innovation.
Goal 10   *Reduced inequalities:* Reduce income inequality within and among countries.
Goal 11   *Sustainable cities and communities:* Make cities and human settlements inclusive, safe, resilient and sustainable.
Goal 12   *Responsible consumption and production:* Ensure sustainable consumption and production patterns.
Goal 13   *Climate action:* Take urgent action to combat climate and its impacts by regulating emissions and promoting developments in renewable energy.
Goal 14   *Life below water:* Conserve and sustainably use the world's oceans, seas and marine resources.
Goal 15   *Life on land:* Protect, restore and promote sustainable use of terrestrial ecosystems, sustainably manage forests, combat desertification, and halt and reverse land degradation and halt biodiversity loss.
Goal 16   *Peace just and strong institutions:* Promote peaceful and inclusive societies for sustainable development, provide access to justice for all and build effective, accountable and inclusive institutions at all levels.
Goal 17   *Partnership for the goals:* Strengthen the means of implementation and revitalize the global partnership for sustainable development.

Adapted from http://www.un.org/sustainabledevelopment/sustainable-development-goals/.

1.2   Scale of the Problem: From City to Building Scale

According to the UN (2015), it took hundreds of thousands of years for global population to grow to 1 billion – then in another 200 years, it grew sevenfold. By 2011, the world population reached 7 billion and in 2015, it increased to about 7.3 billion. This 2015 global population of 7.3 billion is predicted in 2030 to reach 8.5 billion, 9.7 billion in 2050, and 11.2 billion in 2100 (UN DESA, 2015). Growth has been driven largely by greater numbers of people surviving to reproductive age, together with significant changes in fertility rates, increasing urbanisation and accelerating migration. These trends will have far-reaching implications for generations to come (UNPF, 2015).

It is the case that the world is undergoing the largest wave of urban growth in history. More than 50% of the world's population now lives in towns and cities, and by 2030 this number will swell to about 5 billion (UNPF, 2015); it is estimated that by 2050, 66% of the total population will be urbanised (RICS, 2015). Although much of this urbanisation will unfold in Africa and Asia, bringing huge social, economic and environmental trans-formations, all countries and cities will be affected. There will also be migra-tion from densely populated countries, which suffer climate change impacts such as rising sea levels and inundation.

Urbanisation has the potential to usher in a new era of wellbeing, resource efficiency and economic growth, but cities also exhibit high concentrations of poverty and inequality. In some urban areas, wealthy communities coex-ist alongside, and separate from, slums and informal settlements.

Our cities will grow, in many cases faster than ever before. As such, we need planning and governance that delivers transition from one level, scale and type of development, to others at the city scale, ensuring infrastructure can support growing populations and changing land uses. Alongside this adaptation of existing areas to accommodate greater numbers of people, and as the predominant land uses undergo change, we need to consider optimum levels of sustainable development, which includes, at the building level, different degrees of change of use adaptation. Sustainable change of use adaptation is focussed on environmental, social and economic factors; but is affected also by governance and regulatory frameworks. Within these parts the chapters are presented so that city-scale solutions and research is covered first, followed by building-scale solutions.

1.2.1   City-level Challenges

Numerous cities globally are setting up task forces and developing resilience plans. For example, New York published its strategy in 2013. The 100 Resilient Cities (100RC) project has been initiated by the Rockefeller Foundation (100RC, 2016) to assist global cities in their preparations to meet the physical, social and economic challenges we face now and in the future. The 100RC supports the adoption and incorporation of both acute and chronic manifestations of resilience. Acute or shock events include bushfires, earthquakes and floods. On the other hand, chronic stresses undermine and weaken the fabric of a city on a day-to-day or cyclical basis. High levels of unemployment; inefficient public transport systems; endemic violence; and persistent shortages of water and food are examples of chronic stress factors. By addressing both the shocks and the stresses, a city becomes more able to respond to adverse events, and is overall better able to deliver basic functions in both good times and bad, to all populations. As an example, Melbourne, Australia was selected from 372 applicant cities around the world to be among the first wave of 32 cities to join the 100RC network and published its resilience strategy in May 2016.

The 100RC has identified and collated the challenges facing a number of global cities. Table 1.1 shows a selection of those cities, in five different

Table 1.1   Resilience challenges faced in selected cities.

City	Resilience challenges (100 Resilient Cities)
Sydney, Australia	1. Ageing infrastructure 2. Heat wave 3. Infrastructure failure 4. Lack of affordable housing 5. Overtaxed/under developed/unreliable transportation system 6. Rapid growth 7. Rising sea level and coastal erosion 8. Social inequity 9. Terrorism 10. Wildfires
Rotterdam, Netherlands	1. Coastal flooding 2. Drought 3. Hazardous materials accident 4. Heat wave 5. Rainfall flooding 6. Refugees
Chennai, India	1. Aging infrastructure 2. Economic inequality 3. Economic shifts 4. Hurricane, typhoon, cyclone 5. Infrastructure failure 6. Overpopulation 7. Pollution or environmental degradation 8. Pronounced poverty 9. Tropical storms.
Dakar, Senegal	1. Coastal flooding 2. Earthquake 3. Endemic crime and violence 4. Lack of affordable housing 5. Social inequity
New York, USA	1. Heat wave 2. Overtaxed/under developed/unreliable transportation system 3. Rising sea level and coastal erosion 4. Tropical storms

Source: 100 RC, 2016.

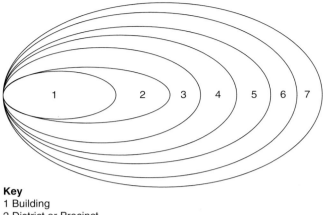

Key
1 Building
2 District or Precinct
3 City
4 Metropolitan area
5 Country
6 Region
7 World

Figure 1.1   Resilience scales. (Source: Rotterdam Resilience Strategy, 100RC, 2016).

continents, and in developed and developing countries, to illustrate both the number of challenges, as well as the similarities and differences that exist. These issues range from social to environmental and economic. Furthermore, some are chronic whereas other issues are acute. Clearly, change of use adaptation sits within these circumstances. It is apparent that different solutions suit different cities and different locations, and also have different degrees of importance.

Resilience scales are the different levels or scales involved, from worldwide to building level. These are illustrated in Figure 1.1, as taken from the Rotterdam Resilience Strategy (100RC, 2016). They are a useful way of understanding how measures taken at the building level impact up to a global level. Above building scale, there is the suburb, district or precinct scale (depending on which part of the world one lives in). After the district or suburb is the city scale, and it is apparent that the scales are now at the level at which policy is made and executed and governance is applied. After the city scale comes metropolitan areas, or the areas immediately around the city. The next scale is the national scale, and it is at this level that national policy and governance decisions are made and executed. After the national scale comes the regional scale, for example Europe, at which some collective decision-making may take place. The final scale after regional is worldwide or global.

1.3   Definitions of Key Terms

As noted above, there are a number of terms that are in current use with respect to 'change of use'. Literally, to change use is where one land use, say for warehousing, is no longer viable in an area. The buildings may become obsolete and thus an alternative or changed land use is a better economic, environmental and social option. For example, on a major river, former Victorian warehouse buildings have been changed or converted to residential or retail use as docks have been relocated to areas where deeper-draught ships can berth. Such patterns of change of use are found in many cities in different countries, such as London, Amsterdam, Toronto, New York and Melbourne.

Change of use is also known as 'adaptive reuse' or 'conversion adaptation' in different parts of the world. In each definition, the key characteristic is that the original land use of the building is no longer economically or socially viable or desirable and a change is required; otherwise the building may be left vacant or, as it is often termed, redundant or obsolete (Baum, 1993). There are many types of obsolescence identified in the literature, from economic, physical, social, environmental and technological, to regulatory or legal. Furthermore, some buildings can be affected simultaneously by more than one type of obsolescence. It follows that the condition of buildings can vary from good to worn out when affected by physical obsolescence (Thomsen and van der Flier, 2011).

Furthermore, when discussing change of use, terms such as retrofit, refurbishment, renovation, remodelling, reinstatement, rehabilitation and recycling of buildings are often used (Wilkinson *et al.*, 2014; Mansfield, 2002; Douglas, 2006; Bullen, 2007). Adaptation occurs 'within use' and 'across use'. For instance, if an office is adapted and remains an office, it is within-use adaptation. If the use is changed to say, residential, this is an example of across-use or change of use adaptation. Adaptation is defined as: 'any work to a building over and above maintenance to change its capacity, function or performance' or, 'any intervention to adjust, reuse, or upgrade a building to suit new conditions or requirements' (Douglas, 2006: 14). The various options for adaptation are illustrated diagrammatically in Figure 1.2 with the change of use or across-use options highlighted.

A second set of key terms requiring discussion is 'decision-making for sustainable change of use adaptation', in other words, *how we identify, model, evaluate and prioritise potential retrofit/reuse, including risk assessment, sustainability and latent conditions.* Throughout this book various models or approaches to decision-making are outlined in the context of environmental, economic and social sustainability criteria. These criteria vary according to circumstances, such as the client and their needs and goals and/or the environmental priorities and regulatory frameworks operating within a city or town. In addition, the budget and/or economic climate will also impact on what is provided. What is required however, is a framework or decision-making tool that enables clients to identify optimum solutions that meet the competing demands and requirements of all stakeholders. Overarching these variables are the resilience issues, which increasingly need to be included to ensure the utmost is done to mitigate the social, environmental and economic impacts of climate-change-related disasters and events.

What is meant by sustainable change of use adaptation? In this case the term sustainability is defined in the framework of the triple bottom line: the economic, environmental and social aspects (Elkington, 1998), which

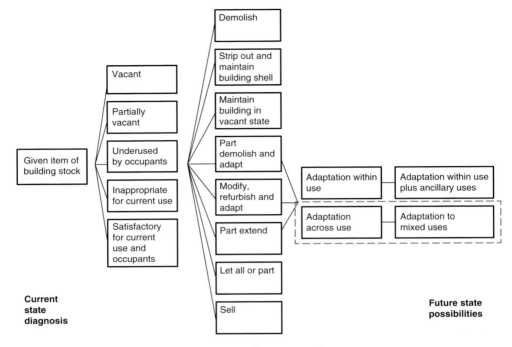

Figure 1.2   Options for adaptation. (Source: Wilkinson, 2011).

are then set within the context and activities of building refurbishment and renovation. Wilkinson (2012), in defining sustainability in the context of political, economic, social, technological, legal, environmental and philosophical thinking and beliefs, has shown there is a wide spectrum of sustainability from very strong to very weak. Furthermore, other studies (Wilkinson 2012, 2015) have revealed, to date, property and construction firms and practitioners generally adhere to and adopt weak sustainability in practice.

1.4   Background and Scope

This book examines the definitions, the best practices and existing guidelines and frameworks for sustainable change of use in building urban resilience in the period to 2050. All commercial land uses, including office, retail and industrial are covered. Case studies and exemplars from Europe, Australia and the UK and several other regions are used to illustrate practical implications of the theory and issues outlined in the chapters.

Adapting the built environment for climate change is now acknowledged as vital, and the implications of inaction are outlined in the IPCC Report of 2013 (Stocker *et al.*, 2013). Globally, organisations, governments, and city governments are setting out plans and strategies for adaptation to mitigate the impacts of climate change. These plans and approaches vary in breadth and depth as well as the climatic conditions that they are addressing. As an example, the Australian Sustainable Built Environment Council (ASBEC) has stated that cost-effective energy efficiency and fuel switching can reduce projected 2050 building-related GHG emissions by half (ASBEC, 2013), with financial benefits estimated at $20 billion by 2030 and a total contribution of 25% of the national emissions reduction target. The challenge is to extend the practices adopted by market leaders to the wider market, and ASBEC recommended strong policy measures, with supporting frameworks and governance, and with minimum mandatory standards, energy market reform, targeted incentives and programmes and a range of education measures, supporting data, information and training (ASBEC, 2013).

1.5 The Notion of Urban Resilience

The notion of urban resilience has grown in recent years and is used in policy and academic discourse (Meerow *et al.*, 2016; UGC, 2013; NSW GPE, 2014). Here, the theory of resilience is used to explain complex socio-ecological systems – urban settlements, cites and buildings – and their sustainable management. Theorists claim that systems are changing continuously in non-linear ways, and that resilience offers a framework for dealing with uncertainties in the future. Another characteristic of 'resilience' is that it is perceived as positive: it involves taking action to make us less vulnerable to climate change, natural disasters and/or manmade disasters, such as economic downturns or collapses. Resilience is an attractive perspective with regards to cities, which are complex adaptive systems (Batty, 2008), and have changed from housing 10% of the population in 1990 to 50% in 2010 (UN DESA, 2010). Urban areas of over 50,000 people account for 71% of global energy-related carbon emissions although they cover only 3% of the area. In accommodating growth and expansion, cities and the buildings within them need to possess resilience. The word 'resilience' is derived from the Latin word *resilio*, which literally means to bounce back. Then, according to Alexander (2013), in the 19th century, the term evolved to embrace the notion of resisting adversity.

Meerow *et al.* (2016) noted that the term has been adopted and used by many disciplines, which each understand and interpret the notion differently. In their extensive literature review of definitions of urban resilience, they found that five themes or attributes emerged as shared qualities of resilience (Meerow *et al.*, 2016). These attributes are listed below and are considered in detail below:

- equilibrium versus non-equilibrium
- positive versus negative conceptualisations of resilience
- mechanisms of system change (from persistence, transitional or transformative change)
- adaptation versus general adaptability
- timescales of action.

A sixth tension exists around the definition of the term 'urban'. The authors posited a definition embodying all the attributes of urban resilience (Meerow *et al.*, 2016):

> The ability of an urban system – and all its constituent socio-ecological and socio-technical networks across temporal and spatial scales – to maintain or rapidly return to desired functions in the face of a disturbance, to adapt to change, and to quickly transform systems that limit current or future adaptive capacity (Meerow et al., 2016).

In contrast, the 100 Resilient Cities project (100RC, 2016) defines urban resilience as 'the capacity of individuals, institutions, businesses and systems within a city to adapt, survive and thrive no matter what kind of chronic stresses and acute shocks they experience'. Both definitions view urban resilience as dynamic and ever-changing. It is necessary to define the word 'urban' and the characteristics of urban settlement. Many definitions examined state that cities and urban systems are complex networked systems (Desouza and Flanery 2013: 91) and conglomerations of ecological, social and technical components. Ernstson *et al.* (2010) claim cities are complex socio-ecological systems composed of networks that are both socio-ecological and socio-technical. Cities and their hinterlands are highly interdependent, with delineation of boundaries problematic. This is because some systems extend beyond the physical city limits, for example water or food supply systems.

Now considering each of the Meerow's five themes in turn:

Equilibrium

An important aspect of urban resilience is equilibrium. Scholars debate issues of single-state equilibrium, multiple-state equilibrium and dynamic non-equilibrium (Davoudi *et al.*, 2012). Single-state equilibrium refers to the ability to return to a previous state of equilibrium after a disturbance. This notion prevails in the disaster management literature, an example being where an area and buildings are reinstated after flooding. Multiple-state equilibrium, however, acknowledges that there can be numerous states of equilibrium in any system. Recently it has been recognised that systems exist in a state of dynamic non-equilibrium: no constant state can exist and there is a continuous state of flux and change. This acceptance has led to the rejection of the notion of resilience as 'bouncing back' in the literal sense of the Latin translation. In this newer understanding of the term, systems are 'safe to fail' as opposed to failsafe, and it is acknowledged that, after a disturbance, cities and the buildings therein may not return to a previous state. Sanchez *et al.* (2016) note that a return to 'normal' may not be desirable and appropriate if the original state was vulnerable; it is undesirable to perpetuate vulnerability. They advocate for a coordinated proactive approach to risk mitigation and adaptation within the urban planning and built environment context.

Positive versus Negative notions

The notion of resilience was perceived as positive in all 25 definitions analysed by Meerow *et al.* (2016): systems possessing resilience were held to be able to maintain basic functions and then to prosper and to improve. However, other studies have questioned whether existing states may be undesirable, for example areas characterised by poor-quality or inadequate housing (Cote and Nightingale, 2011). Hence the debate extends to pose the questions of, for whom and, to what resilience is desired. Furthermore, it should be noted that power inequalities could determine whose resilience agenda prevails (Cote and Nightingale, 2011).

Mechanism of Change

There are three mechanisms of change or ways to resilience. The first is persistent change, where efforts are made to return or maintain the built environment and its systems in an existing state. For example, after a storm, buildings are reinstated (Chelleri, 2012). In this sense, retrofitting or refurbishment could be said to be examples of persistence. The second mechanism is transitional change, which implies some degree of adaptation to a new state or an incremental change, such as the change from warehousing to residential use as an area deindustrialises. The third and most extensive mechanism is transformative change, whereby wide-scale change occurs. An example is where significant change of use adaptation occurs and areas become completely transformed. This change of use adaptation can be an example of transitional systems change and resilience and, collectively, transformational systems change.

Adaptation

The fourth aspect of resilience is adaptation and refers to the differences between specific adaptations, such as high adaptability as against more generic adaptability (Haase *et al.*, 2014). Wu and Wu (2013) argued that too much emphasis on specified resilience undermines system flexibility and the ability to adapt to unexpected threats. Other academics have perceived adaptability as being synonymous with adaptive capacity, and noted the importance of maintaining general resilience to unforeseen threats in addition to specified resilience to known risks. An example might be where there is a known risk of pluvial flooding affecting a city or region. Measures can be taken in the design, construction and adaptation of buildings to reduce the risk of water damage arising and also ensuring faster recovery should pluvial flooding occur. Equally, adopting flexible design and construction in buildings might accommodate a greater variety of alternative uses over time, thereby having adaptive capacity. The Tower of London in the UK is a good example of a building with high levels of adaptive capacity; in its 900-year history, the building has been used as a royal home, a prison, barracks, armoury and now a museum and tourist attraction. Warehouse buildings are another example of building designs with good adaptive capacity, and globally they are now used as residential buildings, hotels, art galleries and retail centres.

Timescale

Finally, there is the notion of timescale within urban resilience definitions. Some studies perceive immediacy and rapidity of recovery as essential characteristics. However, timescale is dependent on whether the focus is on rapid onset events such as storms and floods or more long-term gradual states such as changing climate (Wardekker *et al.*, 2010). Moreover, the measurement of timeframes is unclear and can be measured in hours, months or years. Reinstatement of energy supply following a storm would preferably be delivered within hours, whereas reinstatement of flood-damaged buildings might take many months. Furthermore, there is the question of reinstatement being a return to the 'prior state', or an improved and different state that would be more resilient to the same type of event. Sanchez *et al.* (2016) note that urban transformation requires active engagement in setting long-term goals at city or state level. However, flexibility is a prerequisite, otherwise unintended adverse consequences may result. Although these issues are dealt with at city or state level, it is at building level where many interventions and adaptations will occur.

Although resilience is a complex concept with multiple attributes and levels of interpretation, a definition is proposed above. However, Meerow *et al.* (2016) also suggest it is vital to consider other questions: the so-called '5 Ws'. These are who, what, when, where and why? When considering resilience, it is important to be cognisant of who is determining what is desirable for an urban system, whose resilience is prioritised and who is included or excluded from the urban systems. In respect of 'what', we must ask what should the system be resilient to, what networks/sectors are included in it, and whether the focus is on generic or specific resilience? The question of 'when' relates to whether the focus is on rapid or slow onset disturbances, on short- or long-term resilience, and finally, is it on the resilience of current or future generations? The fourth W covers 'where' and relates to the boundaries of the urban system; whether resilience of some areas is prioritised over others, and whether building resilience in some areas affects the resilience of others. Finally, there are issues of 'why': what is the goal, what are underlying motivations and is the focus on process or outcome (Meerow *et al.*, 2016)? A summary is provided in Table 1.2.

Bosher (2008) identified a built-in resilience environment and noted it was the 'quality of a built environment's capability (in physical, institutional, economic and social terms) to keep adapting to existing and emergent threats'. Thus its focus is on coping with dynamic changes. Sanchez *et al.* (2016) observed that, in interpreting disasters as natural, Bosher (2008) absolved policy-makers and stakeholders from blame. This approach is now changing because many stakeholders, particularly in government, are making

Table 1.2 The 5 Ws applied to resilience in buildings.

The 'Ws'		
Who	1.	Who is determining what is desirable for an urban system?
	2.	Whose resilience is prioritised?
	3.	Who is included or excluded from the urban systems?
What	1.	What should the system be resilient to?
	2.	What networks/sectors are included in the urban system, and this the focus on generic or specific resilience?
When	1.	Is the focus on rapid- or slow-onset disturbances?
	2.	Is the focus on short- or long-term resilience?
	3.	Is the focus on the resilience of current or future generations?
Where	1.	Where are of the boundaries of the urban system?
	2.	Is the resilience of some areas prioritised over others?
	3.	Does building resilience in some areas affect the resilience of other areas?
Why	1.	What is the goal?
	2.	What are underlying motivations?
	3.	What is the focus, on process or outcome?

Source: Adapted from Meerow et al., 2016.

and publishing resilience plans. There are no right or easy answers to these questions, but it is imperative that we are cognisant of them and continue to debate them, as we endeavour to build resilient cities and resilient buildings. Figure 1.3 shows a simplified conceptual schematic of the urban system, showing the socio-ecological and social-technical networks described above. Figure 1.3 also shows where buildings fit into the framework.

Other concepts distinguish between built environment resilience, which refers to the physical built environment that accommodate human activities, and community resilience, which refers to the resilience of individuals or a group of inhabitants and their social constructs. Here the literature is focused on notions of wellbeing, governance and economy. Sanchez et al. (2016) give the example of built environment resilience, with different stakeholders having a different focus. With regards to built environment resilience, engineers are focused on engineering infrastructure and restoring systems to operation as soon as possible after a disaster, whereas community engineering resilience has a focus on social and economic outcomes.

1.6 Synopsis

This book collates the findings of research conducted in Australia, the UK and the Netherlands, although many of the issues and principles are applicable and relevant elsewhere. The authors review aspects of sustainability, and to some extent resilience at various levels from the level of new economic systems and paradigms, to governance and policy, to conversion at masterplan scales, to building-level conversion criteria, to opportunities for top up additions to buildings, to heritage conversion and sustainability in civic buildings, to assessing the potential for office-to-residential conversion,

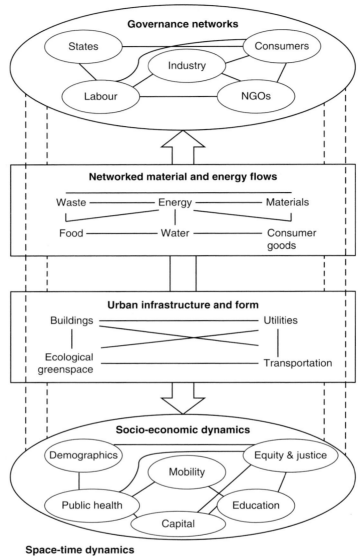

Figure 1.3   A simplified conceptual schematic of the urban system (in Meerow *et al.*, 2016 and adapted from Dickens, 2011).

to the rating tools used in adaptive reuse. Finally, we present a manifesto for the future in respect of adaptive reuse based on the work discussed in the book.

In Chapter 2, Laura Wynne and Professor Chris Reidy of the Institute of Sustainable Futures, University of Technology Sydney examine the concept of the sharing economy and described an operational model applied to adaptive reuse. They assert that adapting cities through urban infill development is a key alternative to urban sprawl, where infill developments and adaptive reuse projects offer spaces for social innovation that can lead to the discovery of new ways of being in the city that are better adapted to sustainability challenges. Such innovations include a reimagining of the way we use spaces and assets and the way we connect with one another. The sharing paradigm captures a broad range of activities and services that are reflective of this reimagining of consumption and ownership. Sharing resources, goods and services can enhance urban resilience by reducing demand for new materials and infrastructure, supporting local economies, and enhancing social networks. This chapter identifies some of the sharing paradigm initiatives that might be enabled through adaptive reuse and infill development in cities around the world.

Chapter 3 explores planning policy instruments for resilient urban redevelopment, and specifically the case of office conversions in Rotterdam. It is written by Assistant Professor Erwin Heurkens and Associate Professors Hilde Remøy and Fred Hobma of Delft University of Technology. Cities all over the world are searching for ways to become more resilient to climate change and related economic challenges. The general consensus seems to be that resilience refers to the ability of a system to respond to exogenous and endogenous pressures. Resilient urban redevelopment through sustainable building adaptation could possibly be a strategy to accommodate endogenous pressures such as socio-demographic change. It changes the economic base of cities and enhances urban environmental quality. Urban resilience can be built in part by reshaping real estate markets, in which institutions and organisations prefer adaptation of real estate over demolition and new building. However, this requires the utilisation of public planning policy instruments, which correspond to changing real estate market demands and private actor needs. This chapter illustrates that making urban areas more resilient by adopting existing real estate to new uses requires an effective mix of planning policy instruments and activities, aligned with market needs at both city and local-development levels. This is achieved by introducing some planning policy instrument classifications, providing case study examples of the utilisation of a variety of planning policies for the adaptation of obsolete office buildings in Rotterdam, and concluding with some general implications for resilient urban redevelopment practice and research.

In Chapter 4, Hannah Baker and Dr Alice Moncaster, from the University of Cambridge, examine how the decision to demolish or adapt existing buildings changes in the context of a masterplan design. UK legislation emphasises the release of brownfield land for new development. The chapter explores adaptation and demolition on larger regeneration sites: for residential developments which will have 200+ dwellings, or over four hectares. These can lead to transformative changes within cities. Decision-making on these larger sites sits within the context of national and local policy, involving higher degrees of complexity than when only the individual building scale is involved. Existing decision-making frameworks focus mostly on individual buildings, and are not generally appropriate for larger scales, the authors argue, for masterplan regeneration sites. The different buildings within the curtilage of the site will often be considered for different adaptation options:

- demolition
- part-demolition and adaptation
- modification
- refurbishment
- adaptation
- part extension.

The inherent complexity of considering multiple buildings at the same time is increased by the additional relationship between the master plan and urban infrastructure, as the consideration of factors such as utilities, ecological green space and transportation affect the decisions being made about individual buildings. Illustrative case studies show how these differences operate and impact in practice.

There is a shift to the building scale in Chapter 5, where Professor Craig Langston of Bond University in Australia examines issues affecting sustainable design and building conversion. Good architecture is something we all seek, but is hard to define. Langston uses Gordon's 1972 definition of buildings that exhibit 'long life, loose fit and low energy'. These characteristics, named by Gordon as the 3 L Principle, are measurable and embody the principle of adaptability discussed in this chapter. Life-cycle cost (LCC) provides a method for accessing the economic contribution or burden created by buildings to the society they aim to serve. No research investigates the connection between 3 L and LCC, and Langston hypothesises that buildings with a high 3 L index may have a low-LCC profile. If this is the case, then LCC may be used to assess 'good architecture'. This chapter uses a case study methodology to assess the durability, adaptability and sustainability of 22 projects that have won architectural design awards. The 3 L criteria are measured and compared with the average LCC per square metre using a long time-horizon (greater than 50 years). Langston claims the research is significant, as it tests a process to assess objectively what is commonly intangible and to determine if LCC is a suitable predictor of 'good architecture'. LCC is suggested as an economic paradigm as part of the consideration of feasibility. It can be used in a cost–benefit analysis to help compute profit. This chapter expands current thinking on economics by proposing a 4P decision-making model based on profit, people, politics and planet as a way forward to greater resilience and sustainability.

Professor Gordon Holden discusses the ecological performance of new additions constructed on top of existing buildings, focusing on apartments. The emerging architectural typology of 'building-top apartments' is discussed as a more 'sustainable' solution to providing urban apartments than conventional 'demolished-site' developments. Apartments built on top of existing buildings avoid demolition of the host building, thereby avoiding waste and improving life-cycle performance. The addition can be built more economically and quickly, as it does not require excavation and footings. Furthermore, it contributes to urban densification, supporting city social and cultural vitality and economic development. Urban densification means that many more people will walk to work, thereby reducing transport congestion and pollution as well as contributing to public health through better fitness. It supports higher numbers of people in the city as casual observers and thereby potentially contributes to reductions in crime. By accommodating a significant proportion of the city's population growth in building-top apartments, land subdivision on the city's boundaries, which consumes energy and resources at a higher rate, is potentially reduced. This emerging urban architectural typology contributes to city sustainability and resilience in terms of having less impact on the environment than conventional development while contributing to better economic performance and to social and cultural endeavours.

In Chapter 7, Rob Geraedts, Theo van der Voordt and Associate Professor Hilde Remøy of Technical University, Delft, examine whether building owners and other stakeholders can adopt different strategies to cope with issues and choices around vacancy, renovation, change of use adaptation, or whether to demolish and build a new building. This chapter discusses how to cope with vacancy through change of use adaptation and gives overviews of the many factors and aspects that enable or hinder change of use adaptation of (office) buildings into housing. They explain how to assess the characteristics of the market, location, building and the stakeholders. They present the 'Conversion Meter', a tool to assess the potential for converting vacant office buildings into housing. The tool is built up from an initial fast appraisal using so called 'veto' criteria, followed by a more detailed assessment of the conversion potential. No single criterion is sufficient to decide if conversion is viable or not; it is the combination of all the criteria that provides a valuable indicator of conversion potential. The next step calculates a conversion potential score as a weighted sum of all the criteria. This is followed by an assessment of financial feasibility and a final check on possible risks, and the opportunities to eliminate them. The chapter concludes with lessons learned from case studies in which the Conversion Meter was applied.

In Chapter 8, Associate Professor Sara Wilkinson of the University of Technology Sydney, analyses the rating tools used to measure adaptive reuse in the context of resilience and sustainability. The literature review evaluates the issues related to sustainability-rating tools and conversion adaptation in different countries and then compares and contrasts approaches. Issues raised in earlier chapters regarding regulations are discussed, as is the question of whether a mandatory or voluntary approach is best for conversion adaptation. Finally, this chapter relates how regenerative infrastructure impacts on resilience and conversion adaptation.

In the final chapter Sara Wilkinson sets out the main conclusions that can be drawn from the preceding chapters and a describes a manifesto for the future.

1.7   Summary

The notion of resilience is being explored actively by many stakeholders, including the UN, city and municipal authorities, developers, urban planners and academics. They hope to gain a deeper understanding of what resilience means and how we can promote a built environment that enhances it. With the largest wave of population and urban growth ever experienced, the built environment has a pivotal role to play in delivering resilience. We must capitalise on the opportunities with our existing buildings, to retain heritage and a sense of place where appropriate, and to increase resilience of existing generations and those to come. The Rotterdam resilience scale shows clearly how buildings ultimately impact up to the global scale. This chapter has also shown there is great potential to learn from different approaches taken in cities globally and also to share experience across the developed and developing world.

Resilience has attributes of equilibrium and non-equilibrium, which means we are in a constant state of flux to some degree and that we need to adopt a 'safe to fail' paradigm, and acknowledge that after a disturbance we will adapt to a new state. We need to be cognisant of whose resilience agenda is prevailing and to answer questions of resilience: 'for whom' and, 'to what'. We should embrace the positive aspects of resilience and be aware that we make changes for the better. It has been shown that adaptation is an example of persistence, whereas adaptive reuse, or change of use adaptation, is a transitional change to a new state. At the city or masterplan scale, where more than one building is involve, the change is transformative. We must also be aware that some retention of system flexibility is useful to cope with the unexpected and there are many examples of buildings that have stood the test of time over centuries. Finally, we note the different timescales in which resilience can be delivered at the different scales. The chapters that follow address all of the issues raised, either explicitly or implicitly, and demonstrate how our collective thinking is transforming and maturing in respect of resilience, sustainability and change of use adaptation.

References

100 RC (2016) 100 Resilient Cities. Retrieved on 24 August 2016 from Http:// Www.100resilientcities.Org/Cities#/-_/.

Alexander, D.E. (2013) Resilience and disaster risk reduction: an etymological journey. *Natural Hazards and Earth System Sciences*, 13(11): 2707–2716.

ASBEC (2016) Low carbon high-performance. How buildings can make a major contribution to Australia's emissions and productivity goals. Report, Australian Sustainable Built Environment Council. Retrieved from on 21st of August 2016 from: http://www. climateworksaustralia.org/sites/default/files/documents/publications/summary_ report_-_low_carbon_high_performance_20160511_1.pdf.

Batty, M. (2008) The size, scale, and shape of cities. *Science*, 319(5864): 769–771.

Baum, A. (1993) Quality, depreciation, and property performance. *Journal of Real Estate Research*, 8(4): 541–565.

Bosher, L. (ed.) (2008) *Hazards and the Built Environment: Attaining Built-in Resilience*. Routledge.

Bullen, P.A. (2007) Adaptive reuse and sustainability of commercial buildings. *Facilities*, 25: 20–31.

Chelleri, L. (2012) From the 'resilient city' to urban resilience. A review essay on understanding and integrating the resilience perspective for urban systems. *Documents d'Anàlisi Geogràfica*, 58(2): 287–306.

Cote, M. and Nightingale, A.J. (2012) Resilience thinking meets social theory: situating social change in socio-ecological systems (SES) research. *Progress in Human Geography*, 36(4): 475–489.

Davoudi, S., Shaw, K., Haider, L.J. *et al.* (2012) Resilience: a bridging concept or a dead end? 'Reframing' resilience: challenges for planning theory and practice interacting traps: resilience assessment of a pasture management system in Northern Afghanistan urban resilience: what does it mean in planning practice? Resilience as a useful concept for climate change adaptation? The politics of resilience for planning: a cautionary note. *Planning Theory & Practice*, 13(2): 299–333.

Desouza, K.C. and Flanery, T.H. (2013) Designing, planning, and managing resilient cities: A conceptual framework. *Cities*, 35: 89–99.

Dicken, P. (2011) *Global Shift: Mapping the Changing Contours of the World Economy* (6th edn). New York: Guilford Press.

Douglas, J. (2006) *Building Adaptation*, Butterworth Heinemann.

Ellison, L. and Sayce, S. (2007) Assessing sustainability in the existing commercial property stock: Establishing sustainability criteria relevant for the commercial property investment sector. *Property Management*, 25(3): 287–304.

Elkington, J. (1998) *Cannibals with Forks: The Triple Bottom Line of Sustainability*. Gabriola Island: New Society Publishers.

Ernstson, H., Leeuw, S.E.V.D., Redman, C.L., *et al.* (2010) Urban transitions: on urban resilience and human-dominated ecosystems. *AMBIO*, 39(8): 531–545.

Haase, D., Frantzeskaki, N. and Elmqvist, T. (2014) Ecosystem services in urban landscapes: practical applications and governance implications. *Ambio*, 43(4): 407–412.

Mansfield, J.R. (2002) What's in a name? Complexities in the definition of 'refurbishment'. *Property Management*, 20(1): 23–30.

Meerow, S., Newell, J.P. and Stults, M. (2016) Defining urban resilience: a review. *Landscapes and Urban Planning*, 147: 38–49.

NSW GPE (2014) A plan for growing Sydney 2014. New South Wales Government Planning and Environment. Retrieved of 21 August 2016 from: http://www.planning.nsw.gov.au/Plans-for-Your-Area/Sydney/A-Plan-for-Growing-Sydney.

RICS (2015) Our changing world: Lets be ready. Royal Institution of Chartered Surveyors. Retrieved on 19 June 2016 from http://www.rics.org/au/knowledge/research/insights/futuresour-changing-world/.

Sanchez, A.X., Osmond, P. and van der Heijden, J. (2016) Are some forms of resilience more sustainable than others? In: *International High-Performance Built Environment Conference – A Sustainable Built Environment Conference*, 2016 series (SBE 16). iHBE.

Stocker, T.F., Qin, D., Plattner, G.K. *et al.* (2013) Climate change 2013: the physical science basis. Contribution of Working Group I to the Fifth Assessment Report of the Intergovernmental Panel On Climate Change.

Thomsen, A. and Van der Flier, K. (2011) Understanding obsolescence: a conceptual model for buildings. *Building Research & Information*, 39(4): 352–362.

UGC (2013) Building resilience task force summary report. June 2013. Urban Green Council, New York City. Retrieved on 21 August 2016 from: http://www.urbangreencouncil.org/content/projects/building-resiliency-task-force.

UN (2015) Transforming our world: the 2030 Agenda for Sustainable Development. Resolution adopted by the General Assembly on 25 September 2015. Retrieved on 21 August 2016 from: https://sustainabledevelopment.un.org/post2015/summit.

UN DESA (2010) World urbanization prospects, the 2009 revision: highlights. United Nations Department of Economic and Social Affairs, Population Division.

UN DESA (2015) World population prospects: the 2015 revision. UN Department of Economic and Social Affairs. Retrieved on 19 June 2016 from http://www.un.org/en/development/desa/news/population/2015-report.html.

UNPF (2015) World population trends. UN Populations Fund. Retrieved on 19 June 2016 from http://www.unfpa.org/world-population-trends#sthash.oMfXUZJO.dpuf.

Wardekker, J.A., de Jong, A., Knoop, J.M. and van der Sluijs, J.P. (2010) Operationalising a resilience approach to adapting an urban delta to uncertain climate changes. *Technological Forecasting and Social Change*, 77(6): 987–998.

Wilkinson, S. (2011) The relationship between building adaptation and property attributes, PhD thesis, Deakin University. Retrieved on 21 August 2016 from http://dro.deakin.edu.au/view/DU:30036710.

Wilkinson, S.J. (2012) Conceptual understanding of sustainability in Australian construction firms. CIB, Montreal, Canada. Available from: http://www.irbnet.de/daten/iconda/CIB_DC25613.pdf.

Wilkinson, S. (2015) Conceptual understanding of sustainability in built environment professionals. In: *Zero Energy Mass Custom Homes International Conference* (ZEMCH), Lecce Italy 22–24 September 2015.

World Bank Group (2015) Building regulation for resilience. Managing risks for safer cities. Retrieved on 21 August 2016 from: www.worldbank.org.

Wu, J. and Wu, T. (2013) Ecological resilience as a foundation for urban design and sustainability. In: *Resilience in Ecology and Urban Design*, Springer.

Precinct-scale Innovation and the Sharing Paradigm

Laura Wynne and Chris Riedy
University of Technology, Sydney

2.1 Introduction

Cities, as centres of human population, production and consumption, are crucial sites for shaping sustainable futures for the planet. In 2014, over half (54%) of the global population resided in urban areas, and by 2050 this will grow to two-thirds of the world's population (UN, 2014). Urbanisation has been strongly entangled with neoliberal agendas and has played a fundamental role in the expansion of contemporary capitalism (Harvey, 2008). As argued by Bauman (1998), Harvey (2008) and countless others, this neoliberal paradigm has reconceptualised citizens as consumers, and strongly encouraged and promoted exponential growth in rates of consumption amongst individuals and households. Rising consumption in our cities has hastened the degradation of our natural environment and resources.

In addition to the impact of this growth in consumption, the standard growth pattern of our cities – urban sprawl, a perpetual outward expansion of urbanised areas – has contributed significantly to the ecological and human cost incurred. Urban sprawl can be linked to two related demographic factors – population growth and household-size decline (Liu *et al.*, 2003), but is also an outcome of planning, market and infrastructure processes. Areas of urban sprawl make greater contributions to carbon emissions than denser, inner-city areas. Sprawl is associated with 8–10 kg of daily per capita emissions from transport alone, compared with between 0 and 4 kg in inner-urban areas (Trubka *et al.*, 2008). Households in areas of suburban sprawl are likely to incur an additional $164 per year in health costs compared to those in moderate- to high-density developments with good access to transport and services (Trubka *et al.*, 2010).

Building Urban Resilience through Change of Use, First Edition.
Edited by Sara J. Wilkinson and Hilde Remøy.
© 2018 John Wiley & Sons Ltd. Published 2018 by John Wiley & Sons Ltd.

As well as influencing environmental impacts, the structure of our cities has a critical influence on the social connectedness that people experience (Leyden, 2003). Cities, when appropriately designed, provide proximity and density that helps to build social capital (Jacobs, 1961). However, long work hours, protracted commutes and single-person households are contributing to what has been identified as a 'loneliness epidemic'. Instead of social connectedness and capital, the structure of our cities might unintentionally facilitate experiences of loneliness and social isolation (Kelly *et al.*, 2012; Jacobs, 1961).

The city is thus a paradox. Cities have great potential to deliver sustainable futures, yet the cities of today fall far short of this potential and may even actively undermine sustainability. We are faced with a messy problem: how to manage the growth of our cities in such a way as to realise their potential and positively benefit both human and environmental health? For Rose (2016, Loc 318), this is a question of restoring balance:

> In a time of increasing volatility, complexity, and ambiguity, the well-tempered city has systems that can help it evolve toward a more even temperament, one that balances prosperity and well-being with efficiency and equality in ways that continually restore the city's social and natural capital.

Our chapter explores one partial response to this problem – the role of adaptive reuse and the sharing paradigm in building urban resilience and restoring balance to cities.

Adapting cities through urban infill development is a key alternative to urban sprawl, with the potential to reduce environmental impacts. Urban infill development has provided high-density housing on former industrial precincts in well-serviced areas of many cities over the last two decades. Examples abound, such as Sydney's Central Park, which has adapted former warehouses, a brewery and worker housing into a mixed-use commercial and residential site, incorporating adaptive reuse of heritage items with new build apartments and office space. Figure 2.1 shows construction work towards the adaptive reuse of the 1911 Irving Street Brewery Building. Formerly the power station providing energy for the brewery, the building has been adapted to house a modern trigeneration facility, which burns natural gas to provide electricity, heating and cooling. The site also hosts community markets every Sunday, making it an important urban node for both environmental and social sustainability. We will return to the example of Central Park later in the chapter.

Urban infill development is most attractive from a sustainability perspective when it conserves resources by adaptively reusing existing buildings, but even infill that only reuses land after demolition and rebuilding has the potential to improve city resilience and sustainability in several ways. First, moribund areas that are no longer contributing productively to the city can be brought back into use, enhancing the productivity of the entire urban system. Second, precinct-scale developments can act as exemplars of sustainable urban form that provide feedback throughout the urban system on

Figure 2.1   Irving Street Brewery Building, Sydney.

what a sustainable, resilient city looks like. They act as nodes around which new ideas and forms of the city can coalesce. Finally, urban infill developments offer spaces for social innovation to discover new ways of being in the city that are more adapted to sustainability challenges. In this chapter, we focus on how urban infill developments can support one particular set of social innovations – the emergence of a sharing paradigm (McLaren and Agyeman, 2015). Sharing resources, goods and services can enhance urban resilience by reducing demand for new materials and infrastructure, supporting local economies, and enhancing social networks. The new sharing paradigm has the potential to make a positive contribution to addressing many of the urban challenges outlined above.

In the next section, we describe the sharing paradigm in greater detail, exploring different definitions and ways of categorising this movement. Following this is a discussion of the benefits that the sharing paradigm can provide for our cities. Finally, we provide some examples and case studies of how urban infill can help facilitate the sharing paradigm.

2.2   The Emergence of the Sharing Paradigm

As the 'loneliness epidemic' has grown, it has been slowly countered by a growing appreciation for community, with some evidence suggesting that 'the age of the individual is being quietly supplanted by a re-emerging collectivism' (Gleeson, 2009). Botsman and Rogers (2010) drew popular attention to this movement, which they labelled 'collaborative consumption'. They saw collaborative consumption as a new paradigm in which reputation, community and shared access to goods and services replace credit, advertising and individual ownership as the key characteristics of consumption practices (Botsman and Rogers, 2010). The drivers included new peer-to-peer technologies, a resurgence of interest in community, environmental concerns and cost consciousness (Botsman and Rogers, 2010). The new paradigm was facilitated by the existence of critical mass or density in cities, idle capacity in the form of unused goods and skills, and the emergence of a 'belief in the commons' and 'trust between strangers' as social innovations.

This paradigm is now more commonly termed the 'sharing economy', but this terminology is arguably too narrow because of its emphasis solely on economic transactions. McLaren and Agyeman (2015) argue that the 'sharing paradigm' is a better term, drawing attention to broader human and social development possibilities that go beyond economic transactions and commercial forms of sharing. We follow their terminology here, recognising that sharing in cities should be about improving human wellbeing in multiple ways.

Defining the sharing paradigm is notoriously difficult, as the boundaries between categories are often fuzzy, and sharing initiatives are constantly evolving. Writing about the sharing economy, Juliet Schor (Schor, 2014) identifies four broad categories of activity. Her first category is 'recirculation of goods'. These initiatives help to get pre-owned goods to people that want them. The category includes online services such as eBay, Freecycle (which prohibits monetary exchanges), Craigslist and Gumtree (an Australian version of Craigslist). Initiatives have even emerged that seek to reutilize perishable goods, such as 'Taste the Waste' which aims to encourage the sharing of food that would otherwise go to waste. The second group of initiatives focuses on 'increased utilization of durable assets'. These initiatives help people to get better value from idle assets, such as cars, homes or tools. Car-sharing services such as Zipcar, Car Next Door and GoGet, and space sharing services such as AirBnB and Couchsurfing are prominent in this category. Sharing services for other assets, such as household tools, have not been particularly successful in Australia to date. They have performed better internationally in dense urban areas. Peerby is an example of such a service in the Netherlands, where expensive, occasionally-required items such as bicycles, luggage, tools and gardening equipment are shared amongst neighbours. The third category comprises 'exchange of services', such as labour and skills. Examples include Airtasker and Task Rabbit, which match people that need jobs done with people willing to do those jobs. The final category – 'sharing of productive assets' – includes initiatives like Landshare, which allows farmers or hobby gardeners to access land on which to grow food. It also includes co-working and cohousing initiatives. WeWork is a prominent international example of co-working, providing subscribers with access to shared office spaces. More recently, WeWork has launched WeLive, providing subscribers with access to shared living spaces. This is a form of cohousing, providing a combination of private and shared spaces for people with mobile lifestyles.

McLaren and Agyeman (2015) also recognize multiple dimensions of sharing: sharing things, sharing services, and sharing activities or experiences. They further note that sharing can happen in individual, collective and public spaces. It can be commercial or communal, and take mediated or more traditional sociocultural forms. All of these notions are gathered up into the sharing paradigm that we consider in this chapter. However, like McLaren and Agyeman (2015), we are particularly interested in the transformative potential of communal forms of sharing in our cities.

The link between adaptive reuse and the sharing paradigm may not be immediately clear. We argue here, however, that a key link can be found in the concept of the circular economy. A circular economy aims to minimise waste, maximise reuse and recycling and identify opportunities for industrial symbiosis (Andersen, 2007), moving from an open-ended, linear model of production-consumption to a circular one, in which wastes are reconceptualised as resources. In a circular economy, goods and materials recirculate without net extraction of materials from the environment. Both the sharing paradigm and adaptive reuse attempt to keep existing materials and assets in use. Proponents recognise the value in existing built and other resources that are no longer utilised for their original purpose, and aim to repurpose and revalorise them. In this way, the sharing paradigm and adaptive reuse are closely aligned phenomena that can contribute to the emergence of a circular economy. However, the sharing paradigm takes in much more than just adaptive reuse and it is by no means guaranteed that an adaptive reuse development will support broader sharing relationships.

If we are to make our cities more sustainable and resilient, we will be compelled to find ways to sustainably redevelop inner city areas *and* to support the full breadth of sharing paradigm initiatives. Inner-city brownfield sites are ideal niches for the sharing paradigm to flourish, as they offer sufficient population density to provide a critical mass of participants and resources to gain and sustain momentum (Botsman and Rogers, 2010).

The impact of the sharing paradigm on the resilience of our cities remains an open question. Many claims have been made for the benefits the sharing paradigm can deliver, but evidence for this remains sparse. In the next section, we examine the potential benefits of the sharing paradigm for cities and precincts.

2.3   Potential Benefits of the Sharing Paradigm for Cities and Precincts

Advocates argue that the sharing paradigm can deliver triple bottom-line benefits. For example, Heinrichs (2013) argues that there is potential for the sharing economy to 'meet expectations regarding effective resource use, strengthening social capital and fostering decentralised value production'.

Some literature also suggests that the sharing paradigm will bring economic benefits to local economies. On the other hand, critical voices have emerged, drawing attention to the ways in which the sharing economy can have negative impacts (e.g. Slee, 2016); much depends on the detail of how sharing is implemented in a particular context.

2.3.1   Reduced Environmental Impact

Activities within the sharing paradigm have been strongly associated – in marketing, literature and the media – with a reduced environmental impact compared to traditional consumption habits. Harvey *et al.* (2014) argue that, by exploiting a spare pool of resources, sharing activities can 'reduce the cost of acquisition and the environmental impact of consumption in comparison to the more typical product lifecycle'. Any resultant environmental benefits are expected to be due to reduced consumption (that is, avoided need to purchase), reduced waste generation (due to increased reuse) or from increased efficiency of use over a product's lifecycle, (due to sharing one product, such as a car or a lawn mower, between multiple consumers).

However, although participation in these activities is 'generally expected to be highly ecologically sustainable' (Hamari *et al.*, 2015: 5), there is little research to provide evidence of any such environmental benefits. Many commercial initiatives operating under the banner of the sharing economy may actually stimulate more consumption and increase environmental impacts (Slee, 2016). For example, Couchsurfing and Airbnb, which may make it cheaper to find accommodation in cities, could encourage increased leisure travel, increasing demand for commercial flights – a heavily emissions-intensive industry. Cities need to facilitate types of sharing that do actually lead to reductions in resource use.

2.3.2   Economic Benefits

The sharing paradigm also has the potential to improve local economic outcomes. Sharing activities, through their largely peer-to-peer nature, can boost local economies by providing alternative and supplementary sources of income. Airbnb, for example, is expected to boost local economies by assisting city-dwellers to meet escalating real-estate costs by allowing them to supplement their income by renting their home (or part of it) to tourists.

However, others warn against embracing the sharing paradigm too quickly, arguing that it has the potential to threaten existing businesses. Airbnb, for example, has been criticised because of its failure to protect consumers through regulatory frameworks like those that apply to hotels (King, 2015), its potential to take business from existing hotel businesses that are large employers (Zervas, Proserpio, and Byers, 2015), its purported potential to inflate residential property prices (Oskam and Boswijk, 2016), and its failure to protect employees due to its 'informal' work arrangements (King, 2015).

When facilitating the sharing paradigm, cities need to take care that people are not made worse off, particularly vulnerable households.

2.3.3   Fostering Social Connections

Much has also been written about the positive social outcomes of the sharing paradigm. Albinsson and Perera (2012: 308) find that sharing events deliver a range of benefits whose scope includes 'not only the goods and services but also the interactions between the individuals who participate in the giving and receiving'. By bringing people together, it is expected that the sharing paradigm has the potential to go some way in addressing the 'loneliness epidemic' mentioned briefly above, by fostering improved social connections.

Social capital may also be fostered through sharing activities. Albinsson and Perera note that these interactions involve the exchange not just of goods but of 'skills, knowledge, space and ideas' (2012: 308), indicating that a broader suite of benefits may result from participating in the sharing economy. McLaren and Agyeman (2015) see the sharing paradigm as having great potential to strengthen communities and build civic participation. On the other hand, critics, including McLaren and Agyeman, raise concerns about the monetisation of sharing; when every social relationship becomes an opportunity for financial gain, social capital may be eroded rather than built. Again, the key is to pay careful attention to the types of sharing that are facilitated in cities and to continually evaluate and adapt to their impacts.

In the next section, we consider three specific ways in which adaptive reuse in cities can facilitate the type of sharing that is likely to deliver the benefits described above.

2.4   How Building and Land Conversions Could Help Enable the Sharing Paradigm

Adaptive reuse and urban infill developments provide important opportunities to shape the urban commons and incorporate the sharing paradigm into the city fabric. This section describes three examples with potential to deliver sustainability benefits in cities.

2.4.1   Cohousing

One of the most obvious intersections between the sharing paradigm and urban resilience is in development of cohousing. Current urban form is biased towards provision of private dwelling spaces. Each private dwelling needs to perform similar functions for its household, such as providing spaces to sleep, cook, eat, wash and relax. This replication is both inefficient and isolating. In cohousing, some of this private space is given up in favour of shared living spaces and facilities. By sharing spaces such as communal kitchens, living areas, laundries and gardens, cohousing developments make more efficient use of space and materials. At the same time, they provide spaces in which social interaction is actively nurtured.

Cohousing is a form of housing that contains a mix of private and communal spaces, 'combining autonomy of private dwellings with the advantages of community living' (Williams, 2005). It can occur at a variety of scales, from multi-unit developments (usually between 4 and 30 households) to small, self-organised clusters of 2–3 households. Most cohousing models attempt to respond to 'triple bottom-line' challenges, by securing the 'three pillars of sustainable lifestyles': social (through being community-oriented and facilitating social interaction), environmental (through efficient design and shared resources) and economic (through striving to achieve affordability) (Tummers, 2015).

Variations on cohousing models abound, but a few key elements appear to be consistently identified across the literature as being common to most cohousing developments. These common factors include:

- resident involvement in the design of the cohousing development (Durrett, 2009).
- self-governance and active participation by residents who manage the community (Brenton, 2013)
- common facilities (Durrett, 2009)
- use of social contact design (Williams, 2005) in planning the development to encourage community interaction
- communality rather than privacy (Jarvis, 2015).

Unlike communes and intentional communities, cohousing does not generally feature:

- a shared community economy (Glass, 2009)
- a common ideology (Williams, 2005).

The design of a cohousing community is generally developed by the residents, led either by the resident group themselves, by a facilitator (such as an architect) or by a developer (Durrett, 2009). Often drawing on principles of deliberative design/development, these processes ensure that the shared values of the community are reflected in the neighbourhood design. Cohousing, through use of extensive communal space and resident management, goes some way to 'combating the alienation and isolation…recreating the neighbourly support of a village or city quarter in the past'.[1]

At the small end of the cohousing spectrum, adjacent suburban blocks can be adapted to accommodate two or three smaller dwellings with some shared spaces, reducing the overall ecological footprint of each household (McGee and Benn, 2015). An example of this kind of adaptive reuse is the redevelopment of two single-storey workers cottages in Balmain, Sydney by Suzanne Benn and her son Andrew Benn (McGee and Benn, 2015).

[1] See http://cohousing.org.uk/.

Suzanne bought the adjacent rundown cottages and the family renovated them into a single cohousing property. The property is now able to accommodate up to three families, or multiple generations of a single family. Gardens, equipment and guest spaces are shared, while the residents retain their own private spaces. This kind of adaptive reuse is still rare and difficult in Australia. The cohousing proposal was initially rejected by the local approval authority due to concerns about the impact on the heritage value of the properties.

Larger, multi-unit cohousing communities use social contact design (or some variant of it) to encourage social interaction in neighbourhoods (Williams, 2005). Social contact design includes principles that are intended to emphasise community and maximise the sharing of resources and experiences. In this way, they differ significantly from standard, speculative development designs that tend to be designed and built with privacy, rather than communality in mind (Jarvis, 2015). Key features of social contact design usually include:

- higher densities to ensure proximity between neighbours
- good visibility of public and semi-private (e.g. porches) spaces
- clustering of dwellings, with entrances near one another
- shared facilities, such as laundries, waste units, gardens, sheds
- car parking located on the periphery of communities to encourage walking (Williams, 2005).

Examples of adaptive reuse into cohousing at a larger scale, particularly at a precinct scale, are scarce. Of the numerous cohousing case studies catalogued by McCamant and Durrett (2011), only three involved retrofitting existing buildings. While there have been many larger cohousing developments, these are typically new buildings on greenfield sites or cleared infill sites. One example is Murundaka in Melbourne, where the members of the Earth Housing Co-operative (a common equity rental housing cooperative) collaborated in the development of 18 private, self-sufficient apartments situated around a common house. The common house contains a commercial kitchen, dining and living space, guest rooms and office space. All the apartments are approximately 10% smaller than they otherwise would have been, offset by the benefit of access to the common house (Daly, 2015). Figure 2.2 shows the communal living area at Murundaka from above, and Figure 2.3 shows the communal kitchen.

Another example in Melbourne is The Commons, which omits car parking space in favour of car sharing and provides communal spaces for the residents to eat, relax and do their laundry. The Commons used a development approach known as 'deliberative development', where residents collaborated with the architect on making decisions about what to incorporate and what to omit from the final design. Invariably, the residents chose to include features that promoted greater sharing and a sense of community for the building.

As well as sharing actual space, cohousing developments provide platforms or hubs for other forms of sharing. The residents of Murundaka share

Figure 2.2 Communal living area at Murundaka, Melbourne.

Figure 2.3 Communal kitchen at Murundaka, Melbourne.

vehicles, have allocated a space for storing materials for reuse, and share food from their communal garden. As such, cohousing developments demonstrate how a sharing paradigm could spread across cities. To date, however, cohousing developments have not been realised at the large scale of a precinct. Further, as noted above, they have rarely involved adaptive reuse. To improve the resilience of our cities, both of these opportunities should be pursued.

2.4.2 Supporting Sharing Businesses

Precinct-scale infill development provides an ideal opportunity for facilitating sharing paradigm initiatives: dense populations of households living in small apartments with minimal storage, little-to-no parking, and a high cost of living will likely be well-situated to participate in sharing activities.

Central Park, a former brewery located next to Central train station in inner-city Sydney, is an example of how adaptive reuse and infill development might encourage sharing paradigm activities. Central Park is a large site of 5.8 ha, a former industrial site in a rapidly growing residential and commercial growth precinct. At completion, the site will include 3000 residences, 65,000 m² of commercial and retail space, and 6400 m² of open green space. It includes the adaptive reuse of former Victorian terrace housing (now repurposed as commercial space, including restaurants and bars), and the brewery's coal loader and an intact warehouse (to be adapted to become a multi-use space for community and commercial use). Although adaptive reuse comprises only a small part of the site, it combines reuse of existing buildings with high-density residential infill and new commercial spaces.

Throughout construction, the developers made available three warehouses on Kensington Street, at the edge of the redevelopment precinct, for shared use as artist studios, exhibition galleries and rehearsal spaces. This was a response to the need to provide affordable spaces for artists and creative industry professionals in the inner-city, recognising that real estate costs often prove prohibitive and provide a disincentive for artists and other creative industry workers to establish themselves in a city. The initiative also recognised the potential of temporary uses of space to provide multiple benefits: such projects can provide a (modest) income stream throughout the pre-development and construction periods, can improve security by reducing the number of uninhabited and unused spaces on site, and can create a draw card for the site even before its final form is realised. The warehouses, known as Fraser Studios, supported dozens of local artists. Brand X, the organisation formed to manage Fraser Studios, now creates opportunities for local artists by identifying and repurposing otherwise-vacant spaces around the city. These warehouses have since been given new commercial uses, such as restaurants and offices (see Figure 2.4). Temporary uses of space such as this demonstrate the synergies between adaptive reuse initiatives and the sharing paradigm, in that both seek to identify opportunities to capitalize on underused infrastructure and facilities, making use of opportunities to foster new initiatives within our cities.

Figure 2.4   Retail reuse of terraces at Central Park, Sydney.

The shopping mall within the Central Park redevelopment includes a community space managed by Brand X. This space allows Brand X to facilitate community events, art exhibitions, installations and creative industry gatherings, provide space and resources for community activities, and support creative and social enterprises to develop.

Central Park has fostered sharing paradigm initiatives that capitalise on its location close to the city and public transport nodes. Located next to Sydney's major bus and rail network hubs, the development's need for resident parking spaces was minimal. By providing a large number of dedicated parking spaces (at least 25 spaces) specifically for car share programs, Central Park has facilitated the sharing of resources and simultaneously avoided the significant development costs that would be associated with providing parking for every apartment in the redevelopment project.

Central Park has also included 'dual key' apartments in its design. Dual key apartments, typically located in inner-city areas where population densities are high, consist of two separate units on the one title that share a lobby and laundry but have their own entrances. Central Park's first phase of development included 18% dual key apartments, with a variety of configurations. These apartments might allow for cohousing with separate households or for adaptation to changing household circumstances (growth in the family or children moving out of home).

Finally, Central Park retained several heritage buildings on the site and incorporated these into the more modern site landscape. Figure 2.5 gives an example, showing the retained Old Clare Hotel with the new One Central Park looming above.

Figure 2.5   The old and the new at Central Park, Sydney.

2.4.3   Coworking

Coworking, like cohousing, is a model that aims to create opportunities for peer-to-peer sharing and collaboration, while eliminating inefficiencies in urban use of space and minimising business costs for freelancers. Coworking, initially fostered within the technology start-up sector and now being adopted across other sectors including the creative industries, brings freelancers, remote workers and small businesses together in a shared workspace. Such spaces usually comprise desk space, meeting rooms and flexible spaces and provide members with a professional, quasi-office set-up that enables them to run their businesses, meet clients and access resources. Coworking spaces respond to a recognition that professionals and companies no longer require the same things from a workspace as they may once have done. Mobility and flexibility are being prioritised over permanence and stability, with workplaces changing to respond to this (Spinuzzi, 2012). Many traditional workspaces have been transformed to reflect these changes, with companies implementing flexible workspaces, 'hot desking' arrangements and recognising that worker productivity is not necessarily linked to time spent in the office.

COMMUNE, a coworking space for creative freelancers in inner-city Sydney, is housed in an adaptive reuse site (see Figure 2.6). The disused warehouses of the former industrial areas of Sydney provide the ideal setting for coworking, with large flexible spaces adaptable to a variety of uses.

Figure 2.6   COMMUNE, a co-working space in Sydney.

Further, such spaces often provide an aesthetic appropriate to the creative and design sector – unpolished floorboards, exposed brick walls and industrial fittings. COMMUNE believes that the very space itself (a former paint factory) is conducive to creativity and design, due to its industrial aesthetics, its high ceilings and its flexible spaces.

Coworking in such shared spaces delivers potential triple bottom-line benefits. Firstly, freelancers and small businesses are able to reduce consumption of resources by sharing facilities such as printers, scanners, projectors and other IT equipment. With paper and other hardware becoming increasingly irrelevant for creative industry jobs, occasional access to such facilities is far more important than ownership of the equipment. This fits with models within the sharing paradigm, which see access to a centrally-managed product being prioritised over exclusive ownership.

Secondly, these spaces can provide a boost to business viability. COMMUNE provides a space to meet clients, to meet potential collaborators and to develop business ideas. These facilities help creative businesses flourish by providing the infrastructure needed to support them. The cost of renting professional office spaces in which to occasionally meet clients and conduct meetings would be prohibitive for many creative industry businesses, especially those that are still in the start-up phase. Coworking spaces provide a leg-up to such businesses, by reducing the cost of accessing professional spaces by sharing resources.

Thirdly, coworking spaces provide freelancers with the opportunity to meet others within their industry, to collaborate and network. Many freelancers work as sole traders, meeting with clients and others only occasionally. This business model can be potentially isolating, involving minimal contact time with others. Coworking potentially reduces the mental health impacts felt by those working alone, by providing opportunities for interaction and connection (COMMUNE, pers. comm.). Further, physical proximity facilitates connectivity and collaboration, increasing the likelihood of shared learning and the realisation of potential opportunities for partnership and collaboration between businesses (COMMUNE, pers. comm.).

2.5 Conclusions: Sharing the City

While much can be achieved at the scale of individual buildings and precincts, the real potential of the sharing paradigm can only be realised when we shift our attention to the scale of the whole city. The city is itself a shared public realm – an urban commons – that can be collaboratively designed and adapted to facilitate a sharing paradigm (McLaren and Agyeman, 2015) and to deliver more resilient cities. However, this requires transformation not only in material infrastructure but in the social, cultural and political engagement of citizens in shaping the city. The public spaces of the city can support a crucial social infrastructure in which democratic deliberation can flourish, or they can narrow social and political interaction into a series of commercial transactions.

Around the world, examples of cities that are actively adapting urban spaces to support social, cultural and political sharing are beginning to emerge. The most prominent example is Seoul, South Korea. In 2012, the Seoul Metropolitan Government declared Seoul a 'Sharing City' and passed the Seoul Metropolitan Government Act for Promoting Sharing. The Sharing City project 'is working to connect people to sharing services and each other, recover a sense of trust and community, reduce waste and over-consumption, and activate the local economy' (Johnson, 2014). Among many initiatives, it has:

- provided grants for establishment of lending libraries, community gardens and tool libraries in apartment buildings
- supported startup companies to catalyse sharing
- opened up public buildings for public use during idle hours
- established the ShareHub online portal for information on sharing opportunities
- pursued intergenerational cohousing
- established car sharing, car park sharing, public wifi and the Seoul Photo Bank (Johnson, 2014).

While government has provided leadership in Seoul, the focus is squarely on public-private partnerships to weave sharing into the urban fabric.

While Seoul remains the leading light in city-scale sharing, the international Sharing Cities Network now has more than 50 member cities. Shareable's Sharing Cities Toolkit contains a wealth of resources for establishing sharing initiatives, from timebanks (programs that allow exchange of services between individuals), to tool libraries, to cooperatives. So far, few cities have even begun to explore the potential to embed sharing opportunities into the urban fabric. Adaptive reuse developments provide an opportunity to experiment with support for sharing and to create sharing nodes or hubs around which sharing cities can crystallise.

Acknowledgements

We would like to thank Sam Ali from COMMUNE for his insights into coworking in adaptive reuse buildings. We would also like to thank our colleague Caitlin McGee, whose work in cohousing and city resilience proved very useful in preparing this chapter.

References

Albinsson, P.A. and Perera, B.Y. (2012) Alternative marketplaces in the 21st century: Building community through sharing events. *Journal of Consumer Behaviour*, 11(4), 303–315.

Andersen, M.S. (2007) An introductory note on the environmental economics of the circular economy. *Sustainability Science*, 2(1), 133–140. http://doi.org/10.1007/s11625-006-0013-6

Bauman, Z. (1998). *Work, Consumerism and the New Poor*. Open University Press.

Botsman, R. and Rogers, R. (2010) *What's Mine Is Yours: The Rise of Collaborative Consumption*. HarperCollins.

Brenton, M. (2013) *Senior cohousing communities – an alternative approach for the UK?* A Better Life.

Daly, M. (2015) Practicing sustainability: Lessons from a sustainable cohousing community. Paper presented at the State of Australian Cities 2015 Conference, 9-11 December 2015, Gold Coast, Queensland.

Durrett, C. (2009). *The Senior Cohousing Handbook*. New Society Publishers.

Glass, A.P. (2009) Aging in a community of mutual support: the emergence of an elder intentional cohousing community in the United States. *Journal of Housing For the Elderly*, 23(4), 283–303.

Gleeson, B (2009) Waking from the dream. *Griffith Review*, 20.

Harvey, D. (2008). The right to the city. *New Left Review*, 53: 23–40.

Hamari, J., Sjöklint, M. and Ukkonen, A. (2015) The sharing economy: Why people participate in collaborative consumption. *Journal of the Association for Information Science and Technology*, 14(4). http://doi.org/10.1002/asi

Harvey, J., Smith, A. and Golightly, D. (2014) Giving and sharing in the computer-mediated economy. *Journal of Consumer Behaviour*, 253–266.

Heinrichs, H. (2013). Sharing economy: a potential new pathway to sustainability. *GAIA: Ecological Perspectives for Science & Society*, 22(4): 228–231.

Jacobs, J. (1961) The *Death and Life of Great American Cities*. Random House.

Jarvis, H. (2015) Towards a deeper understanding of the social architecture of co-housing: evidence from the UK, USA and Australia. *Urban Research & Practice*, 8(1), 93–105.

Johnson, C. (2014). Sharing city Seoul: A model for the world. Available: http://www.shareable.net/blog/sharing-city-seoul-a-model-for-the-world [3 June 2014].

Kelly, J., Breadon, P., Davis, C. *et al.* (2012) *Social Cities*. The Grattan Institute.

King, S. (2015) The three regulatory challenges for the sharing economy. *The Conversation*. Retrieved from https://theconversation.com/the-three-regulatory-challenges-for-the-sharing-economy-37808.

Leyden, K.M. (2003) Social capital and the built environment: the importance of walkable neighborhoods. *American Journal of Public Health*, 93(9): 1546–1551.

Liu, J., Daily, G.C., Ehrlich, P.R. and Luck, G.W. (2003) Effects of household dynamics on resource consumption and biodiversity. *Nature*, 421(6922), 530–3.

McCamant, K. and Durrett, C. (2011). *Creating Cohousing: BUILDING Sustainable Communities*. New Society Publishers.

McGee, C. and Benn, S. (2015). How cohousing could make homes cheaper and greener. *The Conversation*. Available: https://theconversation.com/how-co-housing-could-make-homes-cheaper-and-greener-39235. [20 April 2015].

McLaren, D. and Agyeman, J. (2015) *Sharing Cities: A Case for Truly Smart and Sustainable Cities*. MIT Press.

Oskam, J. and Boswijk, A. (2016) Airbnb: the future of networked hospitality businesses. *Journal of Tourism Futures*, 2(1), 22–42.

Rose, J.F.P. (2016) *The Well-Tempered City* (Kindle edn). HarperCollins.

Schor, J. (2014) Debating the sharing economy. *A Great Transition Initiative Essay*, (October), 1–19.

Slee, T. (2016) *What's Yours is Mine*. OR Books.

Spinuzzi, C. (2012) Working alone, together: coworking as emergent collaborative activity. *Journal of Business and Technical Communication*, 26(4): 399–441.

Trubka, R., Newman, P. and Bilsborough, D. (2008) Assessing the costs of alternative development paths in Australian cities. Report for Parson Brinkerhoff. Retrieved from http://www.earthsharing.org.au/wp-content/uploads/Curtin_Sustainability_Paper_0209.pdf

Trubka, R., Newman, P. and Bilsborough, D. (2010) The costs of urban sprawl-infrastructure and transportation. *Environment Design Guide*, (April), 1–6. Retrieved from http://espace.library.curtin.edu.au/R?func=dbin_jump_full&object_id=160744

Tummers, L. (2015) Understanding co-housing from a planning perspective: why and how? *Urban Research & Practice*, 8(1), 64–78.

UN (2014) World urbanization prospects: the 2014 revision, highlights. Report ST/ESA/SER.A/352, United Nations Department of Economic and Social Affairs, Population Division.

Williams, J. (2005) Designing neighbourhoods for social interaction: The case of cohousing. *Journal of Urban Design*, 10(2), 195–227.

Zervas, G., Proserpio, D. and Byers, J. (2015) The rise of the sharing economy: Estimating the impact of Airbnb on the hotel industry. *Boston University School of Management Research Paper*, (2013–16), 1–45.

Planning Policy Instruments for Resilient Urban Redevelopment: The Case of Office Conversions in Rotterdam, the Netherlands

Erwin Heurkens, Hilde Remøy and Fred Hobma
Delft University of Technology

3.1 Introduction

Cities all over the world are searching for ways to become more resilient to climate change effects: ways that will enable them to thrive socially, economically and environmentally in the future (Pearson *et al.*, 2014). However, resilience in the built environment remains an ambiguous concept; it is not all about responding to climate change or natural hazards (compare, for example, Allan and Bryant, 2011; Van der Heijden, 2014; Gaaff, 2015). It can encapsulate requirements such as (see Wiseman and Edwards, 2012):

- energy efficiency through improvements in urban infrastructure, buildings, transport, food and water systems
- decreases in resource consumption at household, neighbourhood and city levels
- an emphasis on distributed localised energy, water and food production.

Resilience can also relate to (rapid) economic changes (such as financial crises), and the 'short-term ability of economic and social systems to cope with the fall-out of recession and the immediate needs of existing communities and businesses' (Raco and Street, 2012: 1066).

With regard to the above, authors point out that resilience relates to systems' capabilities to respond to exogenous and endogenous challenges. For instance, Newton and Doherty (2014: 7) define resilience as 'the capacity of an urban system – including the natural, built, social and economic elements – to manage change, learn from difficult situations and be in a position to rebound after experiencing significant stress or shock'. Van der Heijden (2014: 5)

Building Urban Resilience through Change of Use, First Edition.
Edited by Sara J. Wilkinson and Hilde Remøy.
© 2018 John Wiley & Sons Ltd. Published 2018 by John Wiley & Sons Ltd.

argues that 'resilience may be considered a descriptive concept that gives insight into the particular properties of a city that make it capable to maintain functioning and recovering from disaster'. Others, like De Jong *et al.* (2015) argue that 'resilience means the ability of a system, community or society exposed to hazards to resist, absorb, accommodate to and recover from the effects of a hazard in a timely and efficient manner, including the preservation and restoration of its essential basic structures and functions'.

The ambiguity of resilience can also be attributed to the fact that cities may face different challenges, driving them to develop different specific planning policies in order to become more resilient in the future. For instance, Newton and Doherty (2014: 15) argue that 'achieving sustainable resilient cities requires a commitment to innovative long-term planning and design, appropriate regulation, nation building, global cooperation and community engagement'. Wilkinson *et al.* (2014: 3) state that 'the drive for climate change adaptation such as carbon neutrality…is prompting city authorities around the world to implement legislation and policy to encourage sustainable building adaptation'.

Note that for such policies to become implemented, governance activities 'undertaken by one or more actors seeking to shape, regulate or attempt to [change] human behaviour' (Van der Heijden, 2014: 6) are necessary. In addition, Roberts (2014: 203) further states that governance for resilient cities should 'be capable of developing integrated approaches to the delivery of policy', which can be done through structures of partnerships and collaboration. This means that resilient policy-making essentially require the cooperation of public, private and civil stakeholders, as policy instruments are aimed to affect market behaviour and decisions. Christensen and Sayce (2014: 125) rightly point out that policies become implemented once 'planners and policymakers…understand the property development process, the risks and rewards that drive property developers and investors'. Moreover, effective policy implementation and governance are often supported by sustainable leadership (Blakely, 2014) and finding (policy) windows of opportunity (Roggema, 2014) to establish change.

To make the need for governance more concrete, we need to consider what type of system we aim to govern or aim to develop policies for. One dominant discourse seems to be that cities need to redevelop existing built-up areas and real estate, as 'with 1–2% of new buildings added to the total stock annually, human-kind needs to adapt its existing buildings, and quickly…as much of the built environment that will exist in 2050 has already been built' (Wilkinson *et al.*, 2014: xiv). Wilkinson *et al.* (2014: 15) also emphasise that 'due to the contribution and impact of the built environment on carbon emissions, adaption [of buildings] is perceived to be an area where significant positive outcomes are possible'. As of now it is understood that 'adaptation is inherently environmentally sustainable because it involves less material use (resource consumption), less transport energy, less energy consumption and less pollution during construction' (Wilkinson *et al.*, 2014: 5).

But can building adaptation also make urban areas and cities more resilient? We argue that urban resilience can be built by reshaping real estate markets (see Heurkens *et al.*, 2015a), by preferring adaptation of obsolete real estate to future uses over demolition and new build (Remøy, 2015). In particular, since adaptations often occur as 'a result of legal, economic, physical, social and environmental drivers' (Wilkinson *et al.*, 2014: 2), a structurally changing (decreasing) market demand for offices, for example, can be considered as an important (endogenous) pressure for real estate markets to become more resilient. In that sense, urban redevelopment through building adaption could accommodate socio-demographic change, change the economic base of cities, and enhance urban environmental quality (Newton and Doherty, 2014).

Considering the above, it comes as no surprise that this chapter considers resilient urban redevelopment as the ability of public and private stakeholders to respond to changes in real estate market demand by adopting existing offices to new usages. This chapter aims to illustrate that making urban areas more resilient by adopting existing real estate to new uses requires an effective mix of planning policy instruments and activities. This must be aligned with market needs at both city and local development levels. Therefore, first we explore various conceptual planning policy instruments that could assist in realising resilient urban redevelopment. Additionally, the effectiveness of such planning policy instruments is demonstrated by case study examples from the city of Rotterdam in the Netherlands. The chapter concludes with some comparative case study lessons for policymakers and general conclusions for research on resilient urban redevelopment.

3.2   Conceptual Planning Policy Instruments

Policy instruments play a pivotal role in the delivery of resilient urban areas. The choice of policy instruments, however, is no easy matter for policymakers and legislators. This section conceptualises policy instruments by elaborating on some of the difficulties involved in choosing the 'right' policy instrument.

3.2.1   Classifications of Policy Instruments

Policy instruments can be classified. Classifications aim to illustrate the variety of policy instruments that can be applied to shape market behaviour in order to realise resilient urban redevelopment through office conversions. In policy terms, the vacancy of offices is a societal problem in major parts in the Netherlands (and many other countries); it has been designated by politicians as a policy problem. To reach its policy objectives, government chooses policy instruments. There are many different classifications of policy instruments. An extensive overview of classifications is given by Fobé *et al.* (2014) and by Schram (2005). Such classifications can be used for the analysis of policy, and can give insight into the instruments that are chosen in practice to steer the actions of actors within a policy area, such as the vacancy and reuse of offices. Thereby classifications also give insights into which instruments were *not* chosen (Fobé *et al.*, 2014: 63).

Table 3.1   Policy instruments: classification of the degree of pressure.

Degree of pressure	Examples of instrument
Coercion	Act, levy
Transaction	Agreement, subsidy
Persuasion	Advice, information

Source: Van den Heuvel, 2005: 23.

Some of the classifications are generic, which means they can be applied to any policy area. This is, for instance, the case for classification by discipline (Van den Heuvel, 2005). This is an often-used classification. It is a generic approach, which can be applied to any policy area in any country. The disciplines are:

- legal
- financial
- communication.

Each of the three disciplines can be subdivided, but for the purposes of this chapter, it not necessary to do so.

Another classification, by degree of pressure, is generic too (see Table 3.1), and can also be applied to any policy field.

Note that a classification by degree of pressure does not coincide with a classification of disciplines. For example, an act and an agreement are both legal instruments, but differ as far as degree of pressure is concerned.

A third and final classification to be discussed here, is by planning policy instruments (see Table 3.2).

This classification is not generic, but specific for the policy area of (spatial) planning, which makes it suitable for the topic of resilience in urban development. The classification of planning instruments is especially useful for the topic of this chapter since it specifies the impact of each of the four instruments on markets. As explained above, markets play an important role in the pursuance of resilient urban development and, in order to improve effectiveness, planners must behave as market actors that strategically deploy planning instruments to influence market behaviour (Heurkens *et al.*, 2015a). A further feature is that the classification of planning instruments incorporates a wide range of planning policy instruments. This includes 'capacity building', which essentially is a multi-governance form of facilitating, which in policy terms can be regarded as a form of policy formation.

3.2.2   Complications when Choosing a Policy Instrument

It is likely that the choice of one or more policy instruments is determined by the effectiveness of that instrument. However, there are complicating factors. The choice of a policy instrument is not entirely free. Some instruments come

Table 3.2 Policy instruments: classification of planning instrument.

Instrument	Impact on markets	Subtypes	Examples
Shaping	Shape decision environment of development actors by setting broad context for market actions and transactions	Development/ investment plans	Public (infrastructure) investment plans
		Regulatory plans	Statutory plans, policies, strategies
		Indicative plans	Non-statutory plans, policies, strategies
Regulatory	Constrain decision environment of development actors by regulating or controlling market actions and transactions	State/third party regulation	Planning permission, property rights
		Contractual regulation	Development agreements
Stimulus	Expand decision environment of development actors by facilitating market actions and transactions	Direct state actions	Reclamation, infrastructure, land acquisition
		Price-adjusting instruments	Grants, tax incentives, bonuses
		Risk-reducing instruments	Policy certainty, place management
		Capital-raising instruments	Loan guarantees, funds, partnerships
Capacity building	Enable development actors to operate more effectively within their decision environment and so facilitate the operation of other policy instruments	Market-shaping cultures, mind-sets, ideas	New perspectives, ways of thinking
		Market-rich information	Market/development process logics
		Market-rooted networks	Formal/informal interaction arenas
		Market-relevant skills	Human capital, individuals

Source: Heurkens *et al.*, 2015a: 631.

with more costs than others. For example, keeping a vacancy register (Dutch: *leegstandregister*) in the framework of a municipal vacancy ordinance (Dutch: *leegstandverordening*) comes with associated costs. High costs may make the choice of a policy instrument unattractive. Furthermore, one policy instrument may have more side effects than another instrument. For example, a subsidy for the demolition of vacant offices may give an incorrect signal to the owners–investors of these offices: the problems will be solved by the subsidy, and there is no need for owners–investors to take measures themselves under this policy instrument.

Moreover, it may be necessary to choose and design the policy instrument in consultation with actors in the policy area. If government is heavily dependent on private actors for the realisation of its policy, it is quite conceivable that these actors influence the choice of instrument(s). For example, if government wants to set up a fund for the demolition of vacant offices and this fund has to be largely filled by contributions from developers of new offices, it is necessary to gain the support of those developers. In sum, the choice of one or more policy instruments may depend on more factors than just the perceived effectiveness of each.

3.2.3   Policy Networks

As stated above, there may be circumstances under which it is necessary for policymakers to choose and design the policy instrument in consultation with the actors involved. Here, the concept of policy networks is useful (Van den Heuvel, 2005: 38; Klijn and Koppenjan, 2004: 11). A policy network envisages a policy problem happening in a network in which both public (municipalities, regional authorities) and private parties (investors, developers, builders, housing associations) are active.

The policy processes around the reuse of vacant offices occur in a policy network. According to Van den Heuvel (2005: 43) policy networks are appropriate:

> For policy problems where the policy actors are dependent on each other and thus co-production is needed, because no one of the policy actors by themselves have enough knowledge, expertise, powers and means to realise the intended policy;
>
> For new and complicated policy problems…;
>
> To steer complex policy areas – where many relationships of dependency exist and the steering of one actor has consequences for the other – from a central point…[1]

The office vacancy problem meets these suitability requirements. As far as the first point is concerned, the knowledge and expertise about vacant offices is spread over different actors. For example, local authorities are experts regarding legal procedures, and owner–investors have expertise regarding market potential. Both fields of expertise are necessary. As far as the second point is concerned, the existence of widespread office vacancies is a relatively new phenomenon in the Netherlands (and many other countries). Certainly, it is not a traditional problem with a proven 'solution'. As far as the third point is concerned, in the area of office vacancies there are many relationships of dependency, in which the actions of one actor can have consequences for another. For example, if a municipality selects locations for the development of new offices, this will be positive for developers, but in principle it will hinder the reuse of vacant offices, to the detriment of the owner–investors involved.

In sum, approaching a policy problem via a policy network appears to be an effective approach to understand actors' goals and move towards effective subsequent policy formation and development. Of course, in a network each actor will have their own goals; each therefore has their preferred policy (Van den Heuvel, 2005: 41). However, public and private actors generally

---

[1] Translation from original Dutch.

realise they are dependent on each other: to achieve their own goals, they will have to cooperate and search for common goals. For instance, on the one hand investors own vacant offices which have a relatively low financial value; they need government action to improve their situation or solve their problems. On the other hand, local authorities are confronted with problems regarding quality of life and safety issues in areas with widespread office vacancies and want to activate owner–investors to tackle these problems by investing in building adaption for new uses. Hence, in a policy network, the parties take note of each other's standpoints. Conflicts of interest will occur and – if things work out well – conflicts can be solved by negotiations and parties will formulate a policy to deal with the common problem (Van den Heuvel, 2005: 41). In effect, a policy network contributes to the successful implementation of policies. It is precisely the mutual dependence of parties that can be regarded as a stimulus to overcome conflicts between organisations. In addition, Van den Heuvel (2005: 39) states that the degree of dependency is also determined by the degree to which actors possess important or indispensable instruments or sources to attain the common policy goal. For example, only the municipality can change land-use plans or grant permits to deviate from a land-use plan (Hobma and Jong, 2016: 55). On the other hand, investors dispose of private investor capital, which is outside the sphere of influence of public organisations.

3.2.4 Effectiveness of Policy Instruments

The effectiveness of achieving urban resilience through office conversions based on the use of policy instruments is a difficult and complex matter to assess. It is often pointed out that the use of a singular instrument has limited effectiveness (Schram, 2005: 192). In many cases, the policymaker decides not to choose one instrument, but several at the same time. Indeed, using several instruments at the same time can be effective in attaining a policy goal. The idea is that instruments complement each other (Van den Heuvel, 2005: 29).

To be more precise, the variety of possible instruments (see Section 3.2.1) raises the question of which instruments are suitable for which situation. Under what circumstances should a particular instrument, or mix of instruments, be chosen? This question lies in the field of instrument theory and – in general – is very hard to answer (Schram, 2005: 190). The work of Klok (1991) shows that many factors influence the success of a policy instrument. One cannot simply say, for situation X, policy instrument A (in combination with policy instrument B) is the most suitable way to achieve a given policy goal. Klok (1991: 403), in his instrument theory, distinguishes three groups of variables that influence the effectiveness of a policy instrument:

1. the characteristics of the actual policy instruments
2. the variables that determine the process of policy implementation
3. the variables that determine the process in the policy field.

So far, this chapter has framed 'resilient urban development' and conceptualised planning policy instruments. After these rather theoretical notions, it is now time to turn to the empirical side of planning policy instruments used for resilient urban development. For this purpose, the case of the city of Rotterdam in the Netherlands is used. Rotterdam can be seen as a national and international frontrunner in the re-use of vacant offices. The city is confronted with substantial numbers of office vacancies, but has been remarkably successful in its policy of having owner–investors re-use vacant real estate (Remøy *et al.*, 2015).

3.3   Planning Policy Instruments in Rotterdam

Rotterdam is the Netherlands' second biggest city. Since 2008, vacancy rates in the office market have increased to almost 20%. The municipality of Rotterdam had the task of choosing policy instruments to combat the vacancy of offices, promote their re-use and thereby increase urban resilience by improved spatial quality and liveability of the city centre. Hereafter, we discuss the various policy instruments and related activities used recently to align public and market interests in relation to office conversion. Then we outline two case studies of office conversion.

3.3.1   Covenant, Land-use Plan and Transformation Team

In this section, we reflect on the Rotterdam 'Covenant for Tackling Office Vacancy' (Dutch: *Convenant Aanpak Kantorenleegstand*) (Karakus, 2011). The Rotterdam covenant was part of the city's vacancy policy from 2011 to 2014 and was reflected in the new programme vacancy policy, wherein the municipality stated its aim to match planned new developments with demand, use new construction to improve urban quality, deploy temporary use and conversions for urban redevelopment, and to continue stimulating and acquiring conversions in collaboration with market parties. This covenant is the central policy instrument that was used by the municipality of Rotterdam to tackle the vacancy of offices. It used a transformation team assigned by the Rotterdam Department of Urban Development to stimulate land-use change developments, including conversions from offices to housing.

The covenant between the municipality and market parties:

- gave targets for floorspace to be converted
- stated that floorspace converted should be higher than square metres for new-build offices
- stated that knowledge sharing between the municipality and market parties should be increased and that the municipality should become a knowledge centre facilitating private parties.

The covenant upheld the concept of 'best-effort obligations'. This means that no 'hard targets' were given for the market parties, and no measures would be taken to penalise parties who did not adhere to the covenant. As such, the covenant was intended to get market parties moving. The municipality had the idea that attaching hard targets to the covenant would result in endless conferring with lawyers but little change, whereas with the covenant, the different actors involved became enthusiastic and took action right away (Remøy *et al.*, 2015).

Meanwhile, during the covenant term, national legislative changes were implemented that favoured conversions. It is necessary to elaborate on these changes as they affect the way other planning tools can be used by municipalities to support conversions. The most important changes were made as part of the Building Decree 2012, which set a new (lower minimum) quality level for conversions and renovations. Another important amendment was made to the Environmental Law Decree 2014 (Dutch: *Besluit Omgevingsrecht*). This effectively enabled the terms of the land-use plan to be waived more easily. Additionally, the required timespan of municipal procedures was shortened. In this way, municipalities gained more freedom to promote conversions. After a change to the Environmental Planning Decree (in November 2014) the land-use plan (Dutch: *bestemmingsplan*) lost some of its effect too. Although the municipality had to approve all land-use changes, the land-use change application (for conversions) no longer had to be accompanied by a spatial quality justification, as was the case before 2012. This means that, although planners can reject a conversion scheme, it cannot be rejected based on the (lack of) quality of the development. Hence, unsustainable and lower-quality conversions can be developed in undesirable places, far removed from social facilities or local infrastructure.

Other important issues for Dutch municipal planning departments with regard to office conversions, are managing the demand for new uses and maintaining or upgrading the architectural and technical quality of the converted buildings. Particularly in central urban areas, the municipality defines spatial and building quality as criteria for land-use change, in order to enhance the attractiveness of the city. However, after recent amendments, changes to the land-use plan cannot be rejected because of insufficient spatial, urban, and architectural quality. Nonetheless, some municipal planning tools still exist to manage urban development. Municipal parking regulations can be used, together with air quality and noise nuisance regulations, the Architectural Review Committee's advice, and, in the case of listed buildings, the Cultural Heritage Preservation Act (which is legally binding). Altogether, though, it has become more difficult for municipalities to steer urban development according to local wishes. Whereas the planning regulations have become simpler on the wider scale, the changes have resulted in less room to manoeuvre for local government.

For the municipality of Rotterdam, stimulating building conversion as an approach to reduce office vacancies, increase housing density and enhance spatial quality in the city centre and wider urban areas has worked out well. Due to the pro-active involvement of the Department of Urban Development, more than 300,000 m² of vacant offices were

Table 3.3 National measures and measures taken by the municipality of Rotterdam to increase conversion potential.

Measures	Aims
Covenant – part of vacancy policy	Match planned new developments with demand, use new construction to improve urban quality, deploy temporary use and conversions for urban redevelopment, and continue stimulating and acquiring conversions in collaboration with market parties
Creation of specific 'transformation team' to increase dialogue, co-creation and cooperation	Increase cooperation, streamline processes, increase private involvement
Building decree 2012; specific quality level for conversion	Reduce costs of conversions
Environmental law decree 2014	Enable the terms of the land-use plan to be waived more easily; shorten time span of procedures
Land-use planning policy amendments	Changes to land-use plan cannot be rejected because of insufficient spatial, urban, or architectural quality

converted into housing and other functions from 2011 to 2015 (Gemeente Rotterdam, 2015). The municipality has so far kept control over planning. At the end of the covenant, all of the initial targets set were achieved. While traditional planning tools, such as strict environmental and land-use plans and building decrees are losing their effect, the municipality of Rotterdam has developed its own planning tools to steer land use, remedying some of the restrictions that the changes enacted by national government have placed on those responsible for planning and development at the local level. These so-called 'soft' tools (Table 3.3)are based on decision-making by agreement and acceptance, in a process consisting of dialogue, co-creation and cooperation. These tools are based on trust and transparency.

Heurkens *et al.* (2014; 2015b) argue that the Rotterdam Department of Urban Development gradually adopted a facilitating role, assisting market actors in the city to make development and investment decisions. The usefulness of this facilitating role is made clear by the fact that cooperation between the municipality and market parties improved significantly in the period in which the covenant was effective (Remøy *et al.*, 2015). The market parties who had signed the covenant felt involved and responsible. All market parties reported being pleased with the work of the 'transformation team' – the team assigned to pull together land-use change developments – and ascribed successful redevelopments partly to its work. Cooperation in urban redevelopment was the main success factor. Although many obstacles to conversions were removed at the municipal level, private parties still see strict building regulations and procedures as bottlenecks.

3.3.2   Examples of Office Building Conversions in Rotterdam

To illustrate the use of policy instruments to change building use, hereafter two office conversion cases in Rotterdam are discussed: Admiraliteit and Student Hotel (see overview in Table 3.4).

The redevelopment of the former Admiraliteit office building (see Figure 3.1) was initiated by two local developers, ABB and U Vastgoed. Together with the Rotterdam municipality they set up a planning team and proposed a land-use plan change. City Pads was added to the team as a concept developer and end-user annex property manager. ABB and City Pads were involved in the development, and IM Bouwfonds was introduced as an investor after completion. City Pads remained property manager. Despite changes in the team, the process went smoothly. The planning team started in July 2013, and the concept design was submitted in September. The final design and the building permit application were completed in June 2014, after which the permit was issued in July 2014. The municipality advised that meetings should be organised to inform neighbours about the project, and these were held by the developer parties. There were two objections to the development. The developer approached the objectors and found acceptable solutions, and the process was not unduly delayed. The municipality had some requirements for the project that were not anticipated by the developer:

- to increase the quality and size of the houses, reducing the number of houses that could be created
- an adjustment to the facade necessary for the exterior appearance of the building.

Specific fire-safety requirements imposed considerable (unforeseen) costs. The municipality was closely involved in the entire conversion process, and

Table 3.4   Office building conversions in Rotterdam.

Project/building	Admiraliteit	Student Hotel – Former premises of Social Affairs and Labour
Address	Admiraliteitskade 40–50–60 3063 ED Rotterdam	Oostzeedijk 182–220 3063 BM Rotterdam
Sqm floor area	31,400 GFA 27,475 converted LFA	8,451 converted LFA
Residential function/ units	587 studios/apartments 2 commercial spaces	Student housing
Initiator	ABB; U Vastgoed	Student Hotel (1st phase) Van Omme and de Groot (2nd phase)
Owner	IM Bouwfonds	Student Hotel

Based on Kops (2014) and Gemeente Rotterdam (2015).

(a)

(b)

Figure 3.1   De Admiraliteit: (a) during construction and (b) after completion (source: Remøy).

drew up the agreement on development contributions for the recovery of infrastructure costs, started the land-use plan changes, supported the developing parties in drafting the environmental building permit application, helped in obtaining the building site permit and guided the construction management.

The conversion to the Student Hotel took place in two phases. The first building was purchased by Student Hotel itself, the second was purchased by local developer Van Omme and De Groot through a public tender held by the municipality, and was sold to Student Hotel after the conversion. The process of the first phase was delayed by a disagreement with the committee for building aesthetics (Dutch: *Welstandscommissie*) and a complaint from a local resident against the new use and changes in the facade. The conversion of the second phase went somewhat better, and things like the environmental studies could be reapplied directly from the first phase. Meanwhile, between the first and second phases, the parking ratio for the area was decreased. The municipality was closely involved in the transformation process, and co-operated in changing the land-use plan, and advised on the process. In addition, the municipality occasionally helped to accelerate the development process by assessing the plan changes informally, to avoid further disagreements with the committee for building aesthetics and the neighbours. Because of this, it took some time before the environmental building permit was obtained. Nowadays, the Student Hotel functions as a popular source of housing for foreign students studying at the Erasmus University, due to its proximity to the university campus, and the high quality of the rooms and the amenities and services.

3.4   Classifying and Evaluating Policy Instruments in Rotterdam

The previous section discussed some of the instruments used in Rotterdam to encourage conversion of offices into housing in order to make the city resilient to economic and market changes. A particular focus was the Rotterdam 'Covenant Tackling Office Vacancy'. This section evaluates the policy instruments used in Rotterdam by classifying them in accordance with the approach in Section 3.2.1. Lessons are then drawn about the effectiveness of the mix of policy instruments used in Rotterdam to reduce office vacancies and increase urban resilience.

3.4.1   Classifying Rotterdam Office Conversion Policy Instruments

Table 3.5 indicates the main policy instruments used in the conversion of offices in Rotterdam from 2011–2015, brought in relation to the main policy instrument classifications used in literature.

The Rotterdam covenant, in terms of discipline, is in the 'legal' policy instrument category. As said, a covenant in essence is an agreement. It can be an agreement between administrative authorities, or between an administrative authority and societal or private organisations (as is the case for the Rotterdam covenant). A characteristic of a covenant is that the status of the agreements (whether or not legally binding) is determined by the covenant itself (Van den Heuvel, 2005: 65). However, the degree to which this covenant binds anyone is small (only an obligation to make an effort, rather than an obligation to achieve an outcome. In terms of the degree of pressure, the Rotterdam covenant belongs in the 'transaction' category, again because a covenant in essence is an agreement. Since the existence of vacant offices is

Table 3.5   Classification of policy instruments used in Rotterdam office conversion.

Policy instrument	Discipline	Degree of pressure	Planning instrument
	(Van den Heuvel, 2005)	(Van den Heuvel, 2005)	(Heurkens *et al.*, 2015a)
Covenant 'Tackling Office Vacancy'	Legal	Transaction	Regulatory; contractual regulation
Policy network 'Platform Market Sector'	Communication	Persuasion	Capacity building; market-rich information
Land-use plan	Legal	Coercion	Regulatory; state/third-party regulation
Transformation team	Communicative	Persuasion	Capacity building; market and development process logics

seen as a planning problem, the Rotterdam covenant is in the 'planning policy instrument' category and can been seen as a 'regulatory instrument', the subtype being 'contractual regulation'. This again follows from the covenant being an agreement.

The policy network around office vacancies in Rotterdam is known as the 'Platform Market Sector' (Dutch: *Platform Marktsector*) (Remøy *et al.*, 2015: 8). In this network, the policy goals and the policy instruments were chosen more or less collectively. The local authorities, in the formulation of the policy and the choice of instrument, did not stand above the other parties, but between them. All parties who undersigned the Rotterdam covenant, are members of the policy network 'Platform Market Sector' (Remøy *et al.*, 2015: 8). The policy instrument that resulted from the inter-actions between the parties in the Rotterdam policy network around office vacancies (as described in the previous section) is the Covenant Tackling Office Vacancy (Karakus, 2011). Therefore, the Platform Market Sector policy network can be classified being communicative, a form of persuasion, and a capacity building planning policy instrument that provided market-rich information to help develop the covenant.

Additionally, in Rotterdam the land-use plan was used to alter the functional destinations of vacant office buildings from office to housing, hotel, mixed-use and so on. This represented 'coercion' as the degree of pressure involved and the 'legal' discipline. In terms of planning policy instruments, the plan can be regarded as a 'regulatory' instrument, used by the local public authority to enable or permit changes of use and actual office conversions. Nonetheless, as can be seen in the Rotterdam case, this regulatory tool was applied flexibly instead of strictly, with an acceleration of the number of office conversion building permits issued the result.

An important policy instrument used in Rotterdam was the municipal Transformation Team. This team acted as a first point of contact for questions regarding office conversions from market actors. Moreover, it played a role in accelerating the city's internal decision-making process on land-use plan changes. This 'soft' instrument can be placed in the 'communications' and 'persuasive' categories. The team aimed to understand market needs and the obstacles regarding office conversions. This made it a 'capacity-building' policy instrument, which enabled public planners to understand the logic of the market and development process.

3.4.2   Evaluating Rotterdam Office Conversion Policy Instruments

In Rotterdam's policy on the reuse of vacant offices there is no use of 'vertical instruments', such as municipal ordinances. As is evident from the evaluation of the Rotterdam covenant, neither the municipality nor the private parties see any use in the deployment of vertical instruments (Remøy et al., 2015: 4). As far as the choice of a covenant as policy instrument for the municipal approach to office vacancy is concerned, 73% of real estate professionals that participated in a survey indicated that a covenant was a very helpful approach (Remøy et al., 2015: 18). In-depth interviews with people involved with the Rotterdam reuse policy revealed, however, that private parties were more positive about the use of a covenant than municipal civil servants. Municipal civil servants were less positive, because with a covenant it is difficult to determine whether changes in vacancy levels are the result of the covenant or unrelated factors (Remøy et al., 2015: 24, 28). Private parties acknowledge this, but value the covenant because it is a good means to bring all parties together. Further, the private parties appreciate that the process of making a covenant implies that they are helping develop municipal policy (Remøy et al., 2015: 24, 28).

In Rotterdam, the interactions between the public and private parties in the policy network around office vacancy led to the use of a covenant as policy instrument. The covenant was evaluated and this proved that it achieved the goals intended for it (Remøy et al., 2015). We conclude – as far as the choice of a covenant is concerned – with the following observations:

- Use of a policy network appears to be a good choice, because the suitability requirements for policy networks were met.
- The choice of a covenant as policy instrument was a logical result of the policy processes in the policy network.
- The chosen instrument, the covenant, was widely supported by the private sector participants, who they did not want strict governmental rules (Remøy et al., 2015: 4).
- Measured in terms of its own goals, the covenant was effective.

It is very difficult to make statements about the effectiveness of the covenant as compared to possible alternative instruments (or mixes of instruments). Nevertheless, the additional use in Rotterdam of policy instruments such as the land-use plan and the transformation team – mostly tailored to individual office conversion cases, in contrast to the city-wide covenant and policy network – reveals that a mix of policy instruments at different decision-making levels might be a precondition for effective office conversions.

3.5 Conclusions

This chapter has elaborated on the use of planning policy instruments for resilient urban redevelopment by examining the ability of public and private stakeholders to respond to changes in real estate market demand by adapting existing offices to new uses. From the literature, it is clear that in order for Rotterdam stakeholders to handle resilience issues in their particular context, they needed to use policy instruments in a cooperative manner, with multi-level governance efforts. Moreover, (public) planners, in their efforts to redevelop urban areas in a resilient manner, should understand markets and deploy planning instruments in such a manner that private actors will make voluntary decisions in favour of office conversions. Office conversions contribute to increasing the societal and economic resilience of the city, by giving space for new target groups and ensuring economic viability. In addition, the literature review illustrates a wide range of policy instruments should be considered so as to achieve effective office conversion practices, and that it is likely that in particular contexts a mix of instruments will be necessary.

The Rotterdam case study illustrates that such conceptual elaborations and assumptions can be empirically justified. What becomes clear is that making urban areas more resilient – with affordable housing for students and new city centre apartments for communities – through converting obsolescent offices to new uses requires an effective mix of hard and soft planning policy instruments. These instruments need to be aligned with market needs at both city and local-development levels, and combines policy formation with policy implementation measures. Generally, this implies that cities and its stakeholders have to search for their own specific mix of planning policy instruments to cope with their resilience challenges. Therefore, different approaches may be needed elsewhere. Additionally, future research in the field might focus on the relationship between public planning policies and private market decisions, as this chapter proves that meeting various built environment resilience challenges necessitates collective efforts, which can partly be achieved by deploying planning policy instruments in an effective manner.

References

Allan, P. and Bryant, M. (2011) Resilience as a framework for urbanism and recovery, *Journal of Landscape Architecture*, 6(2): 34–45.

Blakely, E.J. (2014) Leadership for sustainability and sustainable leadership. In: L.J. Pearson, P.W. Newton, and P. Roberts (eds), *Resilient Sustainable Cities: A Future*, Routledge.

Bullen, P.A. (2007) Adaptive reuse and sustainability of commercial office buildings, *Facilities*, 24(1–2): 20–31.

Christensen, P.H. and Sayce, S.L. (2014) Planning and regulatory issues impacting sustainable property development. In: S.J. Wilkinson, S.L. Sayce and P.H. Christensen (eds), *Developing Property Sustainably*, Routledge.

De Jong, M., Joss, S., Schraven, D., Zhan, C. and Weijnen, N. (2015) Sustainable-smart-resilient-low carbon-eco-knowledge cities; making sense of a multitude of concepts promoting sustainable urbanization, *Journal of Cleaner Production*, 109: 25–38.

Fobé, E., Brans, M. and Wayenberg, E. (2014) *Beleidsinstrumenten: Theoretische perspectieven en keuzemodellen*, Steunpunt Bestuur Organisatie – Slagkrachtige overheid.

Gaaff, E. (2015) Flood resiliency in urban area development: The performance of flood resiliency policies in waterfront development projects – a comparative study of Rotterdam and New York City. Master's thesis, Delft University of Technology.

Gemeente Rotterdam (2015) De Nieuwe Transformatie Aanpak Kantoren Rotterdam 2016–2020, Rotterdam, Gemeente Rotterdam.

Heurkens, E.W.T.M., Hoog, W. de and Daamen, T.A. (2014) De Kennismotor: Initiatieven tot faciliteren en leren in de Rotterdamse gebiedsontwikkelingsprak-tijk. Working paper, TU Delft.

Heurkens, E.W.T.M., Adams, D. and Hobma, F.A.M. (2015a) Planners as market actors: the role of local planning authorities in the UKs urban regeneration practice, *Town Planning Review*, 86(6): 625–50.

Heurkens, E.W.T.M., Daamen, T.A. and Pol, P.J. (2015b). Faciliteren als basis: Lessen uit Rotterdam. *Ruimtelijke Ontwikkeling Magazine*, 33(1), 30–33.

Hobma, F.A.M. and Jong, P. (2016) *Planning and Development Law in the Netherlands; An Introduction,* IBR.

Johnstone, I.M. (1995) An actuarial model of rehabilitation versus new construction of housing, *Journal of Property Finance*, 6(3): 7–26.

Karakus, H. and the municipality of Rotterdam (2011) *Convenant Aanpak Kantorenleegstand*, Rotterdam.

Klijn, E.H. and Koppenjan J. (2004) *Managing Uncertainties in Networks: A Network Approach to Problem Solving and Decision Making*, Routledge.

Klok, P.-J. (1991) *Een instrumententheorie voor milieubeleid; De toepassing en effectiviteit van beleidsinstrumenten*, Faculteit der Bestuurskunde, Universiteit Twente.

Kops, L.H. (2014) Overheidsbeleid bij leegstand van kantoren. Master's thesis, Delft, Delft University of Technology.

Newton, P.W. and Doherty, P. (2014) The challenges to urban sustainability and resilience. In: L.J. Pearson, P.W. Newton, and P. Roberts (eds), *Resilient sustainable cities: A future*, Routledge.

Pearson, L.J., Newton, P.W. and Roberts, P. (eds) (2014) *Resilient Sustainable Cities: A Future*, Routledge.

Raco, M. and Street, E. (2012) Resilience planning, economic change and the politics of post-recession development in London and Hong Kong, *Urban Studies*, 49(5): 1065–1087.

Remøy, H. (2015) Building obsolescence and reuse. In: S.J. Wilkinson, H. Remøy, and G. Langston (eds), *Sustainable Building Adaptation: Innovations in Decision-making*, Wiley.

Remøy, H., Pallada, R., Hobma, F. and Franzen, A. (2015) *Evaluatie Convenant Aanpak Kantorenleegstand Rotterdam: Monitoring, lessen en aanbevelingen*, TU Delft, Faculteit Bouwkunde, Management in the Built Environment.

Roberts, P. (2014) Governance for resilient, sustainable cities and communities: concepts and some cases. In: L.J. Pearson, P.W. Newton, and P. Roberts (eds), *Resilient Sustainable Cities: A Future*, Routledge.

Roggema, R. (2014) The plan and the policy: who is changing whom?. In: L.J. Pearson, P.W. Newton, and P. Roberts (eds), *Resilient Sustainable Cities: A Future*, Routledge.

Schram, F. (2005) *Het sturen van de samenleving: Mogelijkheden van een beleidsinstrumentenbenadering*, Bestuurlijke Organisatie Vlaanderen – Steunpunt Beleidsrelevant Onderzoek.

Van den Heuvel, J.H.J. (2005) *Beleidsinstrumentatie: Sturingsinstrumenten voor het overheidsbeleid*, Lemma.

Van der Heijden, J. (2014) *Governance for Urban Sustainability and Resilience: Responding to Climate Change and the Relevance of the Built Environment*, Edward Elgar.

Wilkinson, S.J., Remøy, H. and Langston, G. (eds) (2014) *Sustainable Building Adaptation: Innovations in Decision-making*, Wiley.

Wiseman, J. and Edwards, T. (2012) *Post carbon pathways: Reviewing post carbon economy transition strategies*, Centre for Policy Development and Melbourne Sustainable Society Institute.

Adaptation and Demolition in a Masterplan Context

Hannah Baker[1] and Alice Moncaster[2]
[1] *University of Cambridge*
[2] *Open University*

4.1 Introduction

Increasing populations and a trend towards urbanisation worldwide are both increasing the pressure on urban areas to provide sufficient housing whilst managing the built environment sustainably (Karantonis, 2008). In the UK, the recently published White Paper and the Housing and Planning Act 2016 emphasise the need to release brownfield land for new development (DCLG, 2017; HM Government, 2016a). Whilst brownfield sites can range from small plots with one building, to larger areas with multiple buildings (Dixon *et al.*, 2008), this chapter explores adaptation and demolition on larger, masterplan regeneration sites, which have the potential to make transformative change within the city (Meerow *et al.*, 2016). 'Masterplan' is a frequently used term, but there is no general definition (CABE, 2011). Often a masterplan will show the concept of a development including the massing of buildings and connections of streets (CABE, 2011). For the purposes of this research, the UK Government's definition of large-scale major developments is used. For example, for residential areas these are developments that will have two-hundred or more dwellings or over four hectares if dwelling counts are unknown (DCLG, 2007; HM Government, 2016b; SODC, 2016).

Decision-making on these larger sites sits within the context of national and local policy and involves a far higher degree of complexity than is required for individual buildings (Baker and Moncaster, 2017; Mok *et al.*, 2015). Current decision-making frameworks, which tend to focus on individual buildings, are generally not appropriate for masterplan regeneration

Building Urban Resilience through Change of Use, First Edition.
Edited by Sara J. Wilkinson and Hilde Remøy.
© 2018 John Wiley & Sons Ltd. Published 2018 by John Wiley & Sons Ltd.

sites (Baker *et al.*, 2017). The different buildings within the curtilage of the site will often be considered for different adaptation options, including:

- demolition
- part demolition and adapt
- modify
- refurbish and adapt
- part extend (Wilkinson, 2011).

The inherent complexity of considering multiple buildings at the same time is increased by the additional relationship between the masterplan and urban infrastructure, as consideration of factors such as utilities, ecological green space and transportation can affect the decisions being made about individual buildings (Meerow *et al.*, 2016).

4.2   Literature Review

4.2.1   Factors Affecting the Decision to Demolish or Adapt

Concerns about how best to decide on demolition or adaptation are increasingly common in the developed world, and there is considerable academic research in this area (Baker *et al.*, 2017; Bullen and Love, 2011; Power, 2008; Wilkinson *et al.*, 2014; Yung and Chan, 2012). Figure 4.1 maps the locations of the primary authors reviewed in this field. The authors are also from a range of disciplinary backgrounds and university departments, including building surveying, civil engineering, construction management, architecture, real estate, and urban economics and sociology. This indicates the multi-disciplinary nature of the topic and suggests a need to look at decision-making in an inter-disciplinary manner.

Several authors consider the different types and levels of adaptation and demolition (Baker *et al.*, 2017; Douglas, 2006; Wilkinson, 2011). Duffy and Henney (1989) developed a model showing the different layers associated with the adaptation of an individual building, which was later updated by Brand (1994) and has been frequently cited since (Borst, 2014; Douglas, 2006; Gosling *et al.*, 2013; Kelly *et al.*, 2011; Lacovidou and Purnell, 2016; Schmidt III *et al.*, 2010; Wilkinson, 2011). This model is adapted in, which reinterprets the layers and plots them against the different time-scales of adaptation identified by Schmidt III *et al.* (2010). One example is building services, which often have a shorter timescale of intervention (7–15 years) and will change more regularly than the facade of the building (20 years) as they require more regular updates and a lower degree of intervention (Schmidt III *et al.*, 2010) (Figure 4.2).

These layers have links to the technical and physical aspects of individual buildings. Wilkinson (2011) suggests that certain physical aspects of buildings can enable adaptation. For example, the optimal building height of office buildings is found to be eleven to twenty storeys, while the most readily adaptable structural system is a concrete frame construction.

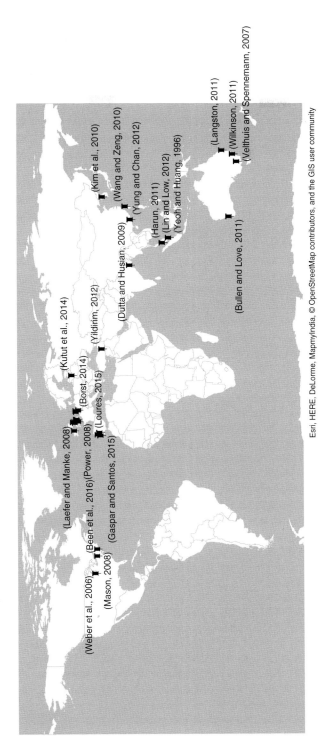

Figure 4.1 Location of primary authors discussing adaptive re-use and heritage value in the academic literature. Source: Baker and Moncaster.

Esri, HERE, DeLorme, MapmyIndia, © OpenStreetMap contributors, and the GIS user community

(Weber et al., 2006)
(Mason, 2008)
(Been et al., 2016)(Power, 2008)
(Gaspar and Santos, 2015)
(Laefer and Manke, 2008)
(Kutut et al., 2014)
(Borst, 2014)
(Loures, 2015)
(Yildirim, 2012)
(Dutta and Husian, 2009)
(Kim et al., 2010)
(Wang and Zeng, 2010)
(Yung and Chan, 2012)
(Harun, 2011)
(Lin and Low, 2012)
(Yeoh and Huang, 1996)
(Langston, 2011)
(Wilkinson, 2011)
(Velthuis and Spennemann, 2007)
(Bullen and Love, 2011)

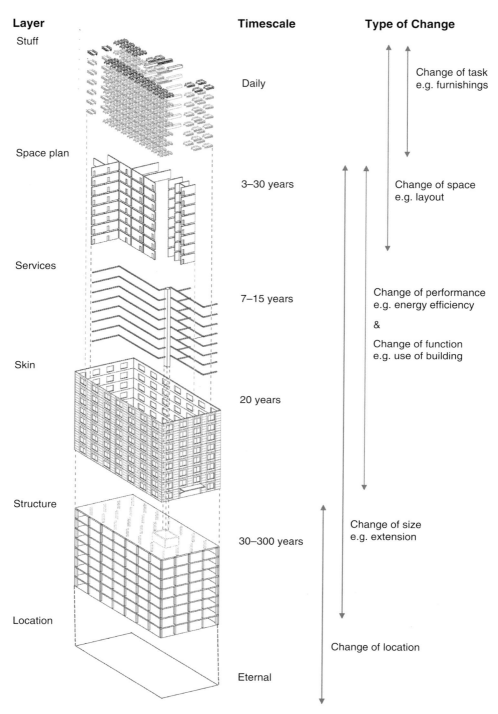

Figure 4.2 An individual building's layers and the associated timescale of adaptation. Source: Baker and Moncaster, adapted and developed from Brand (1994) and Schmidt III *et al.* (2010).

Meanwhile poor building condition is commonly given as the reason for choosing demolition and new build rather than adaptation, which carries associated increases in cost and risk (Bullen and Love, 2011; Plimmer *et al.*, 2008). Reasons for the poor condition typically include rising and penetrating damp, poor workmanship, vandalism, structural instability, age-related deterioration, and outdated services (IStructE, 2008). In practice, technical feasibility and costs are both considered alongside other influencing factors, including aesthetics, historical importance, planning polices, development trends in the area, energy efficiency and life-cycle impacts (Baker and Moncaster, 2017).

4.2.2   Stakeholder Viewpoints

The factors identified in the previous section will have varying levels of importance for the different stakeholders involved in the decision process. There are a range of stakeholders in the decision to demolish or adapt buildings, each with differing priorities and powers (Baker and Moncaster, 2017; Langston and Smith, 2012; Wilkinson, 2011). Although some of these may consider the same criteria as important, this may be for very different reasons. Through interviews with key stakeholders, Baker and Moncaster (2017) found that five different stakeholder groups mentioned designations, planning policies, capital costs, building structures and building condition as important.

However, whilst designations (such as listing a building to protect it from demolition) were regularly mentioned as important by town planners and heritage societies because of the safeguards they represent, some property consultants were concerned that designations might cause delays and extra costs.

4.2.3 Weighting Multiple Criteria

Throughout the academic literature a range of methods have been used to weight criteria. For example:

- Kutut *et al.* (2014) used an analytical hierarchy process consisting of pairwise comparison techniques
- Dutta and Husain (2009) used Barron's rank-order centroid method, which involves selecting the mid-point from a range of weights identified
- Lin and Low (2012) used a seven-point Likert scale.

All of these methods are susceptible to subjectivity and uncertainty, as reflected in the studies by Kim *et al.* (2010) and Bullen (2007). Kim *et al.* (2010) applied a beta distribution to an analytical hierarchy process to reflect the varying preferences (Jalao *et al.*, 2014), whereas Bullen (2007) asked survey respondents to score different factors in decision-making as a barrier or a benefit. The results showed that a factor that some respondents interpreted as negative was seen by others as a positive. For example, just under 60% of respondents felt that the 'planning approval process' was a barrier and approximately 40% interpreted it as a benefit. This links to the comment made above regarding designations and how some will perceive them as a safeguard, whereas others perceive them to be a hindrance in the decision-making process. This factor, in particular, will be heavily influenced by the objectives of the local planning authorities, which can vary by location within the country. In all cases, the stakeholders' perceptions of the factors proposed by Bullen (2007) were influenced by personal preferences and stakeholder roles (Plimmer *et al.*, 2008).

4.2.4   Current Decision-making Tools and Frameworks

To assist with the complexities of the decision-making process, various toolkits and/or frameworks have been developed. These allow users to assess the adaptability potential of buildings (Conejos *et al.*, 2013; Geraedts and Van der Voordt, 2007; Langston and Smith, 2012; Wilkinson *et al.*, 2014). Baker *et al.* (2017) assessed two of these tools, the Transformation Meter (Geraedts and Van der Voordt, 2007) and IconCUR (Langston and Smith, 2012), against five UK case studies, three of which were individual buildings and two of which were multi-building masterplan sites.

The Transformation Meter uses criteria about both the building and the location to score the adaptation potential of individual buildings. One case of a former warehouse was scored by the Transformation Meter as of limited transformability. However, due to the heritage value attached to the building, in real life, the technical challenges were overcome and the building was retained. For the two masterplan case studies, all of the buildings were scored by this tool as having moderate or excellent transformability potential. In reality, 9 out of the 19 buildings analysed across the two sites were demolished. The reasons for demolition were often beyond the tool's framework, as access onto the site as part of the masterplan's transportation network and planning policy, which varies with the geographical context, were often not considered. IconCUR produced the same discrepancies, for similar reasons (Baker *et al.*, 2017). Overall, the studies showed that the tools were appropriate for their intended use of assessing individual office buildings, but that significant adjustments were required when using them on masterplan sites or if different uses were involved.

The increased complexity of decision-making at the masterplan level is emphasised by the Building Research Establishment's Environmental Assessment Method (BREEAM) for Communities 2012 toolkit (BRE, 2012). This framework uses multiple criteria to score a large-scale development using issues relating to sustainable development. Categories which are analysed include: governance; social and economic wellbeing; resources and energy; land use and ecology and transport and movement. One of the issues within the 'resources and energy' category is 'Existing buildings and infrastructure', which has just two credits out of the overall 118 available (Figure 4.3). Although it can be argued that 'existing buildings and infrastructure' is not

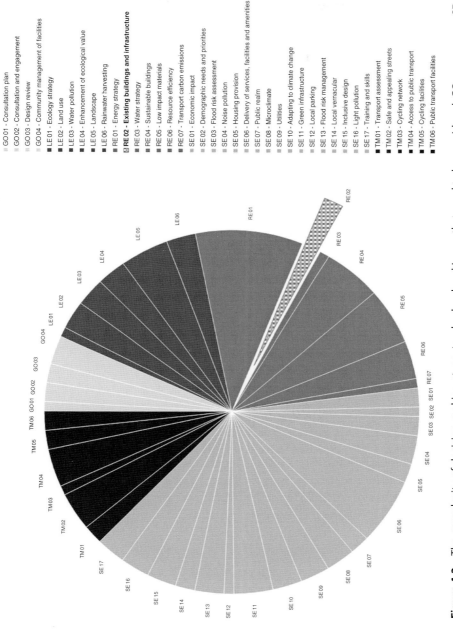

Figure 4.3 The complexity of decision-making at masterplan level and issues that need to be considered. GO, governance; SE, social and economic wellbeing; RE, Resources and energy; LE, land-use and ecology; TM, transport and movement. Image from Baker and Moncaster, BRE (2012).

GO 01 - Consultation plan
GO 02 - Consultation and engagement
GO 03 - Design review
GO 04 - Community management of facilities
LE 01 - Ecology strategy
LE 02 - Land use
LE 03 - Water pollution
LE 04 - Enhancement of ecological value
LE 05 - Landscape
LE 06 - Rainwater harvesting
RE 01 - Energy strategy
RE 02 - Existing buildings and infrastructure
RE 03 - Water strategy
RE 04 - Sustainable buildings
RE 05 - Low impact materials
RE 06 - Resource efficiency
RE 07 - Transport carbon emissions
SE 01 - Economic impact
SE 02 - Demographic needs and priorities
SE 03 - Flood risk assessment
SE 04 - Noise pollution
SE 05 - Housing provision
SE 06 - Delivery of services, facilities and amenities
SE 07 - Public realm
SE 08 - Microclimate
SE 09 - Utilities
SE 10 - Adapting to climate change
SE 11 - Green infrastructure
SE 12 - Local parking
SE 13 - Flood risk management
SE 14 - Local vernacular
SE 15 - Inclusive design
SE 16 - Light pollution
SE 17 - Training and skills
TM 01 - Transport assessment
TM 02 - Safe and appealing streets
TM 03 - Cycling network
TM 04 - Access to public transport
TM 05 - Cycling facilities
TM 06 - Public transport facilities

mutually exclusive from the other categories, the number of issues analysed emphasises that the decision at the masterplan level is part of a complex system whereby many different aspects need to be considered and balanced alongside one another.

4.3 Methodology

The purpose of this chapter is to explore the range of decisions and the reasons behind them when considering demolition and adaptation on a masterplan site in which multiple buildings are affected. The chapter builds upon existing studies on adaptive reuse and demolition at an individual building level (see Baker and Moncaster, 2017). It was recognised by Wilkinson (2011: 56) that, 'the numerous stakeholders and their perspectives do influence individual adaptation cases', and this research uses an interpretative research approach in order to 'capture information about the beliefs, actions and experiences of stakeholders involved in the decision-making process' (Bullen and Love, 2011: 35).

Stakeholder interviews and three case studies provide a rich set of data. Two of the case studies are those initially analysed by Baker *et al.* (2017). For each case study, media articles, planning documentation and other publicly available evidence have been examined alongside interviews with the stakeholders who had an active involvement in the decisions made. The additional 'general interviews' were held with those who had had a similar decision-making role in other projects. All interviews are summarised in Table 4.1.

The case studies were selected to meet the predefined parameters in Table 4.2, and with the necessary collaboration of stakeholders who were willing to share experiences (McLeod, 2014). A brief description of each case study site, including a quantification of the number of buildings demolished and/or retained, is shown in Table 4.3.

Table 4.1 Summary of interviews.

	General interviews	Case study interviews
Architects and urban designers	—	4
Commercial agents and property consultants	4	1
Developers and freehold owners	—	5
Ecologists	—	1
Engineers; building surveyors and regulations officers	4	5
Heritage societies	7	—
Local and regional authority staff	3	5
Members of local campaign groups	—	2
Planning and heritage consultants	3	4
Total	21	27

Table 4.2 Case study parameters.

Parameter	Justification for parameter
Size of site: two-hundred or more residential dwellings or over 4 ha if dwellings counts are unknown; or for other uses, such as commercial, the floor area is over 10,000 m² or more than 2 ha in area	Definition of major large-scale development (DCLG, 2007; HM Government, 2016b; SODC, 2016) – see Section 4.1.
Needs to have some form of planning consent, such as outline planning permission.	If there is a planning application, it will provide the documentation required to provide background information about the buildings and site. If planning permission has not been obtained, it is more likely there will be issues with confidentiality.
Located in England	In the UK there are different planning policies for the different countries.
Should not be completed and demolition and/or construction work should have already started within the site.	Allows for consistency between case studies in terms of the point in time they have been analysed. If a relatively recent project, decisions have been newly made and it is more likely decision-makers can be identified.
Must contain more than one existing building.	Examination must go beyond individual buildings.
Stakeholders can be identified and contacted.	Required to ensure data collection and enable an in-depth review to be undertaken.

Source: Baker and Moncaster.

Participants for the general interviews were selected through similar purposive and opportunistic sampling methods. The intention of both case studies and 'general interviews' was exploratory (May, 2003: 99). The general interviews were held with professionals with chartered status or equivalent professional experience, who had experience of decision-making on masterplan sites, ensuring 'expert elicitation' (Lund Research Ltd., 2012).

4.3.1 Limitations

As with any research, the design has limitations. All of the case studies used are located in England, UK, so the planning policy mentioned is specific to that area. The influence of planning policy will vary from country to country. Rather than using the case studies as exemplars, they are being discussed to demonstrate how the decision in a masterplan context may be different to one for an individual building. Case studies are context specific; those in this chapter are both descriptive and illustrative, providing examples of when decision-making factors could be interpreted differently in a masterplan context (Robson and McCartan, 2016).

Table 4.3 Case study descriptions.

Case study	Local planning authority	Application number	Date of outline planning consent approval	Description	Buildings proposed in outline planning for: Demolition	Retention
CB1 Development	Cambridge City Council, UK	08/0266/OUT	2010	Cambridge is a historic city in the UK with an international reputation. The CB1 development is a major real estate regeneration project around the train station aiming to provide a gateway to the city. Once complete it will provide over 50,000 m^2 of offices, 5000 m^2 of retail, 1250 student units and 330 residential dwellings.	Majority of existing buildings including: partial demolition of a national listed building; 3 buildings of local interest; 3 buildings judged to add townscape character	1 nationally listed building 3 buildings of local interest (due to accidental fire, only 2 retained in final scheme)
Selly Oak Hospital	Birmingham City Council, UK	2012/02303/PA	2013	Former hospital site with buildings dating back to the 1870s. Permission has been obtained to redevelop area to 650 residential dwellings; 1000 m^2 squared of retail space, 500 m^2 of restaurants, cafes and drinking establishments and 1500 m^2 of offices and financial and professional services.	All non-listed buildings and 6 locally listed buildings	8 locally listed buildings
Icknield Port Loop	Birmingham City Council, UK	2011/07399/PA	2013	A former 64.7-acre industrial site dating back to the early 19th Century. Permission obtained to redevelop area for a mix of uses including 1150 residential dwellings; up to 6,960 m^2 of retail, services, employment, leisure and non-residential institution uses, as well as a hotel, community facilities and other associated works.	4 non-designated buildings (before this planning application there had been additional demolition within the curtilage of the site)	2 non-designated buildings

Data sources: Birmingham City Council (2013a, 2013b), Brookgate (2008), Cambridge City Council (2010), GVA *et al.* (2012), Mouchel (2011).

4.4   Analysis

This section discusses the results of the 'general interviews' and case study investigations. The factors identified as drivers for decisions to demolish or adapt within masterplans include national and local policy, place-making and its link to economic viability, technical aspects, and phasing and market changes.

4.4.1   National and Local Policy

Policy is a fundamental aspect of decision-making both at the individual building level and within the context of a larger scheme. In England, as elsewhere in Europe, masterplan sites are subject to regulations under the Environmental Impact Assessment (EIA) Directive (Commission of the European Communities, 1985). As masterplan sites tend to have an increased number of impacts associated with them, as demonstrated by the issues covered in the BREEAM Communities assessment (Figure 4.3), an EIA is often required. For all of the case studies, an Environmental Statement including chapters dedicated to heritage and the decision to demolish or adapt the different buildings was provided.

Decisions at the masterplan level need to consider the relevance of the proposed scheme to national and local authority policy. Although decisions about individual buildings will need to be in accordance with policy, at the larger masterplan level, the local planning authority may have development frameworks that set out the aspirations for the area, including an identification of buildings that make a positive contribution and which efforts should be made to retain. For example, in Cambridge, the local city council developed a Station Area Development Framework (Cambridge City Council, 2004). As part of this document, a conservation area (an area safeguarded due to its special architectural or historical interest) appraisal was undertaken and the local authority's conservation officer identified buildings of significance (Historic England, 2017). The intention was for the framework to be used as a guide for future proposed schemes. However, during the interviews a member of the design team mentioned that the Development Framework had not fully considered design and economic viability. Therefore, the proposal (and later outcome) varied from the appraisal, and included the demolition of buildings identified as making a positive contribution to the area. The first application for planning was rejected by the city council over a number of issues, in particular the over-development of the site. For the second application, the design team felt they had discussed the decisions earlier on with planning officers and this assisted with the process because the officers recommended the scheme for approval. It was then accepted by the elected city councillors.

Pre-application advice and 'front-loading' the council were also discussed in relation to the Selly Oak site and during three of the general interviews. Communication with the council, particularly on larger developments was considered to be vital. A statutory consultee for a heritage organisation (Heritage association statutory consultee, pers. comm.) stated:

> We also try to comment on pre-application as much as possible, so we try to get in touch with developers or they get in touch with us to discuss the proposal before they go for planning permission because that is obviously when you can negotiate the most.

The question of whether or not a building is designated at a national or local level, which can provide protection in the decision-making process, is also linked to policy. In the UK, Historic England (formerly English Heritage) is responsible for national designations, whilst the local planning authorities are responsible for local listings. The National Planning Policy Framework states that the demolition of listed buildings will only be allowed if the applicants can demonstrate that their harm or loss is necessary for public benefit (DCLG, 2012). At the masterplan level, whether a particular building prevents reasonable use of the site is key. During the general interviews, a representative from Historic England discussed a project in which a listed building was allowed to be demolished because it disrupted traffic flow in and around the site. Its demolition therefore led to a public benefit. A similar example was offered by a planning consultant and former planning officer (pers. comm.) in the context of the King's Cross development, a large development project in London, which is cited as a successful example of heritage regeneration (English Heritage, 2010):

> King's Cross...very clearly set out the case for demolishing a listed building because it provides access to the wider site and that I think sets out the scale of arguments that you need. It was a huge site and perhaps therefore was in some ways easier to justify the need to be an overwhelming public benefit.

In the case studies reviewed, a public benefit justification was also used for the demolition of locally listed buildings. On the CB1 site, two buildings – a former hotel and coal-yard office on the industrial site – were demolished to make way for a new transportation network, including a bus route and taxi rank. At Icknield Port Loop, although the heritage consultant felt the facade to a former factory could be retained as part of the masterplan scheme, the Environmental Statement justified its demolition on the grounds of access to the site (Mouchel, 2011). In addition, the Selly Oak masterplan proposes the demolition of 6 of the 14 locally listed buildings; supporting arguments included that they affected legible transportation routes and that they were located in areas of the site that could be used more effectively:

> ...their removal is considered to have clear benefits in terms of achieving the best urban design outcome for the Site, either by better revealing retained buildings of greater architectural and historical significance and/or by improving the ability to integrate those buildings into the Masterplan in a well-designed and viable way' (GVA *et al.*, 2012: 8.11).

Most of the interviewees felt that local listings (assigned by local councils) are currently more negotiable than national listings (assigned by a national government body), particularly for larger schemes on which applicants often argue that the demolition of one building can lead to investment in another. At an individual building level, a justification based on public benefit, in terms of larger infrastructure systems and in particular the choice between investing in one building or another, appears to be less common. These aspects of decision-making relating to policy were broadly identified in the literature review. However, it is fundamental that they are recognised from all stakeholder viewpoints, as applicants will try to show how their scheme, including the demolition and retention of buildings, is in accordance with planning policy, whereas opponents of the development will try to show how it is not in accordance. In general, unless the decision is taken up to appeal at a national level, it is the local authority and the councillors who need to decide whether or not the proposed future of the existing buildings is justified, thus being important decision-makers in the process. Overall, this section has shown that policy is fundamental to consider during decision-making but that the demolition of listed (safeguarded) buildings may be more negotiable when they are considered as part of a masterplan and applicants can demonstrate their loss results in public benefit.

4.4.2   Place-making and its Link with Economic Viability

A simple definition of place-making is given by Wyckoff (2014) stating that it is 'the process of creating quality places that people want to live, work, play and learn in'. It is a concept that is regularly mentioned alongside community viewpoints and the community's social and cultural identifies (Project for Public Spaces, 2009). For existing buildings, it can be seen as the way the different values attached to buildings can help provide a focus or identity for different areas and a connection to the past. It therefore may be, but is not always, related to the heritage value of the building, and it also implies an enhancement of economic value; the Royal Institution of Chartered Surveyors, for instance, found that place-making increased commercial value by 5–50% (RICS, 2015). The concept of place-making was mentioned by almost 50% of the general interviewees. For example, a property consultant referred to the 'sense of place' provided by historic buildings, even those that are undesignated (not listed and safeguarded by policy). In a separate interview, a representative from a heritage society discussed how the demolition of existing buildings, even if not designated, could disrupt the integrity of the masterplan site. Retaining some buildings: 'gives the site some form of identity; the people who would come to live there would have some kind of pride in their neighbourhood' (Heritage society representative, pers. comm.).

An individual building may not be seen as economically viable to retain. However, in the context of a larger scheme, this economic deficit may be offset by the intangible values added by place-making. This concept has previously been acknowledged by Robert Evans from Argent, the developer of King's Cross (English Heritage, 2010). Evans states that the individual buildings 'would not be viable in their own right' but that they 'work because they are part of a greater whole' (Evans, 2016: 44). This idea was reiterated by a property consultant interviewee, who discussed how the cost of knocking one building down within such a large scheme is miniscule. If that building adds value to the site through place-making, the space that could have been utilised by knocking it down could be made up for elsewhere.

Discussions with the urban designer of the Icknield Port Loop development indicated that their principle is to try and save as many historical buildings as possible because they form part of the 'urban grain'. On this project, the two buildings to be retained were identified early on. They were seen as beneficial in providing some character and avoiding monotonous development. During the design process, the existing buildings provided an anchor to work from and provided urban design merit. On the Selly Oak site, the reasons provided for the retention of buildings were that they were judged to be more significant historically and by the community and were located at landmark positions within the site, an aspect relevant to masterplanning. During the interviews, the design team discussed how they wanted the buildings to reflect the former use of the area as a hospital and leave a legacy. In the case of the water tower building (Figure 4.4) these intangible values, including the prominence of the building in the site, were considered to outweigh the technical complexity created by its unique scale (GVA *et al.*, 2012).

On the Cambridge site, three buildings have been retained. The nationally designated main station building and the industrial mill (Figure 4.5) were considered to be landmark features near the centre of the development. They could also be used as a reference point for the new building heights. Although the former coal-yard office, converted to a restaurant, is of modest size (a two-storey building), the heritage consultant and planning officers were keen to retain it, because replacement buildings would have affected the established character of the road. A glazed extension was added at the

Figure 4.4   Selly Oak hospital retained water tower forming a landmark feature on site. Source: Baker and Moncaster.

Figure 4.5   Retained industrial mill converted to residential apartments. New build student and residential site in background. CB1 development, Cambridge. Source: Baker and Moncaster.

back to make the building commercially viable. As recognised in particular in the general interviews, new build can also contribute to place-making and it is important for the new and old to work together.

Linked to creating a 'place' is the 'masterplan vision': the design team's conception of the aspirations for the area, which may include particular design concepts. However, other stakeholders may not always agree with these concepts and this is where there are often divided opinions regarding a regeneration project. For example, within Cambridge City Council's (2004) Station Area Development Framework, three buildings were identified as adding 'townscape value' because they were located at regular intervals along the street, thus creating a sense of 'rhythm'. During the design of the masterplan, the design team's aspiration was to develop this concept further and create a 'rhythm' along the whole street by having building volumes at regular intervals. This was considered to be a key concept by the design team, and required the demolition of a Victorian terrace (Figure 4.6). The terrace is to be replaced by a large modern office building, stepped back from the station building. The proposed building uses the land more efficiently from an economic perspective and is said to retain the 'rhythm' of the masterplan. The design team felt that the terrace would look 'out of place'. Although permission for this concept was granted at the outline planning stage, additional conservation area consent still had to be granted alongside the full application, because the design of the replacement building had been adjusted since outline permission was granted. This resulted in a petition of over 1000 signatures, seeking to save the Victorian terrace (Save Wilton Terrace, 2015). The campaigners disagreed with the justifications given for the demolition of a building, which had been recognised as a building of local interest in the original Development Framework. Although the planning

Figure 4.6 Victorian terrace (top) demolished in favour of a larger office block (model shown on bottom). CB1 development, Cambridge. Source Baker and Moncaster.

office recommended the scheme for approval, the city councillors rejected it three times based on the local campaigners' concerns (Cambridge City Council, 2004). However, after a planning appeal at the national level, permission for demolition was granted, thus providing an example of divided opinions regarding the future of buildings within a masterplan scheme. In contrast, although demolition of a small coal-yard office building on the outskirts of the site was initially considered, its demolition was not seen to be as fundamental to the 'core' of the scheme, and it was ultimately retained.

Heritage value, particularly on masterplan sites, can reach beyond the physical buildings. At an individual building level, the heritage of a demolished building could simply be reflected in the name of the replacement new build. When it comes to the masterplan, this reflection of the area's past can be taken a step further. One heritage organisation discussed how value should be acknowledged in the streetscape and the layout of the site; another interviewee referred to the Liverpool One scheme in the north of England.

Although this development was next to a world heritage site and on a historic waterfront, numerous buildings were demolished and replaced by new builds of a similar massing to the existing ones. The heritage was reflected by maintaining the historic street pattern, and the scheme has been referenced positively by English Heritage (now Historic England) for this reason (English Heritage, 2013). This idea was also seen in the case studies. On the Cambridge site, members of the design team highlighted some of the public art contributed through Section 106 agreements (planning obligations to make a development acceptable). They also retained historic features such as an old crane base and a statue of the goddess Ceres, which had been commissioned by Spillers (a flour milling company) who previously occupied the industrial area (Brookgate, 2008). At Icknield Port Loop, the designers and land-owners explained that their vision had been to create a waterside regeneration project and they wanted to take advantage of the historical canal network. The canal in itself was seen as a heritage asset, which should be enhanced.

These examples show that place-making (creating an area with character) can occur through the retention of historical buildings in the centre of a development but also alongside new build, and through other interventions such as retaining the street pattern, indicators of industrial heritage and place-names. It is the central/core area within the site where the 'design aspirations' for the area will often, but not always, be stronger. Conversely it is the outskirts of the area where more negations can take place regarding demolition and adaptation as the buildings may have less effect on the overall scheme.

4.4.3   Technical Aspects

The technical details of individual buildings, as discussed in Section 4.1.1, are still relevant in a masterplan context. Buildings will often be rapidly assessed to get an overview of their condition and adaptability. Whilst in some cases developers may choose to invest in adaptation, clearly this route is associated with greater risk, especially if the building is in poor condition and has limited technical feasibility for adaptation. The risks are often reflected in cost models, and increase for each building that is retained (property consultant, pers. comm.):

> ...there is inherently risk attached to refurbishment projects; if you have multiple buildings with this and unknown consequences of what might be uncovered, the developers are unlikely to take it.

At Icknield Port Loop, three of the buildings were demolished on technical justifications. Although the site contained an art-deco building constructed in 1932, which was described as 'architecturally the most significant structure on the Birmingham Corporation site' (Grover Lewis Associates, 2011: 19), the building was in very poor condition. The issues included cracks in concrete beams, spalling concrete, corroding reinforcement bars, insufficient concrete cover of reinforcement bars, and water ingress in the roof structure. This building, as well as a two-storey masonry factory on site, were assessed in a condition report (DTZ, 2011). The factory had suffered from water ingress, which affected the roof, internal walls and windows. The report concluded that the buildings had reached the end of their lifespan and were now functionally obsolete. The cost of the conversion for them to meet the requirements of modern day use made them economically obsolete.

From a technical and heritage point of view, the non-listed buildings on the Selly Oak site were never realistically considered for adaptation; the design team considered them to be intrusive and offering no intrinsic value. During the assessment of the locally listed buildings, regulations referring to the technical aspects of the building were considered. The problems highlighted included shallow building depths, layouts inhibiting vertical circulation, irregularity in the plan, and small floor areas. In an interview, a member of the Cambridge design team explained that many of the existing office buildings did not meet modern office demands because they had limited floor-to-ceiling heights, resulting in complications when incorporating raised floors and suspended ceilings. The majority of the other demolished buildings formed part of an old industrial site and were in poor condition. Within the industrial area, an original silo building next to the retained mill had originally been identified for retention in the outline planning permission. During refurbishment, an accidental fire broke out in this building and the majority of the masonry structure collapsed. Although some residents felt that the building should have been rebuilt because of its local listing, the design team felt that this would not be authentic to the heritage and that is would no longer be commercially viable.

Overall, this section has demonstrated that at a masterplan level, despite opportunities for some buildings to be retained because of place-making attributes, in many cases buildings will still be demolished on technical grounds, including their inability to meet modern requirements such as BREEAM (sustainability assessment), linking to higher construction costs and risk.

4.4.4   Phasing and Market Changes

The decision to either demolish or adapt a building is considered at the individual building level as part of the project. However, at the masterplan level the decision becomes more complex. This is partly because, with the development taking place over a longer period, there is more likelihood of changes in both the local market and the wider economy. One common way of addressing market changes for larger and more vulnerable schemes is to phase development appropriately. Several interviewees discussed phasing as a solution, with three suggesting that heritage buildings could act as a catalyst for further regeneration. However, in the case studies, the new buildings were constructed first to provide the necessary cash flows. For example, on the Cambridge masterplan site, new-build student accommodation was completed first. This was because construction began just after the UK's

2008 economic recession. During these times, student accommodation in Cambridge was still in demand. On the Selly Oak site, the provision of housing is being phased and construction continues while the first residents have moved into their new-build properties. Although an interviewee in the general interviews emphasised the importance of investing in existing buildings first to create a community hub, as happened at Kings Cross, this is not always desirable for the developers: new build is often less risky and the proceeds can be used to invest in the existing buildings.

Due to the uncertainty related to large-scale developments and market changes, all of the case studies investigated submitted an outline planning application, to be followed up with a 'reserved matters' application, rather than a full planning application. In England, outline planning can be used at an earlier stage to determine whether planning permission will be granted. These applications include information about the massing, quantity and uses of buildings and are later followed by 'reserved matters' applications, which consider the appearance of the buildings. Outline planning is favourable to developers because it allows for a greater degree of flexibility than full planning and developers can react to any market changes. However, outline planning is not always favoured by other stakeholders. For example, in the case of the Cambridge development, the use of outline planning was criticised by the Commission for Architecture and the Built Environment, who felt that outline planning was inappropriate because the site was a conservation area, containing lots of listed buildings: an outline planning application cannot guarantee the quality of the final development (Cambridge City Council, 2008). Although outline planning can provide flexibility for the developers, some may perceive it as producing uncertainty for the local residents, as they do not know exactly what they are going to get from a complex scheme, where multiple factors come into play. This shows that in larger schemes there is a balance between stakeholder priorities. This section has shown that the decision about demolition and adaptation goes beyond what should happen to the buildings. It must also set out when demolition or adaptation should happen.

4.5   Conclusion

Building adaptation and demolition has previously been researched throughout the developed world and from multi-disciplinary viewpoints. This chapter has highlighted decision-making criteria previously identified at an individual building level about whether to demolish or adapt, including technical aspects such as building condition, floor-to-ceiling heights, floor area, heritage value and associated designations, and planning polices and economics. Stakeholders involved in these decisions will inevitably weight criteria differently and have different priorities. The aim of this chapter was to explore how these decisions can differ in the context of a large-scale masterplan regeneration site, through three UK case studies and additional interviews with stakeholders. The decision-making factors are summarised in Table 4.4 and include national and local policy, place-making and its link

Table 4.4 Summary of decision-making factors and how they are interpreted differently in a masterplan context.

Decision-making factor	How factor is interpreted differently in a masterplan context
National and local policy	▪ Increased importance of pre-application advice with local authority. ▪ Building designations (aimed to safeguard buildings from demolition) more likely to be subject to compromises, such as investing in one building to enable investment in another. ▪ Increased likelihood of arguments justifying demolition for 'public benefit', in particular to facilitate transportation networks. ▪ Heritage can go beyond the physical buildings and be reflected in street patterns or art work around the site.
Place-making and its link with economic viability	▪ On some occasions the intangible values associated with heritage, such as a sense of identity and character, will offset the economic viability of an individual building within the 'greater whole' of the masterplan. ▪ Retention is balanced against to opportunity for new build and to increase floor areas. New build can also contribute to place-making.
Technical aspects	▪ Technical aspects, such as limited floor-to-ceiling heights and poor condition, which are associated with individual buildings are still considered at this level. ▪ Adaptation at an individual level and masterplan level is associated with risk and uncertainty; this will increase with each building retained.
Phasing and market changes	▪ Increased complexity associated with when to demolish or adapt existing buildings. Large-scale regeneration projects often take place over longer time periods, and will be more vulnerable to changing local economies and global market conditions. ▪ General interviews indicate early retention of existing buildings can act as a catalyst for further growth. ▪ Case studies showed investment in new buildings first to create necessary cash flows to invest in existing buildings, associated with more risk.

to economic viability, technical aspects, and phasing and market changes. Although these items are displayed in separate rows, they are not mutually exclusive; the case studies showed that during decision-making, multiple factors will combine: the decision is context dependent and can be influenced by land values, the current market conditions, attitudes within local councils and corporate objectives.

Within England's planning policy, the National Planning Policy Framework indicates that there must be an overriding public benefit to justify the demolition of a listed (safeguarded) building. On masterplan sites, arguments regarding transportation networks and compromises involving demolishing one building to enable investment in another come into play. This was evident in both the Cambridge and Selly Oak case studies. During the general interviews and case studies, it was recognised that the retention of historical assets can add character to an area and contribute to 'place-making'.

While the retention of an individual building may not be economic because of constraining technical aspects, within a larger scheme other values such as heritage may be weighted higher if a building can contribute to the character and identity of the area, the additional cost being offset by the rest of the development. On all the case study sites, historic buildings were being used as notable or landmark features within the masterplan in combination with new build. The case studies and interviews also provided examples of intangible values beyond the physical buildings, such as the retention of the historical canal network at Icknield Port Loop, which was seen as fundamentally reflecting the area's industrial past.

Previous research has investigated what features can enable adaptability in existing structures. At a masterplan level, physical criteria are still important, and the case studies showed examples of buildings being demolished because they were in poor condition, had limited floor-to-ceiling heights and/or shallow floor plans, and outdated services. Existing buildings are associated with higher levels of risk and uncertainty than new build, so it is unlikely that all existing buildings will be kept: risk increases with each building retained. There were examples of technically complex buildings being adapted rather than demolished because of their contribution to place-making, emphasising that the different factors of decision-making are often combined and not independent from one another.

A final consideration for masterplan sites is the phasing of demolition or adaptation of different buildings. On larger developments, construction generally takes place over a longer period, resulting in the project becoming more vulnerable to changing local and global economies; for this reason, phasing is important. During the general interviews, interviewees discussed the benefits of redeveloping existing buildings first, to create a community hub and identity early on. However, in the Selly Oak and Cambridge case studies, new build was constructed first to create the necessary cash flows to allow for investment in the following phases of development.

For all of the factors discussed, it is clear when looking at the decision of adaptation or demolition within a larger site, the complexity of decision-making increases because there are often more influencing factors. When making these decisions, which will have large impacts within an urban area, it is vital the different stakeholder attitudes are recognised and the balance between influencing factors is appropriately considered.

4.6   Planned Continuation of Research

Over the next two years as part of an ongoing PhD project, the three masterplan case studies investigated within this chapter will be expanded and increased to include additional sites. Currently, this research shows what is being done, rather than necessarily what *should* be done. One key aspect missing from the discussion in this chapter is embodied energy, a commonly cited benefit of building retention (Baker and Moncaster, 2017). The embodied carbon of a new building can equal or even exceed the operational carbon over a design life of sixty years. The majority of the embodied carbon is due to the building materials and their initial construction, with an additional impact caused by demolition and processing of demolition waste (Moncaster and Symons, 2013). Therefore the sustainability argument for retaining a building rather than demolishing it and building new is strong. The omission of embodied carbon from decision-makers' concerns is possibly linked to the current lack of ownership, awareness of the issue, or the lack of a simple method of calculation. No regulations yet require the reduction of embodied carbon, unlike that of operational carbon, and there is therefore no implied risk in ignoring it. The omission of an issue which has been demonstrated to be such an important part of sustainable design suggests that current decision-making may also ignore other important issues. These aspects will be explored further.

Acknowledgements

The authors gratefully acknowledge the Engineering and Physical Sciences Research Council (EPSRC) for funding this research through the EPSRC Centre for Doctoral Training in Future Infrastructure and Built Environment (EPSRC grant reference number EP/L016095/1) and would like to thank all those that agreed to be interviewed and contributed to this project.

References

Baker, H. and Moncaster, A. (2017) The role of stakeholders in masterplan regeneration decisions. To be presented at the *World Sustainable Built Environment Conference*, Hong Kong.

Baker, H. and Moncaster, A. and Al-Tabbaa, A. (2017) Decision-making for the demolition or adaptation of buildings. *Proceedings of the Institution of Civil Engineers: Forensic Engineering*, 1–13.

Birmingham City Council (2013a) *2011/07399/PA Land at Icknield Port Loop, Bounded by Ladywood Middleway, Icknield Port Road, and Wiggin Street, Birmingham*. Available at: http://eplanning.idox.birmingham.gov.uk/publisher/mvc/listDocuments?identifier=Planning&reference=2011/07399/PA [1 March 2017].

Birmingham City Council (2013b) *2012/02303/PA Selly Oak Hospital, Raddlebarn Road, Selly Oak, Birmingham, B29 6JD*. Available at: http://eplanning.idox.birmingham.gov.uk/publisher/mvc/listDocuments?identifier=Planning&reference=2012/02303/PA [1 March 2017].

Borst, J.I.M. (2014) NOW HIRING, wanted: user of tomorrow for space of the future, Master's thesis, Delft University of Technology.

Brand, S. (1994) *How Buildings Learn: What Happens After They're Built*. Viking Press.

BRE (2012) *BREEAM Communities – Technical Manual* (No. SD202–1. 1:2012). BRE, Watford, UK.

Brookgate (2008) Chapter 8 – Heritage, townscape character and visual quality. In: *CB1 Environmental Statement*. Brookgate, Cambridge, UK.

Bullen, P.A. (2007) Adaptive reuse and sustainability of commercial buildings. *Facilities* 25(1/2): 20–31.

Bullen, P.A. and Love, P.E.D. (2011) A new future for the past: a model for adaptive reuse decision-making. *Built Environment Project and Asset Management* 1(1): 32–44.

CABE (2011) Creating Successful Masterplans – A Guide for Clients. Available at: http://webarchive.nationalarchives.gov.uk/20110118095356/http:/www.cabe. org.uk/files/creating-successful-masterplans-summary.pdf [1 March 2017].

Cambridge City Council (2004) *Station area development framework*. Cambridge City Council Environment & Planning, Cambridge, UK.

Cambridge City Council (2008) Appendix D – Comments from stat. and non statutory consultees. In: *Planning Committee meeting minutes (15 October 2008)*, Cambridge City Council, Cambridge, UK.

Cambridge City Council (2010) *Planning – Application Summary: 08/0266/OUT*. Available at: https://idox.cambridge.gov.uk/online-applications/applicationDetails. do?activeTab=summary&keyVal=JWSXVIDX04X00 [1 March 2017].

Commission of the European Communities (1985) Council Directive on the assessment of the effects of certain private and public projects on the environment (85/337/EEC). *Official Journal of European Communities*. Report Number: L175/40.

Conejos, S., Langston, C. and Smith, J. (2012) AdaptSTAR model: A climate-friendly strategy to promote built environment sustainability. *Habitat International*, 37: 95–103.

DCLG (2007) *Planning Performance Agreements: a new way to manage large-scale major planning applications – Consultation*. DCLG, London, UK.

DCLG (2012) *National Planning Policy Framework*. Her Majesty's Stationary Office, London, UK.

DCLG (2017) *Fixing our broken housing market*. Her Majesty's Stationary Office, London, UK.

Dixon, T., Raco, M., Catney, P. and Lerner, D.N (eds.) (2008) *Sustainable Brownfield Regeneration: Liveable Places from Problem Spaces*. John Wiley & Sons.

Douglas, J. (2006) *Building Adaptation*, 2nd edn, Elsevier.

DTZ (2011) *Overview condition report. relating to: Unit H factory and art deco garage Rotton Park Street, Icknield Port Loop Birmingham* (No. AMI/DW/je/). On behalf of: British Waterways & HCA, Birmingham, UK.

Duffy, F. and Henney, A. (1989) *The Changing City*. Bulstrode Press.

Dutta, M. and Husain, Z. (2009). An application of multicriteria decision making to built heritage. The case of Calcutta. *Journal of Cultural Heritage*, 10(2): 237–243.

English Heritage (2010) *Heritage Counts 2010 England*. English Heritage, London, UK.

English Heritage (2013) *The Changing Face of the High Street: Decline and Revival*. English Heritage, London, UK.

Evans, R. (2016) A developer's perspective – heritage adds value. In: *Conservation Bulletin – London and the London Plan*. Historic England, London, UK.

Geraedts, R. and Van der Voordt, T. (2007) A tool to measure opportunities and risks of converting empty offices into dwellings. In: *Sustainable Urban Areas Conference*, Rotterdam, Netherlands.

Gosling, J., Sassi, P. and Naim, M., Lark, R. (2013) Adaptable buildings: A systems approach. *Sustainable Cities and Society*, 7: 44–51.

Grover Lewis Associates (2011) *Heritage appraisal of buildings at Icknield Port Loop, Ladywood, Birmingham* (No. GLA-061) for British waterways/DTZ, Newark, UK.

GVA, Environ & University Hospitals Birmingham NHS Foundation Trust (2012) *Volume 2 Environmental Statement – Selly Oak Hospital* (No. UK18–16673 Issue: Final). Birmingham, UK.

Historic England (2017) *Conservation Areas*. Available at: https://historicengland. org.uk/listing/what-is-designation/local/conservation-areas/ [28 February 2017].

HM Government (2016a) *Housing and Planning Act 2016*. Available at: http://www. legislation.gov.uk/ukpga/2016/22/part/6/crossheading/permission-in-principle-and-local-registers-of-land/enacted [9 August 2016].

HM Government (2016b) *Planning Applications Decisions – Major and Minor Developments, England, District by Outcome*. Available at: https://data.gov.uk/ dataset/planning-applications-decisions-major-and-minor-developments-england-district-by-outcome/resource/947477ba-2f91-4c45-bc66-b71d85e76a0a [17 August 2016].

IStructE (2008) *Guide to Surveys and Inspections of Buildings and Associated Structures*. The Institution of Structural Engineers, London, UK.

Jalao, E.R., Wu, T. and Shunk, D. (2014) A stochastic AHP decision making methodology for imprecise preferences. *Information Sciences*, 270: 192–203.

Karantonis, A.C. (2008) Population growth and housing affordability in the modern city-Sydney a case study. Presented at the *14th Pacific Rim Real Estate Society Conference*, Pacific Rim Real Estate Society, pp. 1–14.

Kelly, G., Schmidt III, R., Dainty, A. and Story, V. (2011) Improving the design of adaptable buildings through effective feedback in use. Presented at the *CIB Management and Innovation for a Sustainable Built Environment* Conference, Amsterdam, Netherlands.

Kim, C.-J., Yoo, W.S., Lee, U.-K., Song, K.J., Kang, K.I. and Cho, H. (2010) An experience curve-based decision support model for prioritizing restoration needs of cultural heritage, *Journal of Cultural Heritage*, 11(4): 430–437.

Kutut, V., Zavadskas, E.K. and Lazauskas, M. (2014). Assessment of priority alternatives for preservation of historic buildings using model based on ARAS and AHP methods, *Archives of Civil and Mechanical Engineering*, 14(2): 287–294.

Lacovidou, E. and Purnell, P. (2016) Mining the physical infrastructure: Opportunities, barriers and interventions in promoting structural components reuse. *Science of the Total Environment*, 557–558, 791–807.

Langston, C. and Smith, J. (2012) Modelling property management decisions using 'iconCUR'. *Automation in Construction*, 22: 406–413.

Lin, G. and Low, S. (2012) Influential criteria for building adaptation potential from the perspective of decision makers. Presented at the *48th ASC Annual International Conference*, Birmingham, UK.

Lund Research Ltd. (2012) *Purposive sampling*. Available at: http://dissertation. laerd.com/purposive-sampling.php [19 August 2016].

May, T. (2003) *Social Research: Issues, Methods and Process*, 3rd edn. Open University Press.

McLeod, S. (2014) *Psychology Perspectives*. Available at: http://www.simplypsychology. org/sampling.html [2 June 2016].

Meerow, S., Newell, J.P. and Stults, M. (2016) Defining urban resilience: A review. *Landscape and Urban Planning*, 147, 38–49.

Mok, K.Y., Shen, G.Q. and Yang, J. (2015) Stakeholder management studies in mega construction projects: A review and future directions. *International Journal of Project Management*, 33(2): 446–457.

Moncaster, A.M. and Symons, K.E. (2013) A method and tool for 'cradle to grave' embodied carbon and energy impacts of UK buildings in compliance with the new TC350 standards. *Energy and Buildings*, 66: 514–523.

Mouchel (2011) *Icknield Port Loop – Environmental Statement – Volume 1* (No. 1039706-NaN-001). British Waterways & Homes and Communities Agency, Haywards Heath, UK.

Plimmer, F., Pottinger, G., Harris, S., Waters, M. and Pocock, Y. (2008) *Knock it Down or Do It Up? Sustainable Housebuilding: New Build and Refurbishment in the Sustainable Communities Plan*. BREPress.

Power, A. (2008) Does demolition or refurbishment of old and inefficient homes help to increase our environmental, social and economic viability? *Energy Policy*, 36(12): 4487–4501.

Project for Public Spaces (2009) *What is Placemaking*. Available at: http://www.pps.org/reference/what_is_placemaking/ [1 May 2016].

RICS (2015) *Placemaking and land value*. Information Paper (draft). Available at: https://consultations.rics.org/consult.ti/placemaking [1 May 2016]

Robson, C. and McCartan, K. (2016) *Real World Research*. John Wiley & Sons.

Save Wilton Terrace (2015) *Rt. Hon. Eric Pickles, Secretary of State: Save Cambridge's Victorian Wilton Terrace and stop two tower buildings of 9 and 10 storeys (higher than Kings College Chapel) being built*. Available at: https://www.change.org/p/rt-hon-eric-pickles-secretary-of-state-save-cambridge-s-victorian-wilton-terrace-and-stop-two-tower-buildings-of-9-and-10-storeys-higher-than-kings-college-chapel-being-built [28 February 2017].

Schmidt III, R., Eguchi, T., Austin, S. and Gibb, A. (2010) What is the meaning of adaptability in the building industry? Presented at the *CIB 16th International Conference on Open and Sustainable Building* Conference, Bilbao, Spain.

SODC (2016) Planning applications FAQ. South Oxfordshire District Council. Available at: http://www.southoxon.gov.uk/services-and-advice/planning-and-building/application-advice/general-planning-advice/planning-applic [17 August 2016].

Wilkinson, S. (2011) The Relationship between Building Adaptation and Property Attributes, PhD Thesis, Deakin University, Australia.

Wilkinson, S.J., Remøy, H. and Langston, C. (eds.) (2014) *Sustainable Building Adaptation: Innovations in Decision-making*, 1st edn, Wiley-Blackwell

Wyckoff, M.A. (2014) *Definition of Placemaking: Four Different Types*. Available at: http://pznews.net/media/13f25a9fff4cf18ffff8419ffaf2815.pdf [1 March 2017].

Yung, E.H.K. and Chan, E.H.W. (2012) Implementation challenges to the adaptive reuse of heritage buildings: Towards the goals of sustainable, low carbon cities. *Habitat International*, 36(3): 352–361.

Sustainable Design and Building Conversion

Craig Langston
Bond University, Australia

Sir Alexander John Gordon (1917–1999) argued in 1972, as President of the Royal Institute of British Architects (RIBA), that buildings should be designed for long life, loose fit and low energy (Gordon, 1972). While his peers did not immediately embrace this idea, over time his words became a mantra, potentially defining good architecture and its role in modern society (Murray, 2011). Known for over forty years as the '3L Principle', the idea has continued to gain prominence, particularly in the developed world (Murray, 2011).

The identification of good architecture is a combination of multiple criteria relating to values that individuals may not agree upon. Vitruvius (circa 80–15 BC) insisted that three fundamentals should be present: function, structure, and beauty. Others might argue the relationship of a building with its surroundings, cultural context and society's expectations at the time are also important (see for example, Chan and Lee, 2008). Value for money might be added, based on cost–benefit evaluations, which can include tangible and intangible components (Langston, 2005). Finally, Gordon's 3L Principle provides another lens through which good architecture can be viewed. It sets a base performance level for architectural merit.

The idea of creating a building for permanence, yet incorporating flexibility into it and minimising its energy footprint throughout its physical life, is surely the ultimate holistic objective for the architecture profession (Murray, 2011). Today these objectives may be summarised as three key features: durable, adaptable and sustainable. Good buildings should reflect these

Building Urban Resilience through Change of Use, First Edition.
Edited by Sara J. Wilkinson and Hilde Remøy.
© 2018 John Wiley & Sons Ltd. Published 2018 by John Wiley & Sons Ltd.

properties, and not merely be works of public art or monuments to their designers, the technological prowess involved or the wealth of their owners. Good architecture lies in the care with which buildings are designed to provide long-term benefits to the society they serve, and should transcend the utilitarian and the fashionable in favour of performance and legacy (Buchanan, 2000).

The sustainable development movement arose more than a decade after Gordon coined the 3L Principle, and has continued to gain prominence, particularly in the developed world (Conejos, 2013). Jacobs (1961) made the remark that the greenest buildings are the ones we already have. For this to be true, it implies that their original design must have considered issues of longevity and flexibility, else they would not have anything still to offer in the changing world within which we live. Good architecture must stand the test of time. As Frank Gehry put it: 'architecture should speak of its time and place, but yearn for timelessness'. Yet the focus of the sustainable development movement has been on green building, with less consideration being given to durability and adaptability.

No one has ever demonstrated that long life, loose fit and low energy are mutually exclusive. Nor has it been proven that beauty and performance are incompatible. On the contrary, our greatest buildings should possess all these fundamentals, as well as reflect the culture and achievements of their time. Good architecture should inspire, challenge norms and encourage opinion. Are we able to recognise today what will be understood to be good architecture well into the future? How can we measure good architecture at the outset?

Sustainable development needs to embody Gordon's 3L Principle and treat durability, adaptability and sustainability as equally important. A zero-carbon building with a short life span and no consideration of alternative uses after its original function becomes obsolete is arguably only a minor contribution to modern society. While it might demonstrate technological advance and innovation, it is simply a prototype for ideas that demand integration into a broader and more balanced design solution.

Of course, the question of what makes good architecture cannot be answered unequivocally. Nevertheless, just because a question has many answers does not mean that it should not be asked.

In this chapter, good architecture is evaluated in the context of durability, adaptability and sustainability. Each criterion is capable of objective measurement, and the aim is to find a method for measuring good architecture in terms of these three criteria, and to derive an overall rating. This outcome should be reflected in examples of good architecture that we see around us. Using an analysis of 22 recent AIA award-winning buildings in Southeast Queensland, Australia, the relationship between good architecture and the 3L Principle is tested. The life-cycle costing (LCC) of projects – where cost data are available – can be modelled to demonstrate how their cost profile is influenced by time. Yet this must be placed in context of the bigger picture of urban renewal, where optimisation of a single building conversion may be at odds with neighbourhood policies and objectives involving non-economic criteria.

5.2   Durability: Measuring 'Long Life'

The ISO-15686 series on service life planning for buildings and constructed assets is a useful resource with respect to building durability. However, this standard is more applicable to building components and systems than entire buildings (Langston, 2011). This is because the estimated service life of any component is calculated as its theoretical life multiplied by a series of factors that are each scored in the range 0.8 to 1.2 (1 = no impact). The factors represent:

- quality of components
- design level
- work execution level
- indoor environment
- outdoor environment
- usage conditions
- maintenance level.

Whilst a building is a sum of its parts, such parts can be replaced and hence renewed, leaving the basic structure to determine overall life expectancy. The literature on service life discusses the effect of external and internal actions on building durability, and usually identifies location, usage and design as the main parameters (Langston, 2005).

Obsolescence is the inability to satisfy increasing requirements or expectations (Iselin and Lemer, 1993; Lemer, 1996; Pinder and Wilkinson, 2000). This is an area under considerable stress due to changing social demands (Kintrea, 2007), and brings with it environmental consequences. Yet obsolescence does not mean defective performance. Douglas (2006) makes a further distinction between redundancy and obsolescence. The former means 'surplus to requirements', although this may be a consequence of obsolescence. Nutt *et al.* (1976: 6) take the view that '…any factor that tends, over time, to reduce the ability or effectiveness of a building to meet the demands of its occupants, relative to other buildings in its class, will contribute towards the obsolescence of that building'. A few researchers have also included as forms of obsolescence (Campbell, 1996; Gardner, 1993; Luther, 1988; Kincaid, 2000):

- political changes to zoning
- ascribed heritage classification and other imposed regulatory controls
- changes in stakeholder interest.

To assist in forecasts of physical life, Langston (2011) developed an Excel template to model building age. A series of simple questions gives insights into the longevity of a building according to three primary criteria: environmental context (location), occupational profile (usage) and structural integrity (design). Each category is equally weighted, and comprises ten questions requiring simple yes/no answers. Where information is unknown, blank answers are ignored in the calculation. Three questions under each primary

Table 5.1 Durability star rating.

Physical life (years)	Star rating
250 or above	★★★★★★
200–249	★★★★★
150–199	★★★★
100–149	★★★
75–99	★★
50–74	★
below 50	

criterion are double weighted due to their relative importance. The approach is based on the *Living to 100 Life Expectancy Calculator* (see http://livingto100.com), which predicts human lifespans.

The construction of the calculator was informed by a broad survey of literature (see Langston, 2011), recent ISO-15686 standards and personal experience. It was founded on an adaptive management principle (Gregory *et al.*, 2006; Linkov *et al.*, 2006), which purports to develop a model and then evaluate its robustness through subsequent field-testing and observation. While the results of this testing appear promising, definitive validation arguably can only occur by comparison of estimates with reality, where the latter is measured as the duration of the building before it collapses.

Buildings are judged as lasting 25, 50, 75, 100, 150, 200, 250 or 300 years (shorter or longer durations are not supported) using weighted criteria grouped into environmental context (location), occupational profile (usage) and structural integrity (design). The resultant physical life (years) is then converted into a star rating, as shown in Table 5.1.

5.3   Adaptability: Measuring 'Loose Fit'

For a wide range of reasons, buildings can become obsolete long before their physical life has come to an end. Investing in long-lived buildings may be suboptimal if their useful life falls well short of their physical life (Langston *et al.*, 2008). It is wise to design future buildings for change by making them flexible yet with sufficient structural integrity to support alternative functional uses. The development of a design-rating scheme for adaptation potential, known as *adaptSTAR*, enables building designers to understand the long-term impacts of their decisions prior to construction, and thus enable optimisation for adaptive reuse to occur from the outset (Conejos, 2013). As adaptive reuse potential already embodies financial, social and environmental criteria, the rating scheme would extend traditional operational considerations, such as energy performance, to include churn, retrofit, refurbishment and renewal considerations.

Atkinson (1988) modelled the process of obsolescence and renewal (of housing stock), and developed a 'sinking stack' theory to explain the phenomenon. Comparing total building stock over time produces a rising profile in total stock (accumulating via new construction each year) stratified according to building age (older buildings are at lower layers in the profile strata). New stock is added annually to the top of the stack. It degenerates over time and gradually sinks towards the bottom of the stack as new buildings are created and older ones demolished. If little new construction is added, then the entire building stock will age, and greater resources will be required to maintain overall quality and amenity levels. Certain layers in the stack are likely to represent periods of poor-quality construction, and these layers age more rapidly and absorb greater maintenance resources (Ness and Atkinson, 2001). Each layer in the stack reduces in height with the passage of time. Only the top layer grows because it represents the current rate of new construction. The net effect is a sinking of the stack, a phenomenon that occurs whether or not sufficient maintenance takes place.

The *adaptSTAR* tool is an attempt to rate new building design for future 'adaptivity'. This rating is done when the project is in its design phase, although it can be applied in hindsight based on the latent conditions before a proposed intervention takes place. As such, it reflects the adaptability within a design concept: the potential for change of functional use later in life (Conejos, 2013).

The concept of the *adaptSTAR* design-rating scheme for adaptation potential uses categories of obsolescence derived from literature. These comprise physical, economic, functional, technological, social, legal and political considerations (Conejos, 2013). Each category was broken down into subcriteria that were also assembled from a review of the literature and from expert interviews with the design teams of eleven Australian award-winning adaptive reuse conversions in New South Wales and the Australian Capital Territory, as well as a pilot study involving the Melbourne General Post Office in Victoria. The subcriteria were then rated by a sample of practising Australian architects experienced in adaptive reuse work in order to determine the relative importance of each subcriterion. This then led to the calculation of a weighting for each obsolescence category.

A five-point Likert scale is used to assess subcriteria and to develop an *adaptSTAR* score out of 100. The resultant *adaptSTAR* score is then converted into a star rating, as shown in Table 5.2.

Table 5.2   Adaptability star rating.

adaptSTAR score	Star rating
85 or above	★★★★★★
75–84	★★★★★
65–74	★★★★
55–64	★★★
45–54	★★
35–44	★
below 35	

Source: Conejos (2013).

From this work it has been found that the seven obsolescence categories have reasonably equal weights (Conejos, 2013). The coefficient of variation of the seven criteria weights was just 8.32%. A scoring template was developed to enable new building designs to be rated for the future adaptation potential.

5.4   Sustainability: Measuring 'Low Energy'

In Australia, the Green Building Council of Australia (GBCA, 2010) operates Australia's only national voluntary comprehensive environmental rating system for buildings, known as 'Green Star'. The GBCA established Green Star in 2002 as a rating system for evaluating the environmental designs of buildings. It evaluates the green attributes of building projects in eight categories (with bonus points for innovation). Green Star is largely based on the BREEAM (UK) and LEED (US) approaches, which were developed a decade or more earlier. The GBCA promotes green building programs, technologies, design practices and operations. Rating tools are currently available or in development for most building market segments, including commercial offices, retail, schools, universities, multi-unit residential buildings, industrial facilities and municipal buildings. While strictly not confined to low energy considerations, it takes account of the level of building sustainability using eight categories: management, indoor environmental quality, energy, transport, water, materials, land use and ecology, and emissions – plus extra points for innovation.

The goal of this rating system is to assess the current environmental potential (or sustainability) of buildings. It is a useful tool for property managers when identifying upgrade and retrofit priorities (Wilkinson *et al.*, 2014). The rating system also assists corporate sustainability and environmental reporting efforts. Every Green Star rating tool is organised into eight environmental impact categories and an innovation category. Credits are awarded within each of the categories, depending on a building's environmental performance and characteristics. Points are achieved when specified actions for each credit are successfully performed or demonstrated.

An environmental weighting is applied to each category score, which balances the inherent weighting that occurs through the differing number of points available in each category. The weights reflect issues of environmental importance for each state or territory of Australia and thus differ by region. The sum of the weighted category scores, plus any innovation points, determines the project's rating. Only buildings that achieve a rating of four stars and above are certified by the GBCA. This is similar to LEED and other rating schemes in current use elsewhere in the world. The resultant Green Star score is then converted into a star rating, as shown in Table 5.3.

Table 5.3 Sustainability star rating.

Green Star score	Star rating
75 or above	★★★★★★
60 – 74	★★★★★
45 – 59	★★★★
30 – 44	★★★
20 – 29	★★
10 – 19	★
below 10	

Source: GBCA (2010).

5.5   Case Studies

It is proposed that award-winning buildings, as judged by experts from the architectural community, should demonstrate at least four stars in each of the long life, loose fit and low energy criteria. Twenty-two commercial buildings were selected from southeast Queensland, each of which had received an Australian Institute of Architects (AIA) award in the last ten years. Each was assessed, retrospectively, to determine their star rating for all three criteria, and to compute a combined index based on equal weighting (Langston, 2014).

Independent validation of the models' results by a panel of seven architectural experts drawn from local industry found that there was 62% overall agreement. An example of one of the case studies is shown in Figure 5.1.

Only 4.5% of the dataset scored less than four stars in any criteria. The mean star rating across all case studies was 5.09 for durability, 4.64 stars for adaptability, and 4.55 stars for sustainability. The mean overall index for the case studies was 4.76 stars. All award-winning projects received high scores for durability, adaptability and sustainability. Should the minimum standard be raised to five stars, then 39.4% of the dataset would not qualify. The full results of this study are shown in Figure 5.2.

All of the award-winning projects examined in this research therefore appear to meet Gordon's 'test' for good architecture. The 3L Principle is expected to be inversely proportional to the computed LCC per square metre of gross floor area measured over a 30–100-year life. Unfortunately, since LCC was either never calculated or was confidential, data could only be obtained for Case Study #2 (Figure 5.2). Using a 30-year study period and a 3% discount rate, the comparative LCC for this case study in 2012 terms was AUD$6,536/m^2 (Langston, 2013).

An earlier study based on 30 commercial buildings in Melbourne (Langston, Y.L., 2006) found that the mean ratio of annual operating costs to capital costs was 0.0361. These buildings, which are examples of ordinary projects, had a mean capital cost of AUD$2,540/m^2 and a mean operating cost of AUD$4,175/m^2 over 30 years (in 2006 terms). Adjusted to 2012 prices, this equates to an LCC (capital + operating cost) of AUD$7,924/m^2.

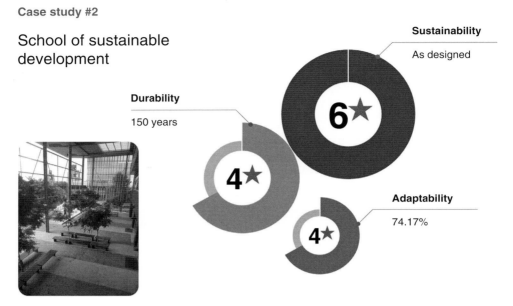

Case study #2

School of sustainable development

Figure 5.1   Bond University School of Sustainable Development (Langston, 2014).

How can we judge good architecture?

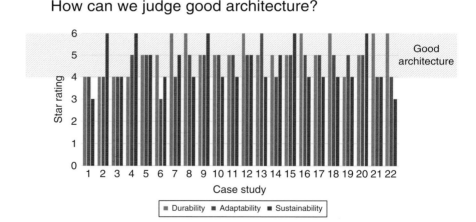

Figure 5.2   Judging good architecture (Langston, 2014).

Case Study #2 has superior durability, adaptability and sustainability performance to the Melbourne data, and therefore suggests that good architecture may lead to lower LCC, albeit with potentially higher capital costs. Case Study #2 had a capital cost of about double the average for Melbourne data and an operating cost of about a third. Clearly one case study is insufficient to define a generic relationship between the 3L Principle and LCC, but it does suggest that higher upfront costs may be offset by savings on recurrent costs, and thus represent good value over a building's life. Further investigation of this relationship is needed. It is possible that good architecture can be judged by LCC.

5.6   A Framework for Evaluation of Urban Renewal Projects

5.6.1   Big-picture Thinking

Urban renewal, including building conversion projects, aims to embrace the ethos of good architecture, so issues of durability, adaptability and sustainability are relevant. Furthermore, if good architecture can be measured by lowest LCC, as suggested in Figure 5.3, then economic evaluation appears fundamental.

However, urban renewal project viability and success are dependent on a number of interdisciplinary factors that are both general and locally specific. Many approaches to or models of urban renewal projects focus on specific issues such as design, cost and neighbourhood amenity, yet often provide discrete qualitative descriptions only (Yung *et al.*, 2015). The evaluation of urban renewal projects, however, is interdisciplinary in nature and must embrace economic, social and environmental criteria, known as the triple bottom-line (Elkington, 1998), as well as the local political context. These criteria must be integrated, well balanced, and capable of objective robust measurement. It is important that a specific compliance threshold is maintained for each criterion.

For urban renewal projects to have significant impact, the project size is preferably of a neighbourhood scale, covering at least four city blocks or eight intertwining streets (Xu *et al.*, 2012). Such projects contribute to improving undesirable parts of cities and rectifying past planning decisions through new urban design theory. They cultivate social cohesion, supporting local employment, delivering economic viability and improving the urban micro-environment. Evaluation is difficult because of the range of dynamic factors at play and the political imperative to push ahead and make holistic decisions that deliver collective utility (Wilkinson *et al.*, 2014).

These problems demand a systems approach that can integrate assessment subsystems grounded in multiple disciplines, and that can be understood and tracked through a quantitative evaluation model. An integrative decision-making model shows how key criteria may influence one another for a particular circumstance, or for a larger system. System dynamics can be used to explore a wide range of project or policy scenarios and identify optimum outcomes.

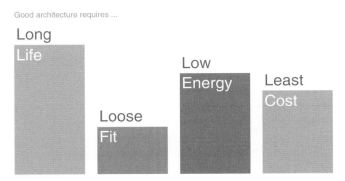

Figure 5.3   LCC as a surrogate for good architecture.

Much work has been done on the factors that affect economic, social and environmental performance for urban renewal projects. Chan and Lee (2008) give these as:

- community contributions
- conservation and preservation
- conservation of existing properties
- daily living provisions
- development strategy
- image building
- integrated design
- land strategic utilisation
- land-use planning
- open spaces design and provision
- provision of welfare facilities
- quality living condition
- quality welfare planning and provisions
- transport arrangements.

Langston (2013) also looked at the role of coordinate-based decision-making for the evaluation of sustainable built environments. This was based on value for money (wealth over resources) and quality of life (utility over impact) as subsystems. In this research, profit, people, politics and planet are conceptualised as the subsystems that form the basis for an integrative (4P) decision-making model. Each criterion is assessed in units that are appropriate for determining a quantifiable score. 'Profit' is the benefit–cost ratio, representing the overall commercial viability and indicative budget. 'People' is a measure of local project support, and represents the level of stakeholder satisfaction that may be expected. 'Politics' is the risk and reward, representing the impact and probability of success of cultural innovation. 'Planet' is the ecological footprint, representing the expected resource depletion and pollution via a life-cycle assessment. Each criterion represents a subsystem that can be explored in a dynamic way, yet can be upwardly assembled into a single decision criterion with respect to specific performance thresholds. There is a fundamental optimisation sequence that can reduce evaluation time. The conceptual framework is shown in Figure 5.4.

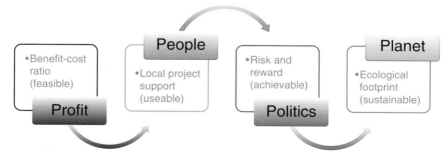

Figure 5.4   4P conceptual framework. Adapted from Beech (2013).

Each criterion has a relationship with the other three. Project or policy selection needs to be based on the combined score of all the criteria (the higher the better), bearing in mind that the profit, people and politics criteria need to be maximised and planet one needs to be minimised, at the same time satisfying all thresholds. This gives rise to the following upper-level algorithm:

$$\text{Overall 4P score} = \frac{\text{profit} + \text{people} + \text{politics}}{\text{planet}}$$

5.6.2   System Dynamics

System dynamics is generally described as a computer-aided approach to policy analysis and design. It applies to problems arising in complex social, managerial, economic or ecological systems that are characterised by interdependence, mutual interaction, information feedback, and circular causality. The approach typically begins with defining problems dynamically, and then proceeds through mapping and modelling stages to building confidence in the model and its real-world implications. Conceptually, circular causality (including system feedback and learning) is at the heart of the approach. Diagrams of loops of information feedback are used to conceptualize the structure of complex systems and to share model-based insights. Yet circular causality by itself is not enough. The explanatory power and insightfulness of feedback understandings also rest on the notions of active structure and loop dominance. The concept of endogenous change is fundamental to a system-dynamics approach. It dictates aspects of model formulation: exogenous disturbances are seen at most as triggers of system behaviour; the causes are contained within the structure of the system itself (Richardson, 2011).

System dynamics has been used in a wide range of applications and industries, including urban planning and sociology (Forrester, 1969). The approach brings with it both an understanding of urban problems and a robust evaluation response that is quantifiable and repeatable. Over time, system models improve and increasingly provide insight into the complex causes and effects seen in real life.

System Dynamics Review, the journal of the System Dynamics Society, is the best source about current activity in the field. Key references on system dynamics include Sterman (2000), Maani and Cavana (2007), Ford (2009), Morecroft, (2007) and Wolstenholme (1990). System dynamics can utilise other techniques, such as the analytic hierarchy process developed by Saaty (1980), to model critical factor relationships.

5.6.3   Model Application

Building on the 4P conceptual framework, a decision-making model can be proposed using system thinking. It applies within an over-arching procurement process and has a geographic information system (GIS) at its heart.

The GIS database feeds four primary subsystems aligned to core decision criteria (profit, people, politics and planet). Algorithms built into each of the four submodels determine benefit–cost ratio, local project support, risk and reward, and ecological footprint respectively.

Ultimately these outcomes are balanced and optimised to provide an objective 4P score that identifies the best combination of variables, informing priorities and enabling intelligent portfolio decisions to be made. The connections between each criterion involve iteration, meaning that past outcomes must be reviewed in the context of new information and decisions. The proposed evaluation and decision processes involved are shown in Figure 5.5.

The overall 4P score for an urban renewal project requires numeric representation of profit, people, politics and planet subsystems. Each of these values is computed on a scale of 0–5 inclusive and so the overall 4P score normally lies somewhere between 0 (worse case) and 15 (best case). But rather than just focus on optimal performance, specific compliance thresholds set boundaries within which optimisation must take place:

- *Profit*: discounted benefits must outweigh discounted costs.
- *People*: positive local support (strengths) must outweigh negative local opposition (weaknesses).
- *Politics*: positive risks (opportunities) must outweigh negative risks (threats).
- *Planet*: project must not exceed moderate (reversible) levels of environmental impact.

The application of the model involves a number of steps. First, each of the four core criteria is explored and the results are integrated in the decision-making subsystems. For example, in regard to the 'profit' subsystem, the model will use the results of a market analysis of existing commercial activity within a neighbourhood to construct a business plan for urban renewal that can be expressed in terms of tangible income and expenditure over the project life cycle. This is used to develop a discounted cash flow and benefit–cost ratio model. External input is required in terms of prices and economic assumptions, such as the appropriate rate of discount to be applied. The benefit–cost ratio is computed as the sum of discounted benefits divided by the sum of discounted costs. A value greater than 1 would indicate that the project is commercially viable. The specific performance threshold is therefore set at 1. Model output can be transferred and presented in Microsoft Excel. Once all four subsystems have been constructed, each with their own numerical model, the connection between them is established.

The next step is integrating the decision-making model to a GIS database from which market, needs, policy and infrastructure data can be obtained and used to inform each of the subsystems. Market analysis captures the demographics of a neighbourhood that might underpin the proposed business plan. Needs analysis determines existing gaps that might undermine a resilient community and demand redress during the project's design. Policy analysis captures the political circumstances and sentiment that might

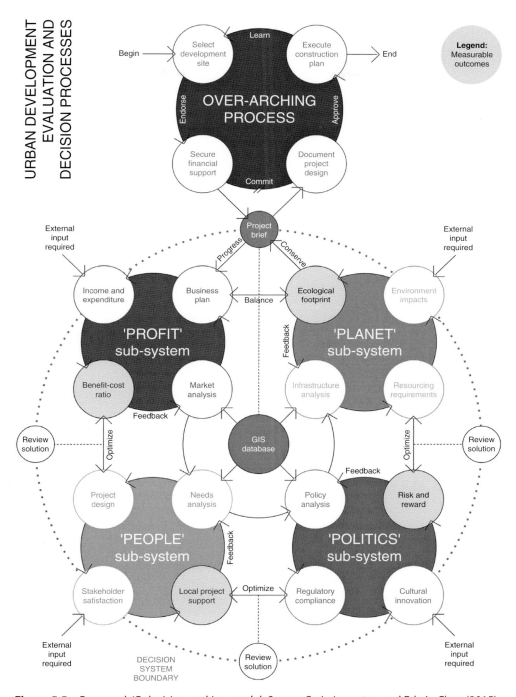

Figure 5.5   Proposed 4P decision-making model. *Source:* Craig Langston and Edwin Chan (2015).

underpin regulatory frameworks and compliance. Infrastructure analysis determines the existing services (transport, energy, water, sewer, telecommunications, etc.) that might underpin resourcing requirements and other environment impacts.

In the final step, core criteria values are computed. These collectively identify an optimal urban renewal outcome capable of further interrogation. The ability to review the solution at various stages of its evaluation based on the sequence described in the conceptual framework is key. This review leads to optimisation of linkages between profit and people, people and politics, and politics and planet criteria. In the final iteration, planet and profit criteria are balanced to ensure that the overall 4P score is maximised and all specific performance thresholds are satisfied. Difference scenarios can be explored.

The application of system dynamics to urban renewal involves scenario modelling, and is illustrated in Figure 5.6. Each subsystem is modelled individually using the Stella system dynamics software package. A number of techniques underpin this process, including discounted cash flow analysis, analytic hierarchy processing, risk analysis and life-cycle assessment. The outcomes for profit, people, politics and planet are then combined to map the 4P score over time. In the example provided, which is a hypothetical scenario construct, it is determined that collectively the specific compliance thresholds are realised only after Year 18 of the project's life cycle. This is called the *acceptance zone*.

Urban renewal project outcomes can be communicated to others via a simple 5-star rating scale. This rating is computed by dividing the overall 4P score by 3, and can be used to compare competing urban renewal scenarios or projects and assess relative priorities. The rating can vary over time, as can the scenario outcomes themselves. It is also a valid optimisation objective to seek strategies to extend the acceptance zone. System dynamics has been shown to suitable for scenario modelling and project or policy formation (see, for example, Cavana, 2010).

5.6.4   Previous Work

Figure 5.7 shows a typical system dynamics model for business operations using a four-subsystem balanced scorecard approach (see http://www.iseesystems.com/). It shows the basic components of model construction: stocks, flows, connectors, converters and feedback loops. Equations and initial values are added to describe the relationships. The model can be 'run' to simulate the outcome of various scenarios over a user-specified time period, to adjust inputs and to provide graphical and tabular output for further analysis.

The integration of a GIS database with Stella has only been reported twice before in the literature. Ahmad and Simonovic (2004) found that research combining GIS and system dynamics could be divided into two limited categories: introducing spatial dimensions in the system dynamics model, which fell short because the spatial dimensions could not be represented

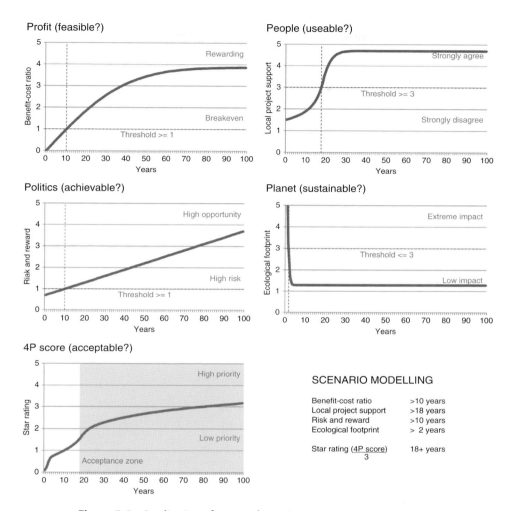

Figure 5.6   Application of system dynamics.

explicitly, and translating system dynamics model equations to run in GIS, which was also limited because changes could not be made during the simulation. Separately, the two severely lacked the other's strength and, by attempting to integrate one into the other, some of the robustness was lost. Therefore, the only way to truly combine the separate strengths of these tools was to run them simultaneously. The spatial system dynamics (SSD) approach first developed by Amhad and Simonovic (2004), however, has not yet been widely adopted. Hartt (2011) undertook research on the impacts of storm damage in Charlottetown, on Prince Edward Island, Canada. He was the second to demonstrate successfully the concept of SSD and was able to extract data from topographic and urban development

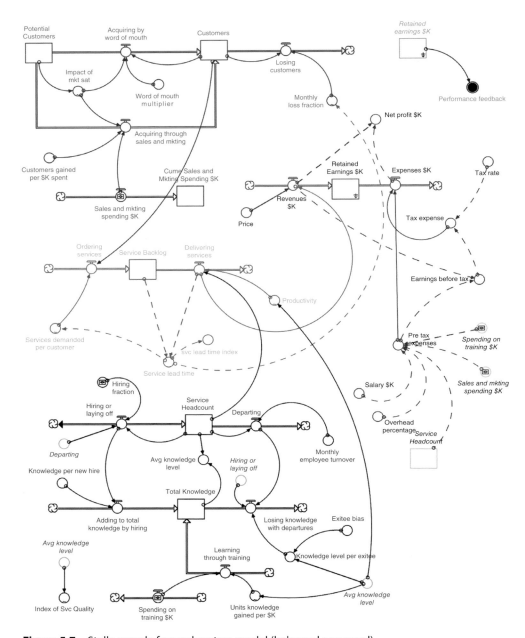

Figure 5.7   Stella sample four-subsystem model (balanced scorecard).

maps, model the effect of various storm surge impacts and then automatically construct a single static overlay that showed flooding and impacts on existing infrastructure. There have been a few similar attempts at software integration since, but it appears the idea of SSD is still very much in its infancy.

Microsoft Excel is used as a means of data exchange between ArcGIS Pro and Stella. In computing, dynamic data exchange (DDE) is a method of interprocess communication under Microsoft Windows. It allows one program to subscribe to items made available by another program, for example a cell in a Microsoft Excel spreadsheet, and be notified whenever that item changes. DDE was partially superseded by object linking and embedding (OLE), but remains used for simple interprocess communication tasks and is more user-friendly than OLE.

5.7   The Application and Implications of Life Cycle Costing

Cost is usually an important factor in building conversion, and a high construction price may well preclude the pursuit of sustainability during design. Yet the costs of buildings can be many times greater when measured over their lives, and good architecture can contribute to lower operational costs even in cases where the initial cost is higher. The technique of LCC converts building costs over many years into a single cost figure today, enabling decisions concerning future value to be more objective. Good architecture cannot divorce itself from the financial implications of acquisition and maintenance, and if it did it would be rendered ineffective in the practical realm.

In terms of big-picture thinking, a systems view of building conversion highlights the need for other objectives than mere economic feasibility. LCC is but part of the consideration of feasibility, as it typically excludes benefits that arise from projects and focuses instead on expenditure. There is an implicit assumption that profit is maximised when cost is minimised in scenarios where overall benefits are constant. But value for money recognises that both benefits and costs can change.

Assessing LCC for building conversion is a process of measuring capital (construction) cost and operating (recurrent) cost, the latter including maintenance, repair and replacement. This is achieved by first deciding on the lifetime the calculation will span. Too short a time horizon will ignore expensive refurbishments required at a later date, and too long a time horizon will reduce the reliability and relevance of the answer. However, the disadvantages of long time horizons are reduced through the process of discounting. This is a fundamental requirement of any comparative cost investigation over more than a short-term redevelopment cycle, and is critical to the capture of the true value of sustainability initiatives (Langston, 2005).

Figure 5.8 provides an illustration of the effects of discounting over time. The data are for the development of vacant residential land for two different types of design: the green roof project reflects 3L Principle thinking in all aspects of durability, adaptability and sustainability, while the traditional project reflects a business-as-usual market-driven solution. Both projects have the same enclosed gross floor area.

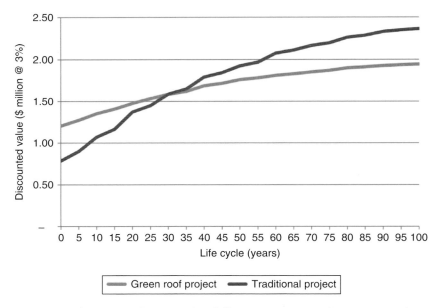

Figure 5.8   Discounted cash flows over 100 years (Langston, 2015)

This example shows that the green project is more expensive initially, but represents better value for money after about 30 years (Langston, 2015). Capital cost of the green roof project is AUD$1,204,376. The traditional project has a 54% advantage. After 25 years the comparative operating cost is modelled as AUD$329,965 for the green roof project and AUD$665,687 for the traditional project, which grows to AUD$556,066 and AUD$1,141,121 respectively after 50 years and AUD$741,659 and AUD$1,577,318 respectively after 100 years. Residual value is based on market value and is assumed to have the same ratio to construction cost after both inflation and depreciation have been taken into account, so can be ignored in the comparison.

5.8   Conclusion: Implications for Future Practice

It is increasingly important to ensure that money spent on renewal of existing built infrastructure is wisely allocated and that maximum social, political and environmental benefits are simultaneously realised.[1] There is a clear need to consider the optimal selection of urban renewal projects,

---

[1] For example, Hong Kong is one of the densest cities in the world, supporting a population of 6690/km² (http://www.gov.hk/en/about/abouthk/factsheets/docs/population.pdf). In the first quarter of 2015, construction expenditure comprised HK$19,965 million (50.3%) on new building construction and HK$19,734 million (49.7%) on repair and refurbishment of existing buildings (HK CSD 2015). Repair and refurbishment is expected to outstrip new construction in the years ahead.

and the decision-making model presented here provides an opportunity to quantify the benefits that flow from urban renewal. This will allow practitioners to pursue projects that provide the highest collective utility and national benefit.

Revitalisation of existing neighbourhoods is likely to be the main source of activity for built environment stakeholders in the future. The redesign of cities and the strengthening of communities to be resilient (both economically and politically) and sustainable (both socially and environmentally) are critical to ensuring rising value for money and quality of life respectively. The core understanding within the model is that urban planning decisions follow an inherent sequence, from the feasible to the useable to the achievable and finally to the sustainable. If a project cannot satisfy any of these 'hurdles', then earlier decisions must be reviewed until the project is acceptable. This approach enables these things to be quantified and combined into an overall performance metric, so that the approach can be applied routinely to new decisions.

An urban renewal decision-making model therefore changes past focus from individual and unique project evaluation to understanding the underlying behaviour of stakeholders and their interactions. Over time, such tools can provide insight into the workings of complex urban renewal scenarios. The proposed urban renewal decision-making model is complex and bespoke. Each subsystem is constructed using system thinking based on a range of possible 'policy settings', specifying performance over time and the number of years necessary before specific compliance thresholds are realised, if at all. From these four connected models, the overall 4P score can then be predicted. Adjustments to base decisions are expected until all thresholds are achieved.

Of note is the nexus formed between urban renewal, system dynamics and multi-criteria decision analysis. Having found no evidence to the contrary, it is suggested that the combination of these three domains has not been attempted before. Perhaps the best example of related work is Macmillan *et al.* (2014) who investigated the societal costs and benefits of commuter bicycling in Auckland, New Zealand. There is no quantitative decision-making model for urban renewal evaluation that includes an objective measurement of project success. The combination of a 4P conceptual framework with GIS-supported integrative decision-making that optimises and balances core criteria in a transparent and objective fashion over time is quite unique.

This 'big picture' approach to the evaluation of urban renewal projects is advocated over past bias towards economic feasibility and techniques, such as LCC, that give a practical yet myopic view of what represents good design within very narrow system boundaries. In the case of building conversion, use of LCC can help to identify the lowest cost of a proposal over a given time horizon, but not necessarily the best value to the owner or indeed to society more generally. LCC is unlikely to expose wider social and political objectives of urban renewal projects, and will assess sustainability only in terms of its cost implications rather than the more important issues of climate change and ecological footprint.

References

Ahmad, S. and Simonovic, S.P. (2004) Spatial system dynamics: new approach for simulation of water resources systems. *Journal of Computing in Civil Engineering*, 18(4): 331–340.

Atkinson, B. (1988) Urban ideals and the mechanism of renewal. In: *Proceedings of RAIA Conference, June, Sydney*.

Beech, D. (2013) Quadruple bottom line for sustainable prosperity. Cambridge Leadership Development. (http://cambridgeleadershipdevelopment/quadruple-bottom-line-for-sustainable-prosperity/).

Buchanan, P. (2000) *Ten shades of green*. Architecture League of New York. (http://www.nationalbuildingmuseum.net/pdf/Ten_Shades_of_Green.pdf).

Campbell, J. (1996) Is your building a candidate for adaptive reuse? *Journal of Property Management*, 61(1): 26–29.

Cavana, R.Y. (2010) Scenario modelling for managers: a system dynamics approach. In: *Proceedings of the 45th Annual Conference of the Operations Research Society of NZ (ORSNZ)*, University of Auckland, 28–30 November, 219–228.

Chan, E.H.W. and Lee, G.K.L. (2008) Contribution of urban design to economic sustainability of urban renewal projects in Hong Kong. *Sustainable Development*, 16(6): 353–364.

Conejos, S. (2013) Designing for future building adaptive reuse. PhD thesis, Bond University, Australia.

Douglas, J. (2006) *Building Adaptation*, 2nd edn. Butterworth-Heinemann.

Elkington, J. (1998) *Cannibals with Forks: the Triple Bottom Line of 21st Century Business*. New Society Publishers.

Ford, A. (2009) *Modeling the Environment*. Island Press.

Forrester, J.W. (1969) *Urban Dynamics*. MIT Press.

Gardner, R. (1993) The opportunities and challenges posed by refurbishment. In: *Proceedings of Building Science Forum of Australia*, Sydney.

GBCA. (2010) What is Green Star? (http://www.gbca.org.au/green-star/green-star-overview/).

Gordon, A. (1972) Designing for survival: the President introduces his long life/loose fit/low energy study. *Royal Institute of British Architects Journal*, 79(9): 374–376.

Gregory, R., Failing, L. and Higgins, P. (2006) Adaptive management and environmental decision making: a case study application to water use planning. *Ecological Economics*, 58(2): 434–447.

Hartt, M.D. (2011) Geographic information systems and system dynamics: modelling the impacts of storm damage on coastal communities. Master's thesis, University of Ottawa.

HK CSD (2015) *Building, construction and real estate sectors: Q1 2015*. Census & Statistics Department, the Government of the Hong Kong Special Administrative Region.

Iselin, D.G. and Lemer, A.C. (eds.) (1993) *The Fourth Dimension in Building: Strategies for Minimizing Obsolescence*. Committee on Facility Design to Minimize Premature Obsolescence, Building Research Board, Washington DC: National Academy Press.

Jacobs, J. (1961) *The Death and Life of Great American Cities*. Random House.

Kincaid, D. (2000) Adaptability potentials for buildings and infrastructure in sustainable cities. *Facilities*, 18(3/4): 155–161.

Kintrea, K. (2007) Housing aspirations and obsolescence: understanding the relationship. *Journal of Housing and the Built Environment*, 22, 321–338.

Langston, C. (2005) *Life-cost Approach to Building Evaluation*. Elsevier (co-published with UNSW Press).

Langston, C. (2011) Estimating the useful life of buildings. In: *Proceedings of AUBEA2011 Conference*, Gold Coast, Australia, April.

Langston, C. (2013) The role of coordinate-based decision-making in the evaluation of sustainable built environments. *Construction Management and Economics*, 31(1): 62–77.

Langston, C. (2014) Measuring good architecture: long life, loose fit, low energy. *European Journal of Sustainable Development*, 3(4): 163–174.

Langston, C. (2015) Green roof evaluation: a holistic 'long life, loose fit, low, energy' approach. *Construction Economics and Building*, 15(4): 76–94.

Langston, C., Wong, F., Hui, E and Shen L.Y. (2008) Strategic assessment of building adaptive reuse opportunities in Hong Kong. *Building and Environment*, 43(10): 1709–1718.

Langston, Y.L. (2006) Embodied energy modelling of individual buildings in Melbourne: the inherent energy-cost relationship. PhD thesis, Deakin University, Australia.

Lemer, A.C. (1996) Infrastructure obsolescence and design service life. *Journal of Infrastructure Systems*, 2(4): 153–161.

Linkov, I., Satterstrom, F.K., Kiker, G., *et al.* (2006) From comparative risk assessment to multi-criteria decision analysis and adaptive management: recent developments and applications. *Environment International*, 32(8): 1072–1093.

Luther J.P. (1988) Site and situation: the context of adaptive reuse. In: R. Austin ed. *Adaptive Reuse: Issues and Case Studies in Building Preservation*. Van Nostrand Reinhold.

Maani, K.E. and Cavana, R.Y. (2007) *Systems Thinking, System Dynamics: Understanding Change and Complexity*. Prentice Hall.

Macmillan, A., Connor, J., Witten, K., *et al.* (2014) The societal costs and benefits of commuter bicycling: simulating the effects of specific policies using system dynamics modelling. *Environmental Health Perspectives*, 122(4): 335–344.

Morecroft, J.D.W. (2007) *Strategic Modeling and Business Dynamics: a Feedback Systems Approach*. Wiley.

Murray, G. (2011) Stirling Prize analysis: long life, loose fit, low energy, e-Architect Newsletter article #125, (http://www.e-architect.co.uk/articles/persistence-of-the-absurb).

Ness, D. and Atkinson, B. (2001) *Re-use/upgrading of existing building stock*. BDP environment design guide, Building Design Professions, Canberra.

Nutt, B., Walker, B., Holliday, S. and Sears, D. (1976) *Housing Obsolescence*. Saxon House.

Pinder, J. and Wilkinson, S.J. (2000) Measuring the gap: a user based study of building obsolescence in office property. RICS Research Foundation.

Richardson, G.P. (2011) System dynamics. In: S. Gass and C. Harris (eds.) *Encyclopedia of Operations Research and Management Science*. Kluwer Academic Publishers.

Saaty, T.L. (1980) *The Analytic Hierarchy Process: Planning, Priority Setting, Resource Allocation*. McGraw-Hill.

Sterman, J.D. (2000) *Business Dynamics: Systems Thinking and Modeling for a Complex World*. Irwin McGraw-Hill.

Wilkinson, S.J., Remøy, H. and Langston, C. (2014) *Sustainable Building Adaptation: Innovations in Decision-making*. Wiley Blackwell.

Wolstenholme, E.F. (1990) *System Enquiry: a System Dynamics Approach*. John Wiley & Sons.

Xu, Y., Chan, E. and Yung, E. (2012) Neighborhood change in semi-urbanized villages: case study of Shanghai. *Journal Urban Planning and Development*, 138(3): 235–243.

Yung E., Chan, E. and Xu, Y. (2014) Assessing the social impact of revitalizing historic buildings on urban renewal: the case of a local participatory mechanism. *Journal of Design Research*, 13(2): 125–149.

Top-up: Urban Resilience through Additions to the Tops of City Buildings

Gordon Holden
Griffith University Queensland, Australia

6.1 Introduction

The focus in this chapter is on recent additions on tops of existing city buildings in developed countries, with particular attention given to apartments. Discussion will centre on the ecological performance of the 'Top-Up', both within its own opportunities and constraints together with the contribution of the typology to wider aspects of urban resilience.

6.2 Top-up Context

Town planning regulations in Western cities have long given attention to limiting the height of buildings. Today's cities establish height zones in order to plan for future population density, a mix of functions and to maintain the provision of services. Central districts typically have the highest limits; buildings on sites below the upper limit are inevitably under financial performance pressures of achieving their potentially highest and best use. Height limits in zones adjacent to city centres are lower. Buildings in such zones are under similar pressures to achieve highest and best use, usually manifest through new buildings constructed up to the height limit. The space above a building's actual height and the zoned height limit is potentially available to accommodate additions to the building, as an alternative to demolition and building anew. It can be shown that in certain circumstances such additions can be more economical than a new building and otherwise may be an interim measure to maintain financial viability until the time is considered right for complete redevelopment. This is especially the case in the lower height zones adjacent to city centres, where potential

Building Urban Resilience through Change of Use, First Edition.
Edited by Sara J. Wilkinson and Hilde Remøy.
© 2018 John Wiley & Sons Ltd. Published 2018 by John Wiley & Sons Ltd.

top-ups are economically and technically feasible. There are numerous constraints to additions on top of existing buildings, which need to be addressed and balanced against the also numerous advantages. These advantages and constraints will be discussed in this chapter, which draws from several previously published works by the author.

Imaginative and productive creation of additions to the tops of existing city buildings in developed countries is a relatively new phenomenon, largely postdating the Second World War, but one that has gained momentum from the 1990s. However, machine rooms, roof-terraces and caretaker/manager accommodation, generally modest in size, on the top of buildings were known from the period between the two World Wars. This is when flat-topped buildings developed, following the era of tapered decorative topping-off of city buildings, of which the Chrysler Building in New York is an exceptional example. Western building history contrasts with other regions. Additions to the tops of buildings are common in cities of many undeveloped countries as well as some more developed ones that have long vernacular traditions of this type The roof-top villages of Phnom Pen, Cambodia, the barrios of Caracas, Venezuela and the inhabited roofscape of urban Athens demonstrate such histories.

Field studies in Australia, Europe and the USA and the limited literature on the subject reveal that a wide range of buildings host these additions, and an equally wide range of functions is seen for the additions themselves (Busch, 1991; Martinez, 2005; Melet and Vreedenburgh, 2000; Bloszies, 2012; Roth, 2012). Host building functions include existing apartments, warehouses, museums, workshops and factories, mansions as well as religious buildings. The scope encompasses single-storey through medium-rise to high-rise buildings. Functions of the additions on top include restaurants, offices, conference centres, museums, art galleries, studios and, commonly, apartments, from single units to multiples. The literature also shows that such additions are global in extent, with many examples across Europe, including the UK, the USA, South America, Asia and Australia and New Zealand. There are also 'hot-spot' cities and regions, where the idea of topping up existing buildings has taken hold and become almost mainstream. Identified hotspots include New York, London, Rotterdam, Wellington, Melbourne and Sydney and several places across Austria, Estonia and Germany.

The examples identified predominately contrast with their host building in design style, form and materials. One such building is the pioneering New York penthouse by famous architect Paul Rudolph (Figure 6.1a). There are some examples that are aesthetically compatible with their host, such as the fine Amsterdam top-up shown in Figure 6.1a. Several top-up examples stand apart, in extreme contrast with their host building and surroundings, and have become talking points both within their community and, further afield, through articles and images distributed by architectural journals.

Constructions on top of existing buildings fall within the 'Heritage' design category in architectural awards: 'This category is for any built conservation project or study developed in accordance with the Australian ICOMOS Burra Charter, or any adaptive reuse of a heritage structure' (AIA, 2017). A relatively recent trend has been to merge 'contemporary design ideas with historical fabric in ways that clearly signals the presence of new life'

(a)

(b)

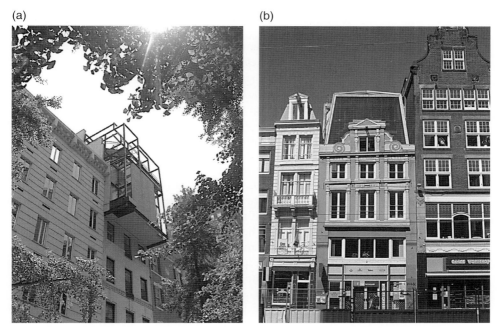

Figure 6.1 Examples of top-ups: (a) Penthouse top-up, New York, 1977–85 (architect: Paul Rudolph); this is a contemporary design style through which Rudolph experimented with materials and space, on top of a 'bland' host building. (b) Penthouse Rokin, Amsterdam 2000 (architects: Archipelontwerpers); this is a contemporary design style conference/meeting centre top-up compatible with its traditional Amsterdam slim canal house host.

(a)

(b)

Figure 6.2 Top-ups that contrast with their host buildings: (a) Apartments, Carlton, Melbourne 2016 (architects: DKO Architecture); a high-contrast top-up on a traditional warehouse host building. (b) RMIT Building 22 Melbourne 2010 (architects: ARM); educational facilities called 'The Brain', subversive in their extreme contrast, top off a heritage-listed host.

(AIA, 2014). This development suggests mainstream architectural acceptance of top-ups, although the subject receives little discussion in the theoretical literature. The vast majority of top-ups in Australia contrast with the host building, several extremely so (Figure 6.2).

6.3   Top-up Typology

Holden (2003) proposed that new apartments constructed on top of existing buildings is an emerging category that has yet to be seriously addressed within architectural theory. The subject receives some attention in the literature, but mainly as an oddity rather than as demonstrating creative possibilities for a new architectural expression and language. This is despite the growing occurrence of roof-top additions, especially apartments providing more housing in otherwise built-out areas. This is especially the case in those inner cities where few vacant sites remain and the existing building stock is performing economically, so there is no pressure to demolish and rebuild. Roof-top apartments as additions, intensifies the city and adds to vitality through accommodating additional city dwellers, who encourage and engage with services and opportunities for work, study culture and socialising. A new technique and aesthetic for architecture and urban design is occurring and this needs to receive greater research and intellectual attention. The city has always been a fertile place for new ideas, and building on top of the existing stock opens up exciting possibilities.

Theoretician Habraken (1998) sees the presence of similar characteristics, such as common functions, as critical in the fundamental classification of a building type. In Habraken's terms, residential dwellings are a prime type, embracing several secondary types: detached houses, duplexes, terraced and townhouses, multi-storey apartments, all of which receive attention in the literature. However, apartments on top of existing buildings are not currently discussed in the theoretical literature. They should be placed in the secondary class and be compared to that class's other dwelling types.

Rowe (1987) adds to the typology discussion the need to investigate types at a detail level through subclass classification. Firstly considering 'spatial distribution of functional parts', an approach which he calls 'organisational typologies', and secondly, to engage with a family of 'standard design responses to parts of buildings', which he defines as 'elemental types'. Organisational typologies for top-up apartments could be based on:

- horizontal or vertical access
- building form and size
- orientation
- the number and size of habitable spaces and their configuration.

The full scope of fundamental, primary, secondary and subclass types and their technical performance for continuing research on building-top apartments is needed to guide future research. Conventional ideas and methods need to be challenged. Innovative industrialised building methods that can involve both assembly and disassembly have potential. Discussion here is confined to introducing elemental types in terms of design style and to testing ecological, technical and economic performance of the emerging typology and its contribution to the city.

Assessment of building-top apartments in Wellington, New Zealand (Holden, 2003) established a classification into two main types, based on the design of the top-up relative to the host building:

- additions where the design is visually compatible with the host building
- additions that contrast with the host building.

Case study analysis suggests that 'contrast' spans a variety of cases, from restrained to extreme contrasts. In both compatible and contrast cases there are further potential subclassifications, relating particularly to structures, materials and colours of the new addition and the host building. This simple style, form and materials agenda was found to be robust and convenient in undertaking field studies and basic codification of building-top apartments, as well as other functional types, when studied in Australia, England, France, Holland and the USA.

6.4 Top-up and Heritage

In classifying new top-up examples across the countries mentioned above, an important dimension was identified, namely the architectural significance of the host building, several of which were heritage listed and subject to assessment and regulation. Design controls in heritage areas of cities tend to adopt a conservative approach to new work, often requiring compatibility between the top-up and the host building. For example, the top-up shown in Figure 6.3a was required to be compatible with the heritage-listed host building. This top-up was confirmed by Wellington city users in a survey as being highly compatible, but the combination of top-up and host was not considered to be aesthetically successful. This suggests that 'compatibility' alone between old and new does not guarantee aesthetic success of the combination (Holden 2005a).

(a)

(b)

Figure 6.3 Contrast as a factor in the success of a top-up: (a) Renaissance Apartments, Wellington, 2000 (architects: Design Group); (b) Blair Apartments, Wellington 2001 (architects: Architecture Workshop).

It is argued that the top-up design should express its own era, 'signalling the presence of new life', as in the AIA quote in Section 6.2. This proposition recognises the approach of contrast rather than compatibility between the host and the new addition. The top-up shown in Figure 6.3b was judged in the Wellington survey as having low compatibility with the heritage-listed host building, but the combination was considered to be highly aesthetically successful. This suggests that design integrity and quality of the top-up is valued. One elderly lady said in the survey 'old is old and new is new, we shouldn't confuse them and want blurring' (Holden, 2005a). As well as extending the life of the host building, there is potential for the top-up to enhance the significance of the host building through its own high design quality, potentially lifting the visual success of the combination. The combination may become more than the sum of the parts.

The retention of heritage buildings through addition of top-ups adds to community cultural assets and importantly extends the useful life of buildings. Retaining a heritage building also contributes to social stability (Costonis, 1989). Such stability derives from retaining a familiar and meaningful built environment in the midst of an increasing pace of life. Underpinning the concept of heritage is social value, which implies social commitment to the heritage item. It is acknowledged that listing as a heritage building in a state or national register, or local environmental plan *per se*, does not prevent the responsible authority from approving a building's demolition. Common practice shows that alteration and adaptation conditions for the retention of heritage-listed buildings are negotiable (ELA, 2017). This is considered to be a reasonable approach; the heritage building is privately owned and despite social value determining heritage classification, no public funds are committed for preservation or upkeep. Private economic viability seems to play an important role in permitting additions, even where the new work is in contrast with the host heritage building.

Central government heritage councils and local authorities have ruled in favour of permitting alterations and additions, both compatible and contrasting with the heritage building. Generally, requirements are set out for doing as much as necessary to care for the place and to make it useable, but otherwise to change as little as possible so that the cultural significance is retained. The key ideas are usability and significance. Rather than allow a heritage building to fall into disrepair, to the extent of being a hazard leading to demolition, the custodians of heritage assets have allowed alterations and additions that are often highly contrasting, provided that the intrinsic aspects that give the host building its 'significance' are retained.

Heritage conservation standards globally are commonly underpinned by the International Council on Monuments and Sites (ICOMOS) principles (ICOMOS, 1978). The underlying philosophy and values of the Burra Charter, Australia's standard for heritage conservation, which is derived from ICOMOS, are that 'Places of cultural significance enrich people's lives, often providing deep and inspirational sense of connection to community and landscape, to the past and to lived experiences. Places of cultural significance reflect the diversity of our communities, and tell us about who we are and about the past that has formed us and the Australian landscape' (Australian ICOMOS, 2013).

While constructing top-ups to heritage buildings is a special case, topping up other city buildings that contribute to the character and history of a precinct achieves similar outcomes, enriching the sense of 'connection to community and landscape, to the past and lived experience' (Australian ICOMOS, 1999). Retaining host buildings, heritage listed or not, and building on top of them contributes to the wider sense of place that strengthens cultural and social endeavours. This is an important underpinning concept for urban resilience.

6.5   Case Studies

6.5.1   Hypothetical Top-Up

Blair Apartments (Figure 6.3b) in Wellington, is the inspiration for a hypothetical investigation (Figure 6.4) of quantifiable matters relating to additions on top of an existing building. This was undertaken and described in detail by Holden and Gjerde (2007).

Indicative costs for three approaches to development of the hypothetical site were produced, based on broad per square metre and per cubic metre costs. These were informed by the New Zealand *Rawlinson's New Zealand Construction Handbook* (Giddens, 2004). It is appreciated that building

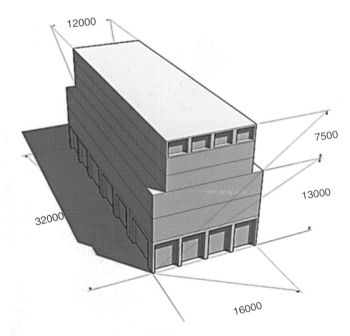

Figure 6.4   Hypothetical case study for development strategy comparison. Modelled loosely on Blair Apartments, Figure 6.3b.

Table 6.1 Cost of three top-up options.

Approach	Description	Cost (NZ$ million)
1	Demolish and build new.	6.8
2	Retain existing unchanged and build on top	3.0
3	Renovate existing and build on top.	4.1

costs vary across cities and countries and change over time, but it is suggested that the figures produced for the time and place of the case study remain valid for comparative purposes. The three approaches are:

1. Demolish the existing building and construct a new one of the same volume.
2. Construct additions on top of the existing building and continue to use the existing building without renovations.
3. Construct additions on top of the existing building and renovate the existing building.

No allowance has been made for a basement level in the costing. Suffice it here to summarise the key findings, recognising that a full feasibility study would need to extend to an analysis of sales and/or letting activity. The total estimated costs for the three approaches are shown in Table 6.1.

At face value, renovating the existing building and constructing additions on top appears to be a cost-effective strategy for development. To demolish and construct a new building (approach 1), which achieves the same volume as renovation and building on top (approach 3), would trigger additional costs associated with demolition, construction and demolition waste and preparing new footings and foundations. There are also implications for embodied energy and life-cycle assessment, as discussed below.

Further, there are financial holding costs that derive from the longer construction time involved in demolishing and building anew compared with retaining the existing building and constructing additions on top. Depending on the construction technique and safety issues, as well as critical path coordination relating to the timing of the new additions, there is potential for a continuing income to be available to the developer through retaining existing tenants in the host building during construction on top. Upon completion, the new top-up apartments could be sold or rented while the host building is being renovated, thereby retaining an income stream throughout the whole of the 'build on top and renovate' development option. A full feasibility study that takes account of these matters would further favour the 'build on top and renovate' financial position over 'demolish and build anew'.

6.5.2 Top-Up and Design and Technical Matters

The most common form of redevelopment in cities is complete demolition and building anew, potentially up to the town planning height limits of the site.

City buildings are rarely dismantled to recover and recycle materials, mainly because of time and labour costs and the long disposal time-line, with implications for storage. Rapid and complete demolition and waste removal frees up the site quickly for new work, with positive impacts on safety and carrying or holding opportunity costs. Complete demolition is likely where the existing building is not an especially good example of its type, where the function is compromised or restricts alterations, where the services are obsolete, where the building fabric has seriously deteriorated and where the building is not sufficiently capable of supporting a top-up, even with structural improvements.

In order to construct top-ups, the host building must be structurally capable of supporting the new work or the existing building's structure must be capable of being strengthened and at acceptable cost. In both cases, there are likely to be weight limits applied to the new work which will impact on the choice of materials of construction. Typically, apartments on top of existing buildings adopt lightweight construction approaches. This is suitable for smaller additions on structurally sound host buildings such as Didden Village, Rotterdam (Figure 6.5a) as well as the examples shown in Figures 6.1 and 6.3. An alternative is where a large-scale addition requires a supporting structure on its own footings penetrating through, but independent of, the host building. An example of this is the Porter House condominium in New York (Figure 6.5b).

For the hypothetical case study, the demolition, waste, preparation of new footings and their implications for embodied energy and life-cycle assessment are discussed in more detail by Holden and Gjerde (2007) than in this chapter. A summary follows.

(a)

(b)

Figure 6.5   Construction approaches to top-ups: (a) Didden Village, Rotterdam 2007 (architects: MVRDV) is a lightweight residential addition, contrasting with the host factory building with workshops on two floors with a residential floor above that gives access to the roof-top additions. (b) Porter House Condominium, New York 2003 (architects: ShoP); a contemporary addition contrasting with the century-old host warehouse building. The additions required independent structure and footings.

Demolition and waste disposal where no materials are recycled is a financial liability. In the hypothetical case this represents approximately 1.5–2.0% of the overall cost to demolish and construct a new building. With demolition, there is also nuisance from noise, dust and vehicles. Waste from demolished buildings is a significant proportion of all waste in developed countries (ranging from 15 to 20%) and cuts across sustainability objectives of governments to reduce waste (Storey *et al.*, 2005).

New footings for the complete re-build in the hypothetical case represent approximately 2–3% of the overall cost, depending on the nature of the foundations. Preparing the footings to take the structure in the hypothetical case is estimated to take from 4 to 6 weeks, adding to financial opportunity costs.

Embodied energy is the total energy used in all activities to create a building and this is used as a *de facto* measure of human impact (Alcorn, 2003). This includes direct energy to make the building and indirect energy embodied to make the materials of the building. Holden and Gjerde (2007) estimate that to retain the existing building and build a top-up would use approximately 16,000 GJ (gigajoules) less energy than demolishing the existing and constructing a new building. Embodied energy is directly linked to greenhouse gases (carbon dioxide, methane and nitrous oxide). It would take an intensive study to determine in what proportions these were produced for the hypothetical building on top, but there are without doubt positive greenhouse gas implications for retaining the host building and adding new apartments on top.

A building life cycle includes extraction of raw material and the making of refined products, transportation, construction and energy use and maintenance throughout the building's life. The longer a building can provide continuing use the better is the per-annum performance. To retain a building and construct a top-up clearly contributes to sustainability and resilience for both the building in question and also for the urban fabric of the city.

Holden (2003) identified several problems with new apartments built on top of existing buildings in Wellington. These mostly relate to the design issues of access, space planning design, and engagement with light and ventilation for interior rooms as well as the technical issues of insulation, and the performance of construction materials. Access was an especially challenging aspect, because of strict fire escape regulations.

The overall quality and performance of many of the cases in Wellington was not considered to be high. The cases studied were what now may be classified as first-generation top-ups, built in the decade from their first occurrence to about 2005. Poor quality is attributed to the lack of experience of architects, developers and builders at the time and the lack of precedent models. Additionally, it is conjectured that many developers involved were looking for minimal financial exposure to a building type that had yet to prove itself in the marketplace. Nevertheless, top-ups have proved to be a viable alternative to the conventional demolish-and-build approach in providing additional residential accommodation. Top-up apartments in Wellington now range widely in resale value, depending on location, access, the quality of construction, finishes and fittings of the host building as well as the new additions. For example, the Blair Apartments (Figure 6.3b) are in the upper value range. Further research and guidance on top-ups will improve future generations of their design and construction.

6.6   Urban Resilience

6.6.1   Urban Renewal and Intensification

It is recognised that positive outcomes of constructing apartments on top of existing buildings may also be achieved through demolition and constructing new buildings. Both urban renewal approaches share attributes of increasing the habitation density of city environments. Such increases strengthen the city's economy, efficiency, vitality and culture. Density increases in some western cities can be achieved without increasing demand on utilities and services. For example, the inner suburbs of the city of Brisbane, Australia had a household occupancy of over five in the 1960s, dropping to less than half that number in the 1990s due to lifestyle changes (Brisbane City Council, 1990). Infrastructure for water, sewerage, power, gas and transport built decades ago remain capable of servicing the earlier occupancy level (with normal upgrades), thereby providing an opportunity to permit intensification of residential housing levels today. Constructing apartments on top of existing buildings can, in many instances, be accommodated without seriously impacting on city infrastructure.

Habitation densification, either through new buildings on demolished sites or through constructing additions on top of existing buildings within the city centre, contributes to curtailing city-edge residential development (McIndoe *et al.*, 2005). Continued residential expansion of city edges has attendant negative impacts on sustainability, in particular through the infrastructure and range of services that are needed for new areas. There are also social and cultural engagement deprivation impacts that derive from city-edge isolation as well as public health problems that derive from high car usage at the expense of personal exercise. City-edge expansion also consumes productive agricultural land, leading to further challenges to urban resilience (Newton, 2004).

6.6.2   Urban Renewal Case Study: Te Aro District, Wellington, New Zealand

Wellington's Te Aro district population has substantially increased over the past 25 years, from approximately 800 residents in 1991 to almost 11,800 in 2017. The population is projected to be about 19,800 by 2043 (Wellington City Council, 2017). Habitation growth to date has been accommodated mainly in new apartment buildings on demolished sites, but also through top-ups, which contribute residences for approximately 2000 (17%) of today's population. There is further potential for building-top apartments to make a considerable contribution to accommodating projected population growth over the next 25 years.

Te Aro is adjacent to Wellington city centre and is approximately 1000×800 m in extent. Because of its proximity to the city centre and to a wide range of workplaces, education facilities, services, recreation and amenities, the area hosts a high number of apartment buildings, all capped at the eight-storey (27 m) height limit for the area. Convenience makes Te Aro a desirable location to live. The area is highly conducive to building-top apartment development and building conversions, due to the numerous well-made older buildings, typically of three floors (12–15 m) that served functions that are now obsolete. Many of these buildings are capable of supporting additions on top, possibly involving structural strengthening and certainly requiring service upgrades. As a result, Te Aro is home to approximately three quarters of the city's one hundred or more building-top apartments (Figure 6.6a). This includes a high proportion that have converted parts of the host building into apartments, many with retail functions at street level and some also with offices above ground floor (Figure 6.6b).

Te Aro benefits from a resurgence in the residential population, which has given additional vitality to the area. It also benefits from the establishment of a new visual layer on top, while maintaining a large degree of the original character at street level. The trigger for the resurgence is multi-dimensional. Te Aro is one of the areas first settled by Europeans, who arrived from the mid-1800s. At this time, it was home to mainly working-class residents. Most of the area slowly evolved over its first century to become focused on manufacturing, warehousing, retail and entertainment, functions that all declined under successive economic challenges to the country as a whole. By the 1970s, the area was in disrepair, with many unoccupied buildings. There were few permanent residents in Te Aro at the time.

In the early 1990s New Zealand introduced several initiatives that collectively contributed to Te Aro's renaissance. A national building performance

(a)

(b)

Figure 6.6 Te Aro top-ups: (a) View over part of Te Aro showing several top-up apartments, from a single contrasting example in mid frame, foreground called 'sky-box' to more compatible examples in the left and right foreground. (b) Top-up apartments on an existing office building, converted to apartments with ground floor retail and car-parking above.

code was introduced which allowed lightweight timber-framed construction for apartment buildings (New Zealand Legislation, 1991, 1992). Soon afterwards, the Wellington 1994 town plan froze subdivision of city boundary perimeter land for residential purposes, thereby forcing developers to look back into the built areas of the city for investment opportunities. A subsequent town planning initiative removed strict single-use zones in the city, allowing mixed uses for buildings (Wellington City Council, 1994). New Zealand established a moratorium period within which the strengthening of buildings was required to meet new earthquake resistance codes, but the government also provided financial subsidies to assist owners to meet the new standards. Some buildings that were considered to be substandard structurally were demolished by their owners, leaving vacant sites waiting for development. In this era, two universities – Victoria and Massey – established faculties in Te Aro and elsewhere in the city centre area, introducing many students and staff members into previously quiet, underused urban areas, with many buying residences close to their places of work. These people were joined by an increasing array of expatriate New Zealanders returning from abroad and new immigrants from overseas urban cultures, with positive experiences of inner-city living.

Multiple ingredients were in place for the renewal and revitalisation of Te Aro, with an emphasis on residential development. Without it being anticipated, building-top apartments evolved and even flourished in this climate.

Three quarters of the Te Aro area accommodates buildings and vacant sites; the other quarter is allocated to roads, paths and parks. Approximately 5–6% of the buildings are considered to be suitable for two- or three-storey lightweight additions on top. This could generate approximately 1000 new apartments, which at the average occupancy for Wellington suggests that about 2500 additional people could be housed through top-ups. This would contribute about one-third of the projected population growth over the next 25 years. In all, this could enhance the city's economy and vitality at lower cost than by providing similar apartments through demolition of existing buildings and building new apartments.

6.6.3 Health, Safety and Vitality in the City

Te Aro's residents mainly walk to their places of employment, education services, cultural activities, recreation, and entertainment, and to social occasions (Wellington City Council, 2009). At 20% Wellington has one of the highest percentages of commuter walking trips in the western world, and the highest by far across Australia and New Zealand (Wellington City Council, 2008). Walkers contribute positively to traffic and pollution reduction by not travelling in vehicles and they contribute to the economy of a place through local spending (Litman, 2003). Walking also contributes positively to public health, with the individuals engaged are generally fitter and healthier than sedentary private car commuters (McIndoe et al., 2005; Woodward, 2002). With the increased residential and visitor populations and the wide mix of services and functions in Te Aro, there are more 'eyes on the street' over longer day-night periods. This adds to a greater sense of personal safety. A preliminary analysis of crime statistics in Wellington shows that per-capita crime rates have decreased over the period of substantial population growth discussed here (Statistics New Zealand, 2016).

The Lonely Planet (2011) guide to New Zealand states that Wellington 'is crammed with more bars, cafes and restaurants per capita than New York'. This confirms the sense of vitality that comes with the population density. With the high numbers of people out and about in Te Aro both day and night comes expectation of better urban environments and facilities than before. The city has responded upgrading many parks, public places, streets, and cultural facilities. The business community has responded likewise by providing a wide range of improved outlets and services. Te Aro's character and lifestyle attracts increasing numbers of residents from other parts of the city, as well as out-of-town visitors, further adding to the vitality and the wellbeing of the citizens. Through new apartments on top of existing buildings, together with other apartment buildings on the sites of demolished obsolete buildings, the increased population contributes to city vitality, a strong economy, cultural progress and improved public health and safety (Holden 2005b).

6.7   Conclusion

While the concept and definition of 'urban resilience' remains a work in progress, it is generally accepted that it may be understood as a measure of a city's capacity to survive, adapt and grow under stress. This triggers numerous dimensions, many of which are addressed more fully in other chapters. Constructing apartments on top of existing buildings engages mainly with the big-picture resilience concepts of sustainable growth and wellbeing of citizens, within which several subtopics have been explored in this chapter.

Building-top apartments can be seen as already contributing to urban resilience in numerous ways through the principles revealed in the cases discussed, none of which independently would be seen as outstanding or a 'silver-bullet' solution. There are, however, many transferable lessons, not the least being the sharing of opportunities and constraints across national and city government leaders, public servants, financiers and entrepreneurs, professionals, developers, and the community as a whole. With such a combination in creative interaction, urban resilience must surely be strengthened.

References

Alcorn, A. (2003) *Embodied Energy and CO$_2$ Coefficients for NZ Building Materials*, Centre for Building Performance Research, Victoria University of Wellington.
AIA (2014) National Architecture Awards 2014: Let's look at the heritage finalists. *www.theconversation.com/national-architecture-awards-2014-lets-look-at-the-heritage-finalists*.

AIA (2017) National Architecture Awards. www.architecture.com.au/events/national/awards/enter-the-awards. Australian Institute of Architects.

Australia ICOMOS (1999) *The Burra Charter*, Australia ICOMOS

Bloszies, C. (2012) *Old Buildings, New Designs: Architectural Transformations.* Princeton Architectural Press.

Brisbane City Council. (Loder and Bayly Consultants) (1990) *Inner Suburbs Action Plan.* Brisbane City Council.

Busch, A. (1991) *Rooftop Architecture – The Art of Going Through the Roof.* Henry Holt.

Costonis, J. (1989) *Icons and Aliens: Law, Aesthetics and Environmental Change.* University of Illinois Press.

ELA (2017) Case studies. Environmental Law Australia, Federal Court of Australia. envlaw.com.au/category/case-studies/.

Giddens, C. (ed) (2004) *Rawlinsons New Zealand Construction Handbook*, Rawlinsons Media.

Habraken, N.(1998) *The Structure of the Ordinary*, MIT Press.

Holden, G. (2003) *New Apartments on Tops of Existing Buildings – An Emerging Typology.* In: *Proceedings of 'The Planned City' International Conference*, Bari, Italy, July 2003.

Holden, G. (2005a) With a twist on top. In: Sanders, P. *et al.* (eds), *Proceedings of AASA Conference 'Drawing Together Convergent Practices in Architectural Education'*, Brisbane.

Holden, G. (2005b) Residential palimpsest – a novel dimension to city sustainability. In: Kungolos, S. et al. (eds), *Sustainable Development and Planning II*. WIT Press.

Holden, G. and Gjerde, M. (2007) Urban sustainability –comparative value of building-top apartments. In: Homer, M *et al.* (eds), *Proceedings of International Conference on Whole Life Urban Sustainability and its Assessment*, SUE-MOT, Glasgow.

ICOMOS (1978) ICOMOS Statutes adopted by the Vth General Assembly on 22 May 1978 in Moscow. ICOMOS.

Australia ICOMOS (2013) The Burra Charter – The Australian ICOMOS Charter for Places of Cultural Significance.

Litman, T. (2003) Economic value of walkability, In: *Walk 21-IV Conference*, Portland, Oregon.

Lonely Planet (2011) *Lonely Planet New Zealand.* Lonely Planet Publications Ltd.

Martinez, A. (2005) *Dwelling on the Roof.* Editorial Gustavo Gili.

McIndoe, G., Chapman, R., McDonald, C. *et al.* (2005) *The Value of Urban Design*, Ministry for the Environment, Wellington.

Melet, E. and Vreedenburgh, E. (2000) *Rooftop Architecture – Building on an Elevated Surface.* NAI Publishers.

Newton, P. (2004) Reshaping the future of cities. *Ecos, Jan-Mar*: 9.

New Zealand Legislation (1991) *Building Act 1991*, New Zealand Government

New Zealand Legislation (1992) *Building Regulations 1992*, New Zealand Government

Roth, M. (2012) *Roof Architecture and Design*, Braun Publishing.

Rowe, P. (1987) *Design Thinking*, MIT Press.

Statistics New Zealand (2016) *New Zealand Crime Data 1975–2014.* Stats NZ, Wellington.

Storey, J. Gerde, M. Charlseson A. and Petersen, M (2005) The state of deconstruction in New Zealand. In: Chini, A (ed.) *Deconstruction and Materials Reuse – an International Overview.* CIB.

Wellington City Council (1994) *Wellington City District Plan*, Wellington City Council.

Wellington City Council (2008) *Wellington City Council Walking Policy*, Wellington City Council.

Wellington City Council (2009) *Central City Apartment Dwellers Survey*, Wellington City Council.

Wellington City Council (2017) Te Aro Population, dwellings & ethnicity, profile. idnz.co.nz

Woodward, A. (2002) The Motor Car and Public Health – Are we exhausting the Environment? in, The Medical Journal of Australia, Vol 177, No 11/12.

Woodward, A. (2002) The motor car and public health – are we exhausting the environment? *Medical Journal of Australia*, 177(11/12): 592–593.

Conversion Potential Assessment Tool

Rob Geraedts, Theo van der Voordt and Hilde Remøy
Delft University of Technology

Property owners have various possible strategies for dealing with vacant office buildings: consolidation, rent reduction, to retain current tenants or to attract new tenants, selling the building, renovation or upgrading, demolition and new-build, and conversion to new functions (Remøy and van der Voordt, 2014). Most owners choose consolidation: keep the building as it is, searching for new tenants and waiting for better times. Mothballing a building or temporarily allowing use to keep squatters out are usually not permanent solutions for coping with structural vacancy but may precede renovation, redevelopment and conversion. Mothballing and anti-squat may both result in damage to the building and make repair and redecoration necessary before the building can be rented out. Lowering rent can attract tenants, but is no structural solution in a real estate market with supply being higher than demand for the current function. Selling is often not an option either. The value of office buildings is based on the potential rental yield and hence the sale of a vacant building often yields less than its book value. Most owners are not willing to accept this financial loss. Likewise, new investments for renovation or upgrading the building are difficult to explain to investors who have already lost money on a property. Although smaller renovations are performed every five years (Douglas, 2006; Vijverberg, 2001), at some point the building requires major adaptations (Wilkinson, 2011). In markets with high vacancy levels, there is a risk that the benefits of upgrading the building for continuation of the current function will be less than the intervention costs. Demolition and new-build creates possibilities for a good fit with current and future users' needs. However, redevelopment takes time and causes interruptions to income streams. If the building is technically in

Building Urban Resilience through Change of Use, First Edition.
Edited by Sara J. Wilkinson and Hilde Remøy.
© 2018 John Wiley & Sons Ltd. Published 2018 by John Wiley & Sons Ltd.

a good state, redevelopment is a waste of resources and conflicts with global aims for sustainable development. If the building has a particular cultural or historical value or adds value to the identity of the location or a wider area, demolition is not an appropriate strategy either. Conversion to new use may be more appropriate. Conversion may sustain a beneficial and durable use of the location and building, implies less income disruption than redevelopment, and can have high social and financial benefits (Bullen, 2011). However, conversion may be expensive and requires the willingness of various stakeholders to adapt the building for other functions. Besides, the future market value of accommodating a new function must be higher than for continued use with the same function.

So, important questions are:

- Which factors enable successful conversion to other functions?
- Which factors hinder adaptive reuse?
- What are the main opportunities and risks, and how can they be reduced or eliminated?

In Section 7.2 we present an overview of relevant factors and aspects. Section 7.3 presents a tool to assess the opportunities and risks of conversion of office buildings to housing: the Conversion Potential Meter, abbreviated to 'the Conversion Meter'. This tool is illustrated with case studies. Section 7.4 presents important opportunities and risks found in 15 Dutch cases. Finally, Section 7.5 presents concluding remarks related to resilience and how to prevent high levels of vacancy in the future.

7.2 Opportunities and Risks

The most appropriate strategy to cope with vacancy depends on the current and future real estate market (demand and supply), the characteristics of the location, the characteristics of the building or a portfolio of a number of buildings, and the interests, preferences and prerequisites of various stakeholders. These factors have a large impact on the conversion potential of a (vacant) building and opportunities and risks of conversion to other functions. The functional, cultural (aesthetics, architectural-, cultural- or historical value), technical, legal and financial aspects must all be taken into account (Geraedts and van der Voordt, 2007, Remøy and van der Voordt, 2014). All these factors may have an impact on the opportunities and risks of conversion and sustainable adaptive reuse of (office) buildings. They are all relevant to assessing the conversion potential of a particular building, a real estate portfolio, or sustainable area transformations of, for instance, inner cities, suburbs or brownfield sites (see Table 7.1).

The matrix in Table 7.1 can be used as an overall framework to assess different strategies to cope with vacancy. Next, we discuss the four levels – market, location, building and stakeholders – more generally and where appropriate discuss the impact of the five factors.

Table 7.1   Factors that may influence a strategy to cope with vacancy.

	Levels			
Factors	Market	Stakeholders	Location	Building
Functional				
Cultural				
Technical				
Legal				
Financial				

7.2.1   Market Potential: Opportunities and Risks

Adaptive reuse is an option to cope with vacancy in case of:

- an oversupply of vacant buildings: the level and duration of vacancies are high, and are expected to be high in the future
- sufficient demand for new functions
- good financial possibilities of adaptive reuse: the return on investment is sufficient to stimulate property owners or other parties to invest in buying a vacant building and convert it to a new function.

We next consider each of these in turn:

Level and duration of vacancy The longer a building has been vacant, the more likely it is that continuation of its current function is not viable and adaptive reuse may be a more successful strategy. A vacancy level of 4–5% is perceived as necessary to enable companies to move (Keeris, 2007). During the movement of the end user to another building the current building will be vacant for a while, the so-called 'frictional' vacancy. However, when too many buildings are structurally vacant – that is, are vacant for over three years – is an indication of a serious quantitative and/or qualitative misfit between demand and supply.

Demand for new functions Without sufficient demand for other functions, adaptive reuse will not be successful. It is therefore important to assess the demand for space of prospective target groups and their needs and preferences. Table 7.2 shows a number of relevant characteristics of the location and the building that should be taken into account in conversions of vacant buildings into housing. On a more detailed level, it is relevant to make a distinction between subgroups, such as students, first-time buyers, young families, young urban professionals, and elderly people. These subgroups have different demands regarding costs and quality, due to their different phases in life and different income levels, which affect the rent level or purchase price they will pay. In cities with many students and other young people, conversion into low-cost accommodation may be a good choice. For high-rise office buildings, conversion into accommodation for seniors and families can be seen to be increasing in large

Table 7.2   Relevant aspects on the demand side of residential accommodation.

Location (housing environment)	Building (residential)

1. Atmosphere
    a. Nature of built environment
    b. Social image
    c. Liveliness
    d. Available green space
2. Facilities
    a. Shops
    b. Restaurants, bars, etc.
    c. Schools
    d. Bank/post office
    e. Medical facilities
    f. Recreative facilities
3. Accessibility public transport
    a. Distance to bus stop
    b. Frequency and times
    c. Distance to tram/underground
4. Accessibility by car
    a. Distance to motorway
    b. Congestion level
    c. Parking facilities
	1. Dwelling type
	2. Access
	3. Dwelling size
	    a. Number of rooms
	    b. Living room
	    c. Kitchen
	    d. Bedrooms
	    e. Sanitary facilities
	    f. Storage space
	4. Arrangement of dwelling
	5. Level of facilities
	6. Outside space (garden, etc.)
	7. View from dwelling, privacy
	8. Environmental aspects
	    a. Heating
	    b. Ventilation
	    c. Noise
	    d. Exposure to sun/daylight
	    e. Energy consumption
	    f. Materials used
	9. General conditions
	    a. Accessibility
	    b. Safety
	    c. Flexibility
	    d. Adequate management
	10. Costs
	    a. Purchase price/rent
	    b. Other costs

cities. Market research to define the specific demand for dwellings may help to define which conversions are most appropriate to the needs and preferences of potential target groups.

Costs and return on investment Current and expected future vacancy levels may have an impact on rent levels and the financial value of the building. The appraised market value of office buildings is normally based on the rental income. Although structurally vacant buildings generate no income and have no perspective of future tenancy, appraisal of structurally vacant buildings is often based on potential tenancy of the property using either the cap rate or discounted cash flow methods (Hendershott, 1996; Hordijk and van de Ridder, 2005; Ten Have, 1992). The accounted value is usually too high for redevelopers, who calculate land and existing building value residually. As long as these two ways of calculating the value of structurally vacant office buildings are not compatible, the price will be seen as too high by redevelopers and too low by owners. A purchasing price that is too high has a negative impact on the conversion potential.

7.2.2 Influence of Stakeholders

The most important stakeholders in adaptive reuse are owners, developers, investors and local and national government. If the owner is not willing to adapt or sell the building to a developer, adaptive reuse will not be realised. Investors and developers will only be willing to buy and transform a building when this fits with their real estate strategy and provides sufficient return on investment. The government plays an important role by creating stimulus through planning regulations and allowing new functions by changing zoning plans if the current plan does not incorporate the new function(s). An important factor is the city council's policy. If municipalities want to strengthen the residential function in the inner city or in other areas, conversion of office buildings into housing may be a successful option. However, when an area is designated as an office area or is a so-called 'office axe' (a linear zone allocated to offices), continuation as an office building may be more appropriate. So, a check on the current zoning plan and willingness to adapt is important. In some cases, there are grants available for conversion projects.

Other actors, such as the inhabitants of surrounding dwellings, may have an impact as well. Because buildings-in-use contribute to the local economy and/or contribute to a safe and lively environment, neighbours will usually accept adaptive reuse. However, if the current building is highly appreciated due to its architectural appearance, cultural-historical value or its identity, much resistance to change may be experienced.

7.2.3 Location Potential

Adaptive reuse requires that the location fits with the requirements of the new target group: prospective new users and owners. Worldwide, properties in city centres, housing areas or edges of such areas are converted into housing, while conversion of buildings in business parks and peripheral areas rarely happens. Building conversions in city centres can be valuable additions to the housing stock. Considering the functionally realisable apartment types as well as the location of office buildings, interested target groups (buyers or renters) can be found. Office buildings in mono-functional business parks, however, are not regarded as suitable for conversion into housing. When structurally vacant office buildings are situated in such locations, transformation of the area is necessary (Avidar, 2007, Smit, 2007, Koppels, 2011).

7.2.4 Building Characteristics

The functional adaptability of vacant buildings is of critical importance to its conversion potential. This depends, *inter alia*, on the measurements of the buildings' structural grids (Douglas, 2006, Geraedts and van der Voordt, 2007). For instance, post-war office buildings were designed as 'cockpits, fitting closely around the function they were meant to accommo-date (Brand, 1994). This tight fit threatens the functional feasibility of con-version into housing.

A high architectural or cultural-historical value and being marked as a monu-ment will hinder demolition and favour adaptive reuse (Benraad and Remøy, 2007). Most office buildings are not listed though, as many are relatively new and not known for their interesting architecture (Remøy and van der Voordt, 2009). In these cases, the main driver for conversion is not to protect the current building but to get it reused, in order to contribute to the quality of the environ-ment and the future value of the location and the building itself. Requirements to keep and preserve a national or municipal monument can hinder adaptive reuse, for instance because balconies cannot be added to the facade.

A poor technical condition forces intervention to improve the building to the required quality level, which is a hindering factor for conversion due to the high costs.

Legal aspects can also reduce the financial feasibility of conversions, for instance due to strict building code regulations, planning rules or zoning plans that allow particular functions and limit or forbid other functions, or regulations limiting the maximum building height. As the requirements for residential buildings and other buildings that accommodate overnight stays are stricter than for day-use functions such as offices, changes to building structures, stairways and facades are often needed.

Usually, building characteristics do not make conversion impossible, but they can influence financial feasibility substantially (Mackay, 2009). When conversion costs become too high compared to the expected benefits, con-version may be financially unfeasible. Mackay *et al.* (2009) studied several Dutch conversion projects and found a clear relationship between building costs and the alterations of specific building elements. The major cost gen-erator for most office-to-housing conversions is facade alterations (27% of the total building cost), followed by interior walls (17% of total building cost) and contractor costs, a group of costs in Dutch estimates combining site costs, general costs of the contractor and his profit (15% of total build-ing cost). Whereas the costs for interior walls depend on the new function and can easily be predicted, the costs related to the facade depend on the building shape, technical state and quality of the existing building, and on the demand for external appearance, comfort and quality of the converted building. The necessity for facade alterations should therefore be thoroughly assessed when studying office-to-housing conversion potential.

7.3 Conversion Meter

To assess the opportunities and risks of conversion of vacant office buildings to dwellings and to define its conversion potential in a systematic, efficient way, the factors and aspects mentioned above have been integrated in con-version potential assessment tool, known as the Conversion Meter, and for-merly as the Transformation Meter (Geraedts and van der Voordt, 2002, 2007; Geraedts *et al.*, 2004). The Conversion Meter consists of a series of checklists to appraise the potential of vacant buildings for conversion to

Step	Action	Level	Outcome
Step 0	Inventory market supply of unoccupied offices	Stock	Location of unoccupied offices
Step 1	Quick Scan: Initial appraisal of unoccupied offices using veto criteria	Location Building	Selection or rejection of offices for further study; Go/No Go decision
Step 2	Feasibility scan: further appraisal using gradual criteria	Location Building	Judgement about transformation potential of office building
Step 3	Determination of transformation class	Location Building	Indicates transformation potential on 5-point scale from excellent to not transformable

Further analysis (optional, and may be performed in reverse order if so desired):

Step	Action	Level	Outcome
Step 4	Financial feasibility scan using design	Building	Indicates financial/economic feasibility Sketch and cost-benefit analysis; Go/No Go decision
Step 5	Risk assessment checklist	Location Building	Highlights areas of concern in transformation plan; Go/No Go decision

Figure 7.1 Conversion meter process.

residential use. This appraisal takes place in a number of steps, from more superficial to more detailed and specific; see Figure 7.1. Methods to develop this tool included a literature review, interviews with experts, such as developers and housing associations, with practical experience in converting office buildings to housing, and case studies to test preliminary versions of the tool. The first version, Transformation Meter 1.0, was developed during the late 1990s, when the Netherlands suffered from high levels of office vacancy. Since then, many graduation students from the Faculty of Architecture at the Delft University of Technology and students from other universities have conducted case studies to test and evaluate the tool. Most theses have been written in Dutch, with a few exceptions in English. These practical applications allowed us to further improve and refine the transformation potential meter. Two new steps – the financial feasibility scan and the risk assessment checklist – have been added to permit further investigation of the feasibility of a conversion project. In this section, we describe the principle of the new transformation meter and its position in the Go/No-Go decision-making process in the initial phase of a conversion project: The Conversion Meter.

Step 0: Inventory of supply at city, district or portfolio level

As a pre-step before actually starting to use the Conversion Potential Assessment Tool, an inventory may be needed of the market supply of office buildings in a particular municipality, area or portfolio, covering those that have been unoccupied for a long time or may be expected to become vacant in the near future. Information may be obtained from a literature survey, from real estate agents or the investigator's own observations. For consideration of a particular vacant building, Step 0 is skipped.

Step 1: Quick scan: first impression, evaluation based on veto criteria

The instrument offers the user the possibility to perform a quick initial appraisal of the conversion potential. This process is quick and does not require much data. It makes use of six veto criteria under the headings 'Market', 'Stakeholders', 'Location' and 'Building'; see Figure 7.2. Failure of a building to meet these criteria means that it does not have sufficient conversion potential and thus leads to a no-go decision. If not satisfied

STEP 1 QUICK SCAN: Initial appraisal of unoccupied offices using veto criteria

Common target group independent criteria.
Answer 'Yes' (score = 1) is positive for conversion into homes. Answer 'No' (score = 0) is negative for conversion into homes
The user of this checklist could reconsider if these criteria actually lead to a veto decision.
If one of the veto criteria concerned lead to the assessment 'No', the conversion into housing is cancelled.
In that case the next step 2 (Feasibility scan: further appraisal using gradual criteria) is no longer applicable.

ASPECT	VETO CRITERION	DATA SOURCE	ASSESSMENT	
VETO CRITERIA MARKET			Yes	No
1 Demand for housing	1 There is a demand for housing of local target groups	Estate agent or municipality		
VETO CRITERIA STAKEHOLDERS				
2 Initiator (advisor)	2 Presence of enthusiastic influential instigator	Local investigation		
3 Developer	3 Does meet criteria for region, location, accessibility	Property developer		
	4 Does meet criteria on size and character of building	Property developer		
4 Owner	5 Willingness to sell the building	Owner		
5 Investor	6 Willingness to buy and transform the building	Investor		
6 Municipality	7 Positive attitude of the municipality	Municipality		
VETO CRITERIA LOCATION				
7 Urban location	8 Zoning plan permits modification	Zoning plan, policy of municipality		
	9 No serious public health risk (pollution, noise, odour)	Estate agent or on site inspection		
VETO CRITERIA BUILDING				
8 Dimensions of skeleton	10 Free ceiling height > 2.60	Estate agent or on site inspection		
		RESULT QUICK SCAN:	0	0

Figure 7.2   Step 1: Quick scan with veto criteria.

(if the answer to the relevant question is 'No'), a veto criterion leads to rejection of the residential conversion option. Further detailed study is not necessary. This is thus an effective means of scrutinising promising conversion candidates. The veto criteria apply to all target groups. Criterion 5, at location level, concerns the situation of the building within the urban fabric. If the building is located at an industrial site where serious public-health hazards have been discovered, or if the authorities do not allow any modification of the zoning plan at this location, there is little point in taking the investigation of the conversion potential any further.

Step 2: Feasibility scan based on gradual criteria

If the results of the quick scan indicate that there is no immediate objection to conversion (no single question is answered 'No'), the feasibility of conversion can be studied in greater detail by assessing a number of 'gradual' criteria: criteria that do not lead to a go/no-go decision but express the conversion potential of the building and its location through a numerical score. Taken together, these criteria provide an overall picture of the conversion potential of the project. The feasibility scan at location level (Figure 7.3) includes 7 main criteria, subdivided into functional, cultural and legal aspects, and 23 subcriteria. The feasibility scan at building level (Figure 7.4) comprises 14 main criteria, subdivided into functional, cultural, technical, and legal aspects, and 29 subcriteria. A 'Yes' answer to any question indicates somewhat higher suitability for conversion. At the end of the scan, the number of 'Yes' responses is added up to obtain the overall conversion potential score – the higher the better. This is described under Step 3 below. It may be noted that the criteria vary somewhat, depending on the target group considered. For example, students will prefer to live in the city centre where there is more nightlife, while young families with children will tend to opt for a peaceful suburban environment.

Step 3: Determination of the conversion potential class

The results of the feasibility scan can be used to calculate a conversion potential score, based on which the building can be assigned to one out of five conversion classes ranging from 'No transformation potential' to 'Excellent transformation potential'; see Figure 7.5. Depending on the results, this may lead to a no-go decision or to further refinement of the feasibility study in two subsequent phases.

The total scores for the location (result 'A' in Figure 7.3) and the building (result 'B' in Figure 7.4) are determined by multiplying the number of Yes responses in the respective tables by a weighting factor, which has provisionally been chosen as 5 for the location and 3 for the building to reflect the greater relative importance of the location in these considerations. The maximum possible score for the location is thus $23 \times 5 = 115$, and for the building $298 \times 3 = 87$, summing up to a grand total of $115 + 87 = 202$

STEP 2 FEASIBILITY SCAN: Further appraisal using gradual criteria

Answer 'Yes' (score = 1) is positive for conversion to homes. Answer 'No' (score = 0) is negative for conversion into homes
The user of this checklist could reconsider if on of these criteria actually has to be a veto criterion. If so, then this criterion switches to Step 1 and the other way around.

LOCATION

ASPECT	GRADUAL CRITERION	DATA SOURCE	ASSESSMENT	
FUNCTIONAL			Yes	No
1 Urban location	1 Building in suitable area (not remote industrial or offices area)	Town map/ Google Maps		
	2 Good daylight/sunlight possibilities	On-site inspection		
	3 Good view from building, >75% floor space	On-site inspection		
2 Distance and quality of facilities	4 Shop for daily necessities <500 m.	Local investigation/ Google Maps		
Remark:	5 Neighbourhood meeting-places (square, park) <500 m.	Local investigation/ Google Maps		
The quality of facilities can be described in terms of quality, a wide variety and the number of	6 Food service industry (bar, café, restaurant) <500 m.	Local investigation/ Google Maps		
	7 Bank / post office <5 km.	Local investigation/ Google Maps		
different facilities	8 Basic medical facilities (practice, health centre) <2 km.	Local investigation/ Google Maps		
	9 Sports facilities (fitness, swimming pool, sports park) <2 km.	Local investigation/ Google Maps		
	10 Educational facilities (from kindergarten to university) <2 km.	Local investigation/ Google Maps		
3 Accessibility by public transport	11 Distance to railway station <2 km.	Town map/ Google Maps		
	12 Distance to bus, train, underground <1 km.	Town map/ Transport services		
4 Accessibility by car and parking facilities	13 Good flow, normal street quality	Local investigation/ Google Maps		
Obstacles: bottlenecks or thresholds in roads, bridges	14 Distance to parking sites <250 m.	Local investigation/ Re-design		
Flow: 1-way traffic, no parking, traffic jam	15 >1 parking lot/100 m2 office space	Local investigation/ Re-design		

Figure 7.3   Step 2: Feasibility scan using gradual criteria at location level; answer 'Yes' (score = 1) is positive and answer 'No' (score = 0) is negative for conversion into homes.

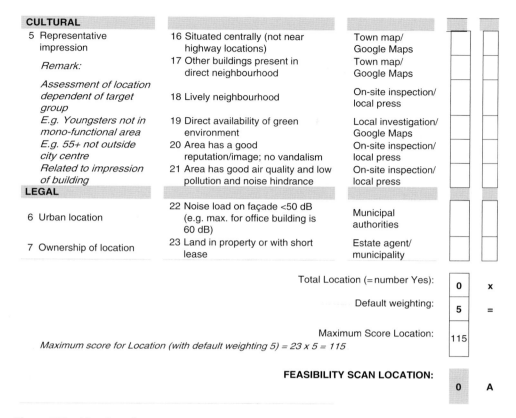

CULTURAL

5 Representative impression

Remark:

Assessment of location dependent of target group
E.g. Youngsters not in mono-functional area
E.g. 55+ not outside city centre
Related to impression of building

LEGAL

6 Urban location

7 Ownership of location

16 Situated centrally (not near highway locations)
17 Other buildings present in direct neighbourhood

18 Lively neighbourhood

19 Direct availability of green environment
20 Area has a good reputation/image; no vandalism
21 Area has good air quality and low pollution and noise hindrance

22 Noise load on façade <50 dB (e.g. max. for office building is 60 dB)
23 Land in property or with short lease

Town map/ Google Maps
Town map/ Google Maps

On-site inspection/ local press

Local investigation/ Google Maps
On-site inspection/ local press
On-site inspection/ local press

Municipal authorities

Estate agent/ municipality

Total Location (= number Yes): | 0 | x

Default weighting: | 5 | =

Maximum Score Location: | 115 |
Maximum score for Location (with default weighting 5) = 23 x 5 = 115

FEASIBILITY SCAN LOCATION: | 0 | A

Figure 7.3   *(Continued)*

(see Figure 7.5). The minimum score is zero, which would indicate that no single feature of the location or the building is considered suitable for conversion.

Buildings in Conversion Class 1 (scoring lower than 40) are assessed as not suitable for conversion to residential accommodation, while those in Class 5 (scoring higher than 161) are perceived as extremely suitable for conversion. In the examples of Figures 7.3 and 7.4, no assessment scores for Location and Building have been filled out yet, and as such the total scores in Figure 7.5 is 0, corresponding to Conversion Class 1: Not transformable.

The total score is an indication of the conversion potential but does not define the final decision. In practice, some criteria can be more important than others. Decision-makers are free to adapt the default weight values of 3 (building) and 5 (location) if that fits better with the particular circumstances.

Determination of the conversion class of an office building completes the first three steps of the Conversion Meter. If the results indicate that the

STEP 2 FEASIBILITY SCAN: Further appraisal using gradual criteria

Answer 'Yes' (score = 1) is positive for conversion to homes. Answer 'No' (score = 0) is negative for conversion into homes
The user of this checklist could reconsider if on of these criteria actually has to be a veto criterion.
If so, then this criterion switches to Step 1 and the other way around.

BUILDING

ASPECT		GRADUAL CRITERION	DATA SOURCE	ASSESSMENT	
FUNCTIONAL				Yes	No
1	Year of construction or renovation	1 Building >3 years	Year of construction		
		2 Building renovated >3 years	Year of last renovation		
2	Vacancy	3 Complete building is vacant	Estate agent		
		4 Building vacant >3 years	Estate agent		
3	New housing	5 Capacity building >20 1p-units/50 m2	≥1000 m2 floor space		
		6 Lay-outs adaptable for local target groups	Sketch design		
4	Extendibility	7 Horizontal extension building possible (neighbouring buildings)	On-site inspection/ Google Maps		
		8 Vertical extension building possible (no inclined roof/light construction)	On-site inspection/ estate agent		
		9 Possibilities for constructing basement	On-site inspection/ estate agent		
CULTURAL					
5	Representative impression *Related to impression of location*	10 Identifiable compared to surrounding buildings	On-site inspection		
		11 Own identity realisable	On-site inspection/ re-design		
6	Cultural heritage	12 Being not a cultural heritage: Simplifies transformation	Municipality/ Authorities		
7	Access (entrance, elevators, stairs)	13 Clear, safe and clarifying building entrance	On-site inspection/ re-design		
TECHNICAL					
8	Condition of maintenance	14 Well maintained; maintenace up-to-date	On-site inspection/ facades		
9	Dimensions of support structure *E.g. Facade grid size determines location inner walls*	15 Depth of building <10 m.	On-site inspection/ estate agent		
		16 Grid support structure >3.60 m	On-site inspection/ estate agent		
		17 Height dimension between floors <6.00 m	On-site inspection/ estate agent		
10	Support structure (walls, columns, floors)	18 Condition support structure is good / not hazardous	On-site inspection/ estate agent		

Figure 7.4   Step 2: Feasibility scan using gradual criteria at building level; answer 'Yes' (score = 1) is positive and answer 'No' (score = 0) is negative for conversion into homes.

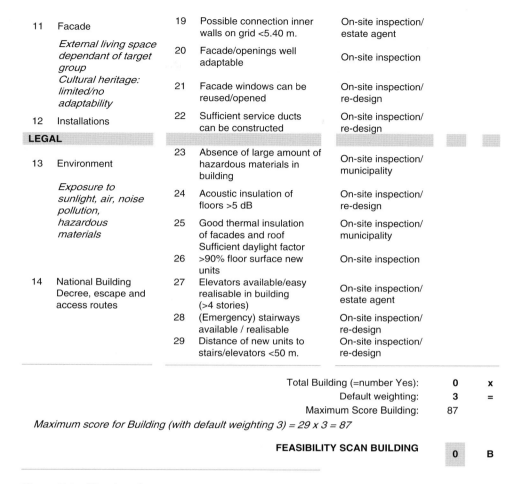

11	Facade	19	Possible connection inner walls on grid <5.40 m.	On-site inspection/ estate agent
	External living space dependant of target group	20	Facade/openings well adaptable	On-site inspection
	Cultural heritage: limited/no adaptability	21	Facade windows can be reused/opened	On-site inspection/ re-design
12	Installations	22	Sufficient service ducts can be constructed	On-site inspection/ re-design

LEGAL

13	Environment	23	Absence of large amount of hazardous materials in building	On-site inspection/ municipality
	Exposure to sunlight, air, noise pollution, hazardous materials	24	Acoustic insulation of floors >5 dB	On-site inspection/ re-design
		25	Good thermal insulation of facades and roof	On-site inspection/ municipality
		26	Sufficient daylight factor >90% floor surface new units	On-site inspection
14	National Building Decree, escape and access routes	27	Elevators available/easy realisable in building (>4 stories)	On-site inspection/ estate agent
		28	(Emergency) stairways available / realisable	On-site inspection/ re-design
		29	Distance of new units to stairs/elevators <50 m.	On-site inspection/ re-design

Total Building (=number Yes): 0   x
Default weighting: 3   =
Maximum Score Building: 87

Maximum score for Building (with default weighting 3) = 29 x 3 = 87

FEASIBILITY SCAN BUILDING 0 B

Figure 7.4 (*Continued*)

STEP 3: DETERMINATION CONVERSION POTENTIAL CLASS OF OFFICE BUILDING

CONVERSION SCORE	CONVERSION CLASS		
Conversion Score Location + Building = 0–40	Class 1: No transformation potential	**Total Score Feasibility Scan A + B:**	0
Conversion Score Location + Building = 41–80	Class 2: Hardly any transformation potential	Maximum Score Location + Building	
Conversion Score Location + Building = 81–120	Class 3: Limited transformation potential	= 115 + 87 =	202
Conversion Score Location + Building = 121–160	Class 4: High transformation potential		
Conversion Score Location + Building = 161–202	Class 5: Excellent transformation potential	**CONVERSION CLASS**	1

Figure 7.5 Step 3: Determination of conversion potential class of office building.

building has sufficient potential for conversion – if it falls into Conversion Class 4 or 5 – the analysis can be continued in two additional steps:

- determining the financial feasibility of the conversion project (Step 4)
- a risk assessment for further planning (Step 5).

Depending on the nature of the project involved, Step 5 may come before Step 4.

Step 4: Financial feasibility scan

The financial feasibility scan aims to obtain an indication of the viability of a conversion project, based on key figures regarding the costs of conversion and revenues from rental income. It is not yet meant as a detailed calculation based on the costs of all construction elements, materials, labour costs and so on. The financial feasibility depends, among other things, on the acquisition costs, the current condition of the building, the level of renovation or modification work required, the finish and comfort level of the housing, the number of (extra) dwelling units that can be created in the building and the project yield by rental income and/or sales prices (Gelinck et al., 2013). On the revenue side, the key figures are the number of dwellings that can be created for the intended target groups, and the rent level or purchase price these target groups might be willing to pay. A sketch plan of a possible layout of the building after conversion is useful to get an indication of the number and types of dwellings that can be incorporated in the current building. The financial feasibility can be improved by increasing the size of the building, say by adding extra floors on top, by a horizontal extension, or by the inclusion of commercial functions (usually at ground level). On the expense side, it is necessary to know the acquisition costs for the premises, including the land price, and the conversion costs: the building and installation costs. Relevant questions to be asked are, for instance:

- What is the current condition of the building?
- Which parts can be reused, and which will have to be demolished?
- What is the ratio of facade surface area to gross floor area (GFA)?
- To what level should the building be finished?
- To what extent can the existing stairways, lifts and other means of access and the facade proportions be maintained?

These issues are all included in a residual-value approach to adaptive reuse. The approach is stepwise:

- The potential yield of the new use is calculated.
- The costs for the building adaptation are determined.
- The residual value results from the yield minus the costs calculation.

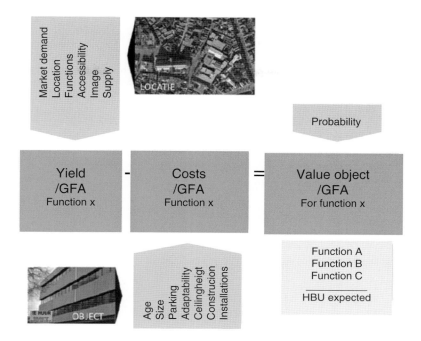

Figure 7.6 Approach to defining the residual value of an office to residential conversion.

The calculation can be performed on different potential new uses. As a final step in the residual-value approach, the residual value of the different options can be compared, to decide on the 'highest and best use' of the adaptive reuse. Step 1 is calculated from the yield-generating characteristics: market demand, location functions mix, accessibility, image and available supply. Step 2 is based on cost generating characteristics like those already described in the feasibility criteria: building age, size, parking, adaptability, ceiling height, construction and installations. Figure 7.6 outlines the residual approach: if one knows the purchase price and conversion costs, and defines the required return on investment, one also knows the investment budget that is available for conversion of the building.

After an approximate cost–benefit analysis has been made on the basis of a sketch of the way in which various dwelling types and layouts can be fitted into the existing office building, the data can be used as input for the development plans of the property developer. Many reference documents are available with key cost figures or rental prices and project costs for various building types. Unfortunately, most cost data refer to new-build projects. Less cost–benefit information is available for conversion projects. The reason is probably that conversion costs and purchase prices and benefits from rental income or selling price are affected by many factors, including the national and local current real estate market and the level of intervention that is needed to convert the current office building into housing of sufficient quality. For instance, the construction costs for transforming the facade are dependent on the condition of the current facade and the possibility of

Table 7.3 Indication of conversion and purchase costs based on 12 cases from the Netherlands.

Dwelling type and residents	Low level of intervention		High level of intervention	
	Construction costs	Purchase costs	Construction costs	Purchase costs
	€m/m2 GFA	€m/m2 GFA	€m/m2 GFA	€m/m2 GFA
Student room	460–620	230–310	550–740	140–190
Studio	620–930	310–460	740–1110	190–270
2/3-room apartment, young couples	770–1030	380–520	930–1230	190–260
4-room apartment, young couples	770–1150	380–570	930–1380	270–400
3-room apartment, senior citizens	370–560	180–270	450–660	110–170
4/5-room apartment, senior citizens	500–1150	250–570	600–1380	140–340

GFA, gross floor area. All costs include VAT.

reusing part or all of it. The state of the supporting structure and foundations can also have an impact on conversion costs differences between projects. Each conversion project is unique (Mulder, 2015). As a consequence, the key cost figures of conversion projects span a huge range.

Table 7.3 shows some key conversion and purchase cost figures, which determine the total investments costs. They are based on 12 projects of the Stadswonen Housing Association in Rotterdam, the Netherlands. The data originate from 2002 and have been updated to 2016 by P. de Jong, Delft University of technology (February 2017). A distinction has been made between conversion projects with a low or a high level of required intervention. The cost differences between the most expensive and least expensive projects are shown to be determined to a large degree by the costs of (conversion of) the facade. The inner walls are on average more expensive, but these costs are less variable and thus have less influence on the overall level of the structural costs. The current supporting structure also has a significant influence on the total costs.

Table 7.4 shows an overview of monthly rental income and residual investment budgets per unit and per square metre of lettable floor area (LFA) or gross floor area (GFA), for different dwelling types and target groups (Geraedts et al., 2004; De Vrij, 2002). The data are based on the same 12 projects as in Table 7.3 and also have been updated by P. de Jong, TUD, February 2017. The target groups define the required type of home, the number and layout of the rooms, access, appeal and the size of the outdoor area. Using this data, floor plans can be drawn and matched to the existing building. When drawing up floor plans, existing stairs, lifts, access paths, design lines and facade boundaries must be respected. Based on the layout of the homes, the number of homes can be estimated and an indication of the rental price or selling price can be established.

To better understand the large range of key cost figures of conversion projects, use can be made of form figures (Pinder et al., 2013). An example

Table 7.4   Feasible rental income and investments per unit, based on 12 cases from the Netherlands.

Dwelling types and residents	Rent/ month €	Feasible investment per unit €000	Feasible investment per m²/RFA €	Feasible investment per m²/GFA €
Student room	176–242	36–53	1,100–1,460	770–1,010
Studio	242–352	53–77	1,460–2,170	1,010–1,540
2/3-room apartment, young couples	605–825	130–178	1,920–2,300	1,300–1,720
4-room apartment, young couples	825–1100	178–237	1,920–2,5,50	1,300–1,900
3-room apartment, senior citizens	440	89	940–1,200	590–950
4/5-room apartment, senior citizens	605–1210	130–261	1,300–2,550	830–1,900

is the ratio between LFA and GFA. This ratio explains how much floor area is used for construction, facilities and circulation areas. The higher this ratio is, the better the space utilisation of the building. A project with less efficient floor plans is usually less financially feasible. Small homes are often easier to fit in existing buildings, which increases the efficiency. For tower blocks, the division into dwellings is less efficient than for elongated buildings. In the tables above an efficiency ratio of GFA/ LFA between 1.3 and 1.55 is assumed. Other key data are layout shape and the percentage of open and closed parts of the facade. Square layouts have less facade surface than elongated floor plans.

The adaptive capacity of buildings may have a large impact on their future value. Today's methods for determining the financial feasibility of building conversions do not consider this future value sufficiently. The adaptive capacity of a building can only be valued in the use phase of the building when functional and structural adaptions are required. To make buildings that are adaptable in the future usually requires extra initial construction costs. When only taking into account the initial construction costs, an adaptable building is less attractive than a 'non-adaptable' building (Hermans et al., 2014). Therefore, not only should investment costs be taken into account, but also the total lifecycle costs. A lifecycle cost approach focuses is on housing costs and benefits during the whole lifecycle. The following elements are taken into account (Hermans et al., 2014):

- the added value of adaptability through lower operating costs
- the added value of adaptive capacity, through lower adaptation costs in the future
- the contribution of adaptive capacity to better lettability and/or market value
- reduction of total cost of ownership and asset management
- incorporation of circular economy principles.

Circular economy concerns require maximum reuse of construction components and natural resources to prevent elimination of value. Each construction component has a residual value through reuse, and this value needs to be considered in the financial feasibility. Applying circular economy principles also means increasing resilience, as these buildings are adaptable and resilient to environmental, societal and economic changes.

Step 5: Risk assessment checklist with possible solutions

Step 5 is a scan of possible risks and ways to mitigate them. It is of great importance to be aware of the possible bottlenecks and risks that may come to the fore. Table 7.5 presents a risk assessment list with possible solutions at market and location level, including from the point of view from some important stakeholders. Table 7.6 presents a risk assessment list with possible solutions at building level. Both tables list the possible risks under the same headings as those used in the quick scan and feasibility scan i.e. functional, cultural, technical, legal and financial. The checklists are based on experience gained in a large number of projects.

Example of risk at stakeholders' level: zoning plan

Risk: The local authorities are not ready or willing to approve any changes in the zoning plan required for success of the project. This is one of the points that need to be thoroughly explored in advance by consulting and convincing the authorities concerned.

Solution: try to convince the municipality of the benefits of conversion to the new functions and use the power and interests of involved stakeholders and prospective tenants.

Example of risk at location level: noise pollution

Risk: Excessive noise level at facade. According to the Dutch Noise Pollution Act, this value should not exceed 60 dB for offices and 50 dB for dwellings. Similar levels are used internationally.

Solution: Many office locations are situated near major roads, railways or industrial premises. If the properties are rezoned for residential use, they will have to meet much more stringent requirements and quite extensive measures may be needed to ensure compliance. Some of these measures will involve modification of the building, but noise screens placed round the source of the noise may also be effective. Another option is to locate rooms where less stringent noise standards apply, such as workshops or bathrooms, where the noise load is highest.

As an example of risk at building level, we can consider poor financial feasibility: where the acquisition price or renovation costs are too high, or the small size of the building means that the costs have to be recovered from a limited number of tenants. In general, for conversion of office buildings to residential accommodation, the larger the project, the easier it is to make financially viable. The investments needed to make the existing building suitable for residential purposes can be partially financed by extending the size of the building, horizontally and/or vertically (by adding new storeys on top).

Table 7.5   Risk assessment checklist at market/location level: possible solutions and important stakeholders.

Market and location		Risk	Possible solution
1. Functional	1	Insufficient parking places	Dependent on target group; consultation about parking rules, consider basement parking
	2	Lack of facilities	Local facilities in building; collaboration with other stakeholders
	3	Lack of public transport	Consulting public transport companies; collaboration with other stakeholders
	4	Unclear route to building	Analysis of neighbourhood; replacement or extra entrance
2. Cultural	5	Bad reputation or unsafe neighbourhood	Improvement of neighbourhood in collaboration with other stakeholders; choice of specific target group
3. Technical	6	Odour	Specific insulation of facades
	7	Noise	Extra noise insulation facades; extra membrane on facade
4. Legal	8	Zoning plan change/ procedure	Consulting local authorities; assessment of local policy and regulations
	9	Land possession/lease	Unfavourable for development; try to amend ground lease
	10	Ground pollution	Clear ground declaration by owner; negotiating lower land selling price due to clean-up costs
	11	Restricted maximum building height	Research possible horizontal extension
5. Financial	12	Purchase price of dwellings to high	Extra benefits through combination with commercial functions; redesign plot; other target groups
	13	Bad lettability of dwellings	Improve price/quality ratio; consider other target groups
	14	Necessity for new facilities	Enhance financial feasibility by adding commercial functions
STAKEHOLDERS			
1. Initiator	15	Absence of enthusiastic influential initiator	Search for experienced instigator at other successful locations, realised projects
2. Developer	16	Does not meet criteria for region, location, accessibility	Consulting and convincing property developer; search for other property developer
	17	Does not meet criteria on size and character of building	Consulting and convincing property developer; search for other property developer
3. Owner/investor	18	Not willing to sell the building	Consulting and convincing owner on realistic costs and benefits of building remaining vacant

Table 7.6   Risk assessment at building level: checklist with possible solutions.

Building	Risk		Possible solution
1. Functional	1	False expectations of building possibilities	Analyse form factors, key ratios, data, gross/net floor area; extension possibilities (horizontal/vertical)
	2	Building depth too shallow (front to back)	Adapt layouts; enlarge by new foundations/facades; add external corridor
	3	Building depth too large	Adapt layouts; add open interior space (daylight), centralise entrances
	4	No basement available for parking, storage	Add basement (dependent on foundations and access)
	5	Floor height too large	Use lightweight mezzanines and interior walls
	6	Windows cannot be opened	Replacement windows; facade renovation
	7	Less connection possibilities for inner walls at facades	Connectable inner walls until facade renovation complete
	8	Lack of outdoor space	Target group dependent; French balconies; recessed parts of facade; interior garden
	9	Insufficient elevators/stairs (access and escape routes)	New elevators/staircases within or external to building
	10	Insufficient access possibilities	Analyse different access possibilities (portico, gallery, inner corridor, central)
	11	Qualitative/quantitative insufficient existing inner walls	Adapt existing walls; add new walls (future adaptability)
	12	Bathrooms insufficiently waterproof	Waterproof floors; use prefab (plastic) bathrooms
2. Cultural	13	Limitations due to heritage status	Early consulting with heritage agency and local government
	14	Insufficiently distinctive building	Add new facade (parts), balconies, dwelling entrances
	15	Insufficient distinguishability of building entrance	Emphasise by louvre or similar; replace in another location
3. Technical	16	False expectations of quality of construction	Analyse construction status onsite (design, condition, finishing, maintenance)
	17	Insufficient air-conditioning	Replacement/renewal, adjusted to dwellings
	18	Insufficient piping, tubes and shafts	Extension (fire-resistant walls between dwellings; holes in existing floors)
	19	Insufficient water supply	Extend facilities (individually controllable and metered)
	20	Insufficient electric facilities	Extend facilities (individually controllable and metered)
	21	Insufficient noise insulation of floors	Double floors and/or double ceilings
	22	Insufficient thermal insulation of facades	Extra insulation outside or inside facade (monumental status); mind adapting windows
	23	Insufficient thermal insulation of windows	Replacement by double glazing; extra secondary frame; extra membrane facade Inside or outside)

Table 7.6   *(Cont'd)*

Building	Risk		Possible solution
	24	Insufficient thermal insulation of facades of roof	Insulate existing roof (inside/outside); replacement by new roof; combine with vertical extension
	25	Presence of moisture, humidity	Analyse causes: humidity, leakage, condensation
	26	Bad flushing in facades	Clean facade; new flushing (where required)
	27	Insufficient daylight and sunlight (<10% floor surface)	Implement inner corridors, extra holes in floors, bay windows, new large windows; ask for dispensation
	28	Bad/dangerous support structure	Reconstruction, reinforcement with steel, gunned concrete, secondary construction
	29	Limited carrying capacity or bad foundations	Reconstruct (extra piles, foundations)
	30	Insufficient carrying capacity for vertical building extensions	Use lightweight construction (steel or timber frame) for new floor levels
4. Legal	31	Presence of asbestos	Negotiate lower selling price, demand asbestos-free declaration by seller
	32	Restrictions from (local) regulations	Dispensations re outer space, ceiling height, entrance/access, daylight, insulation
	33	Uncertainty/vagueness about building permit	Early local communication about demands and information to be delivered
	34	Inadequate incorporation of fire safety requirements	Early local communication about access, fire escape routes, etc.
5. Financial	35	Building difficult to buy/acquire	Step-by-step purchase: at first ground lease, then in a later stage possession; collective purchase with other stakeholders
	36	Large investment in initial phase	Financial feasibility study
	37	Difficult feasibility (say, building is too small)	Analysis of extension possibilities; combination with other (commercial) stakeholders; search for subsidies
	38	Risk of vacancy, impoverishment (say, long development required)	Limit vacancy period through temporary let of (parts of) building

One advantage of adding new built premises is that the extra land costs are basically zero. If new floors are added, the building's supporting structure must be strong enough to bear the extra load, or must be reinforced to this end. Horizontal extensions must fit in with the location and usually permits must be obtained from the municipal authorities (town planning, building control, fire safety). Another possible way of improving the financial feasibility is to rent out retail, business or office space on the ground floor or to rent out parking space. Usually, exemptions from particular building regulations are granted by national and local authorities.

7.4   Conversion Meter Case Studies

The conversion meter was developed by use of case studies. Two of the case studies that were used for developing the conversion meter are presented here.

7.4.1   Puntegale

Puntegale is one of the icons of conversion, designed by Stadswonen, Rotterdam, in the Netherlands. This former tax office, built in 1940–1946, was converted in 1999 into dwellings for students and starter homes for young people entering the housing market (Figure 7.7). The drivers to convert were the high demand for housing, a housing association in search for inner-city building locations, the attractive appearance of the building, the beautiful entrance hall, and the expected increase of the value of assets due to revitalisation and upgrading of the whole area. Hindering factors were the low return on investment, noise nuisance, and a lack of permission to add balconies to the facade due to its status as a municipal monument.

Figure 7.7   Puntegale, Rotterdam (source: Stadswonen, Rotterdam).

Figure 7.8   Atlantic House, Rotterdam (source Remøy et al., 2015).

Thanks to a clever redesign, the final result was a successful conversion that suited current user requirements, and complied with regulations for new buildings in the Building Code, and sustainability principles.

7.4.2   Atlantic House

The conversion of the national listed office building Atlantic House was initiated by the property developers Van Herk and HD and completed in 2009 (Figure 7.8). The street facade, the roof and the public indoor spaces, including the restaurant, had to be conserved as part of the monument listing. The original flexibility concept was brought back in the project, apartments were developed as lofts, and adaptations were reversible. The building was sustainably converted; original building parts were reused and energy saving measures were applied. The success factors of the project were the location near to Rotterdam city centre, the characteristic external appearance, the flexibility of the layout., and the cooperation with the municipality and their willingness to co-create new solutions for this project.

7.5   Lessons Learned from Case Studies

7.5.1   Applicability of the Conversion Meter in Practice

Versions of the Conversion Meter have been used in many case studies, to explore its applicability and options for further improvement, to investigate the conversion potential of the building(s), and to explore which opportunities and risks come to the fore in practice. The checklists have been shown to be widely applicable. No missing factors came to the fore. However, the predictive power of the conversion potential score is limited. Some cases with a low conversion potential according to the criteria were converted successfully, whereas some cases with a high conversion potential score were not converted due to insurmountable obstacles. In cases with a high conversion potential score, some risk factors frustrated actual conversion. These findings confirm that the scores of 0 (No) or 1 (Yes) per criterion and the allocated default weights that were mentioned in Section 7.3 (for the location and building levels) can be different in practice, depending on the local context. The cultural value of a vacant building or a misfit with the current parking standard may in practice be more significant, amounting to veto criteria in the success or failure of an intended adaptive reuse (Remøy and van der Voordt, 2014, Baker *et al.*, 2017). On the other hand, a number of veto criteria in the first version of the tool were found to be too stringent, such as a project size of less than 20 dwelling units (2000 m²), a building being partially occupied, a duration of vacancy of less than three years, or a building less than three years old. In later versions of the Conversion Meter these former veto criteria were skipped or reclassified as gradual criteria.

7.5.2   Adaptability

Markets increasingly demand for flexibility and sustainability. There is also as a growing understanding of the importance of a circular economy. A direct connection can be made between adaptive building and sustainability (Wilkinson and Remøy, 2011). The longer a building is kept in its function instead of becoming vacant or being demolished, the more sustainable it will be. The more flexible a building is, and the more adaptable to changing user demands, the longer it will keep its function, and the lower the total lifecycle costs will be (Hermans *et al.*, 2014). The adaptive capacity of a building includes all the characteristics that enable it to keep its functionality through changing requirements and circumstances, during its entire technical lifespan and in a sustainable and financially profitable way. The adaptive capacity is considered a crucial component when looking into the sustainability of real estate stock (Geraedts, 2016).

7.5.3   Opportunities and Risks Found in 15 Dutch Cases

Remøy and van der Voordt (2014) tested 15 cases on conversion potential 'from offices to housing' by using the Transformation Meter version 2.0. In their analyses some recurring opportunities and risks came to the fore and are discussed below.

Opportunities

The short development time-span, from the first sketch till delivery of the apartments, was considered an opportunity. One project took just two years from the first sketch to completion. While still working on the design, the building was stripped to its structural frame, stairs and elevator. Not only was time saved because the main structure was already there, but because of this approach, fewer days were lost due to bad weather. The 'WYSIWYG-factor' – 'What You See Is What You Get' – contributed to this advantage. In many cases, display apartments were furnished before the reconstruction started. Whereas most people cannot interpret architectural drawings, display apartments inform potential buyers better and boost sales. Financial feasibility was improved by selling the apartments before construction started, leading to lower financing costs and risks. Moreover, in various cases conversion costs were lower than for demolition and new build. The conversion costs varied considerably. High conversion costs were caused by demand for high quality in the external and internal finishes and demands for comfort from the target group (in particular, acoustic and thermal insulation). Low conversion costs were achieved when few changes were made to the facades (particularly in student housing) and when the floor plan was easily adaptable.

The conversions studied received few objections from neighbours. Redevelopment was thought positive in the cases of a building in an area with high vacancy and dilapidation. This improved the financial feasibility of the projects. Finally, conversion of vacant offices was considered a sustainable alternative to demolition and new build, saving building materials and transportation, and producing less waste than demolition and new construction. A frequently heard argument for demolition is that older buildings are not sustainable. However, the performance of the case study buildings was adapted to the Dutch building code and to the level of comfort expected by the relevant user group. Table 7.7 summarises the key opportunities found in the Dutch cases.

Risks

Asbestos was found in seven of the fifteen projects. Asbestos removal follows strict rules and involves high costs. In all the projects, asbestos removal was accounted for in the building assessment. In a few cases, apartment sales were challenging; in one case, luxury apartments without private outdoor spaces and with low ceilings (in breach of the building rules) were sold only after the prices were lowered significantly. In another case, apartments with daylight from the north only were not sold for the initial asking price. The characteristics of these apartments clearly did not correspond to the preferences of the target group. Even in a tight housing market, quality and willingness to pay was found to correspond, especially in the top segment of the housing market.

Table 7.7   Conversion opportunities in 15 Dutch case studies.

Aspect	Opportunities
Functional	
	1 Sufficient parking places
	2 Existing floor plan easily adapted
	3 Extra "left-over space", not available in new developments
Cultural	
	4 Historical value, strong architectural appearance
	5 Positive impact on surrounding area
Technical	
	6 Reuse of large parts of existing building (facade and construction)
	7 Strong floors, possible to add extra weight
	8 Strong foundation, vertical extension possible
Legal	
	9 New function fits zoning plan
	10 Conversion preferred by neighbours
	11 Measures fit with building code requirements
Financial	
	12 Low purchasing price
	13 Preselling implies lower financing costs
	14 Commercial activities in plinth (ground level)

Three out of five buildings constructed before 1950 and three of the five buildings constructed between 1950 and 1965 were not built according to drawings and the construction materials and measurements were different per floor. The reason was that, in the first years after the Second World War, housing was prioritised over commercial buildings in the Netherlands. It was difficult to get building materials, and in many cases contractors used the material they could find without altering the drawings. Buildings constructed after 1965 showed no such differences.

In one of the 15 projects, the main structure was in an unsatisfactory state. The concrete in the external columns was deteriorating; hence it was repaired and reinforced. This repair added extra costs to the project, but as a result of the repairs the columns became wider, and the design needed modification. In other projects, concrete deterioration and steel corrosion was found but required only minor repairs. In most cases, this kind of technical problem was assessed in the preliminary phase. Office buildings are constructed to carry more weight than housing, and in most cases, additional floors can be carried by the existing structure.

Apartments require more vertical shafts for electricity, water and plumbing than offices. In buildings constructed before 1965, floors were penetrated and shafts installed without problems. After 1965, pre-stressed concrete was commonly used, making larger spans possible. The problem of pre-stressed concrete though, is that it loses strength when the steel is cut. In three of the five buildings constructed after 1965, pre-stressed concrete was used.

Structural grids in buildings constructed before 1965 were small and came with thin, lightweight floors. Although these floors are strong, acoustic insulation was poor and needs improvement to meet modern standards. This was achieved by adding floating floors and suspended ceilings. The Dutch building code requires better thermal and acoustic insulation for facades of residential buildings than offices. Buildings from the 1980s onwards have double-glazing. The thermal insulation of the facade is sufficient for housing, but the acoustic insulation is often not. The facades were replaced in eight of the buildings. In seven projects, the thermal and acoustic insulation of the facades was improved; in five of these it was not possible to change the facade because the buildings were listed monuments.

In several cases the zoning plan and the refusal of the municipality to allow exceptions were considered a problem. Slow regulatory procedures slow the project and delay the first income, threatening the financial feasibility. In most projects, however, the municipality was quite co-operative because conversion into a well-functioning building was found to improve the image of the environment and reduce risks of vandalism and feelings of fear.

Most of the risks revealed were technical. Several influence the financial feasibility. A lowered ceiling and floating floor were placed; structures were repaired, shafts were cut through reinforced concrete floors and legal procedures were fought before permits were obtained. But the conversion costs rose as a result. Developers who were interviewed complained about overrunning budgets and too many hours spent to develop specific solutions to problems that occurred during the construction. Still, the projects were financially feasible. Table 7.8 summarises the most striking risks found in the Dutch cases.

Table 7.8   Risks found in 15 Dutch cases.

Aspect	Risks
Functional	
	1 Present grid does not fit with measurements required for new purposes, resulting in waste of space or costly adaptations of the technical structure
	2 Private outdoor space impossible
Cultural	
	3 The appearance of the building does not suit its new function
Technical	
	4 Incorrect or incomplete building structure assessment
	5 Poor state of main structure/foundation (rotten concrete or wood, corroded steel)
	6 Insufficient shafts available; construction allows no extra shafts to be constructed
	7 Insufficient thermal and acoustic insulation in the floors and facades
	8 Insufficient daylight for housing
Legal	
	9 Zoning law: impossible to meet municipal requirements, zoning law, city policy
	10 Building code: impossible to meet requirements, say for noise-level and fire-safety; municipality unwilling to cooperate
	11 Heritage legislation: status forbids adaptations required for future users
Financial	
	12 Development costs: slow handling of procedures (loss of income, high interest)
	13 Vacancy: reducing income from exploitation or sale of the apartments
	14 Owner not willing to sell for a reasonable price due to high book value

7.6   Concluding Remarks

Although the Conversion Meter has been developed to assess the conversion potential of vacant office buildings to housing, many follow-up studies have shown that the underlying principles and criteria are applicable to other types of conversion as well – for example to functions other than housing, or conversion of buildings other than offices, such as empty schools, healthcare facilities, churches and industrial heritage sites – with only minor changes.

Figure 7.9 shows an example of the temporary conversion of a vacant office building into a care home, for use while the care organisation was preparing a new building elsewhere. After conversion, the building accommodated 114 care apartments, a recreation area, a library, medical support facilities and a social-cultural neighbourhood centre. A stimulus to the conversion was the need for housing with care in this particular neighbourhood. Hindering factors were the different languages of care organisations, developers, and the construction industry, a lack of skills to test the building plans for financial feasibility, and rapidly changing government policy regarding how to finance care homes.

7.7   Next Steps

The Conversion Potential Assessment Tool has been developed for use in a Dutch context. A next step is to examine its applicability in other countries.

Figure 7.9   Utrecht, de Zusters (The Sisters). Source: Remøy and van der Voordt (2011).

Further testing of the new Conversion Meter in current Dutch cases is relevant too. Additional case studies in the Netherlands and in other countries will provide a better insight in the impact of national and local legislation and the economic and cultural context. The same counts for the financial feasibility scan (Step 4 in Section 7.3) and financial ratios.

A broader analysis with further case studies may further increase the validity of the tool and reliability of the cost data. Financial benefits from rental income or sales should be tested for other types of conversion, for both the current function (not only offices) and the function after adaptation (other than housing). It would be interesting to include the costs and benefits (including environmental criteria) of alternatives such as demolition and new construction in the feasibility scan as well (Barrett, 2009, Watson, 2009, Wilkinson *et al.*, 2014, Conejos *et al.*, 2015). The checklist could be extended to cover the extra risks that may appear from additional project analyses or interviews with parties who have practical experience of conversion projects.

The practical applicability of the Conversion Meter may be improved by digitising the tool and by adding photos, sketches and boxes with lessons from case studies to illustrate the criteria and risks checklist. Another topic is to explore the need for extra modules looking at particular issues such as sustainability (see, for instance, Mohamed *et al.* (2017). Finally, the criteria could be linked to tools for adaptable buildings in order to make future conversions functionally and technically simpler and less expensive (see for instance Remøy and van der Voordt, 2011; Geraedts, 2016). Buildings that support the possibilities of adaptive reuse are more ready to change and make it easier to cope with an ever-changing real estate market and as such will contribute to a more resilient built environment (Hassler and Kohler, 2014).

Note 1: Most TU Delft publications and MSc theses can be downloaded from tudelft.repository.nl.
Note 2: The Conversion Meter may be used for free. Your experiences or comments are welcome at the authors of this chapter.

References

Avidar, P., Havik, K. and Wigger, B. (2007) Gentrification: stromen en tegenstromen. *Oase*, 73: 9.

Baker, H., Moncaster, A. and Al-Tabbaa, A. (2017) Decision-making for the demolition or adaptation of buildings. *Proceedings of the Institution of Civil Engineers – Forensic Engineering, 2017: 1–13.*

Barrett, K.J. (2009) The key issues when choosing adaptation of an existing building over new build. *Journal of Building Appraisal*, 9(1): 14.

Benraad, K. and Remøy, H. (2007) Belevingswaarde. In: Van der Voordt, D.J.M., Geraedts, R.P., Remøy, H. and Oudijk, C. (eds) *Transformatie van Kantoorgebouwen Thema's, Actoren, Instrumenten en Projecten.* 010 Publishers.

Brand, S. (1994) *How Buildings Learn; What Happens After They're Built.* Penguin Books.

Bullen, P.A. and Love, P.E.D. (2011) Factors influencing the adaptive re-use of buildings. *Journal of Engineering, Design and Technology*, 9(1): 14.

Conejos, S., Langston, C., Smith, J., Lavy, S. and Lai, J.K. (2015) Enhancing sustainability through designing for adaptive reuse from the outset: a comparison of adaptSTAR and Adaptive Reuse Potential (ARP) models. *Facilities*, 33(9/10): 531–552.

De Vrij, N. (2002) Measuring is knowing. Working paper, Delft University of Technology.

Douglas, J. (2006) *Building Adaptation*. Butterworth-Heinemann.

Gelinck, S., Van Zeeland, H. and Van Dijk, G., (2013) *Transformatie Wijzer: van kantoor naar woonruimte. Perspectief, financiën en regelgeving*. Stichting Bouwresearch.

Geraedts, R.P. (2004) Transforming empty office buildings into homes. In: *International Workshop Tokyo Metropolitan University*. Tokyo: Tokyo Metropolitan University.

Geraedts, R.P. (2016) FLEX 4.0, a practical instrument to assess the adaptive capacity of buildings. *Energy Procedia*, 96: 12.

Geraedts, R.P. and van der Voordt, D.J.M. (2002) Transforming offices into homes. In: *CIB W104 Open Building Implementation, Balancing Resources and Quality in Housing*. Mexico City: Mexican Institute of Architects, The Housing Institute of Mexico City, Universidad Autonoma Metropolitana (UAM); the Universidad Iberoamericana; Habitat International Coalition, and TAVI.

Geraedts, R.P. and van der Voordt, D.J.M. (2007) The new Transformation Meter; A new evaluation instrument for matching the market supply of vacant office buildings and the market demand for new homes. In: *Building Stock Activation 2007*. Tokyo.

Geraedts, R.P., van der Voordt, D.J.M. and de Vrij, N. (2004) Transformation Meter revisited; Three new evaluation instruments for matching the market supply of vacant office buildings and the market demand for new homes. In: *10th Annual Conference CIB W104 Open Building Implementation, Open Building and Sustainable Environment*. Paris: CIB W104.

Hassler, U. and Kohler, N. (2014) Resilience in the built environment. *Building Research & Information* 42 (2): 11.

Hendershott, P.H. (1996) Valuing properties when comparable sales do not exist and the market is in disequilibrium. *Journal of Property Research*, 13 (1): 57–66.

Hermans, M., Geraedts, R., van Rijn, E. and Remøy, H. (2014) *Determination Method Adaptive Capacity of Building to Promote Flexible Building* [Bepalingsmethode Adaptief Vermogen van gebouwen ter bevordering van flexibel bouwen]. Brink Groep.

Hordijk, A. and van de Ridder, W. (2005) Valuation model uniformity and consistency in real estate indices: The case of the Netherlands. *Journal of Property Investment & Finance*, 23: 165–81.

Keeris, W. (2007) Gelaagdheid in leegstand. In: Van der Voordt, D.J.M., Geraedts, R.P., Remøy, H. and Oudijk, C. (eds) *Transformatie van kantoorgebouwen*. 010 Publishers.

Koppels, P.W., Remøy, H. and El Messlaki, S. (2011) The negative externalities of structurally vacant offices: An exploration of externalities in the built environment using hedonic price analysis. In: Jansen, I. (ed.) *ERES 2011, 18th Annual European Real Estate Society Conference*. Eindhoven.

Mackay, R., De Jong, P. and Remøy, H. (2009) Transformation building costs; understanding building costs by modelling. In: Wamelink, J., Prins, M, and Geraedts, R.P. (eds) *Changing Roles*. TU Delft.

Mohamed, R., Boyle, R., Yang, A. and Tangari, J. (2017) Adaptive reuse: a review and analysis of its relationship to the 3 Es of sustainability. *Facilities*, 35(3/4): 138–154.

Mulder, K. (2015) Tijdelijk bewoond [Temporarily Inhabited]. TU Delft.

Pinder, J., Schmidt-Iii, R. and Saker, J. (2013) Stakeholder perspectives on developing more adaptable buildings. *Construction Management and Economics*, 31: 19.

Remøy, H.T. and van der Voordt, D.J.M. (2011) Zorg voor leegstand. Herbestemmen van leegstaande kantoren naar zorggebouwen [Transformation of vacant office buildings to health care buildings]. BNA, TU Delft.

Remøy, H.T. and van der Voordt, D.J.M. (2014) Adaptive reuse of office buildings: opportunities and risks of conversion into housing. *Building Research & Information*, 42: 9.

Remøy, H.T. and van der Voordt, D.J.M. (2009) Sustainability by Adaptable and Functional Neutral Buildings. In: Dobbelsteen, A.V.D. (ed.) *3rd CIB International Conference on Smart and Sustainable Built Environment*. Delft University of Technology: Delft, The Netherlands.

Smit, A.J. (2007) Transformatie van verouderde bedrijventerreinen. In: van der Voordt, D.J.M., Geraedts, R.P., Remøy, H. and Oudijk, C. (eds) *Transformatie van Kantoorgebouwen*. 010 Publishers.

Ten Have, G.G.M. (1992) *Taxatieleer Onroerende Zaken*. Stenfert Kroese.

Vijverberg, G. (2001) *Renovatie van kantoorgebouwen; literatuurverkenning en enquete-onderzoek opdrachtgevers, ontwikkelaars en architecten [Renovation of office buildings; literature survey clients, developers and architects]*. DUP Science.

Watson, P. (2009) The key issues when choosing adaptation of an existing building over new build. *Journal of Building Appraisal*, 4: 9.

Wilkinson, S.J. and Remøy, H. (2011) Sustainability and within use office building adaptations: A comparison of Dutch and Australian practices. In: *Pacific Rim Real Estate Society Conference*, Gold Coast, Qld. Pacific Rim Real Estate Society, Bond University.

Wilkinson, S.J., Remøy, H. and Langston, C. (2014) Reuse versus demolition. In: Wilkinson, S.J. and Langston, C. (eds) *Sustainable Building Adaptation. Innovations in Decision-making*. John Wiley & Sons.

Rating Tools, Resilience and Sustainable Change of Use Adaptations

Sara Wilkinson
University of Technology Sydney

8.1 Introduction

Rating tools endeavour to provide a benchmark and an objective indication of the level of sustainability of a building or a precinct for users, occupants, owners and investors. Since 1990, many building rating tools have been launched, for example ATHENA, BEAT 2002, BREEAM, LEED, Green Globes, CASBEE and Green Star, to name just a few (Poveda and Lipsett, 2011). The tools were developed by a mix of government and/or private bodies and focus on a limited number of issues, such as energy and water, or a wide range of metrics including social and environmental criteria. As such, some may be part of a mandatory requirement imposed by government, for example the Australian Building Energy Efficiency Certificates (BEECS) and the European Energy Performance Certificates (EPCs). One of the aims of the tools in the commercial property market, and to a lesser extent in the residential market, is to create added value for investors (Newell *et al.*, 2011. Hurst and Wilkinson, 2015). The premise being, all other things being equal, that a 6-star Green Star office property (the highest rating possible) will have a higher value than a non-rated or lower-rated equivalent. Evidence exists across Europe, the USA and Australia and other markets that premium offices with green building ratings do achieve higher capital and rental values, experience less vacancy and higher absorption (Fuerst and McAllister 2011; Newell *et al.*, 2011). The evidence in the residential market is less clear, with pockets in some cities appearing to value some aspects or attributes of sustainability, such as energy efficiency (Hurst and Wilkinson, 2015. Brounen *et al.*, 2012). However, overall, traditional attributes of proximity

Building Urban Resilience through Change of Use, First Edition.
Edited by Sara J. Wilkinson and Hilde Remøy.
© 2018 John Wiley & Sons Ltd. Published 2018 by John Wiley & Sons Ltd.

to schools and other amenities typically have a higher significance for buyers and renters (Hurst and Wilkinson, 2015).

Another dimension of the various tools is that some measure design and construction sustainability whereas others focus on operational or in-use sustainability. In Australia, for example, NABERS, the National Australian Building Energy Rating tool, focuses on energy in design, whereas Green Star, the tool developed and promoted by the Green Building Council of Australia (GBCA), covers issues including water consumption, materials specification, provision of amenities such as cycling facilities and so on. BEECS and their EU equivalent EPCs, measure operational energy use within a building.

A number of questions must be posed with respect to rating tools used to evaluate the sustainability and resilience of buildings. For example, who uses existing rating tools and why? What choices are available to people in respect of adaptive reuse? Which markets do the various existing rating tools cover? Where are these tools found? When and how are they used in the market? And finally, given the focus here, do any of the tools explicitly or implicitly incorporate resilience considerations?

This chapter provides an overview of the use of ratings tools in some key markets, such as Europe and the UK, Canada and the USA, and Australia. Some of the well-known tools are evaluated, such as BREEAM and LEED, whilst other less well-known tools such as One Planet and the Living Building Challenge are also discussed because they appeal to different markets, or offer a different perceptive and a different framework. Conejos *et al.* (2012) proposed the AdaptSTAR tool for sustainable adaptive reuse, but the market, where the more established tools are dominant, has not taken this product up. AdaptSTAR does identify specific issues relating to adaptive reuse and hence a brief description is provided. Resilience issues identified by the Rockefeller Foundation are also outlined. Finally, there is a critical analysis of the effectiveness and scope of the tools and we consider whether gaps exist in respect of addressing resilience issues. The chapter concludes with an appraisal of where we currently sit and where gaps in scope and details exist in some of the current rating tools for adaptive reuse and resilience.

8.2 Sustainability in Building Adaptation: Drivers and Barriers

Using a Canadian market survey of green building and rating tools as an illustration, it is possible to better understand the drivers and barriers that affect their use in the commercial market. In Canada 'doing the right thing' and 'client demand' were found to be main drivers for increased green building activity, and were selected by 42% as one of the top three drivers (CAGBC, 2016). In the 2016 survey, 24% of the respondents ranked 'doing the right thing' as the number one when selecting their top three drivers, followed by 18% who opted for 'client demand' as the top driver in the commercial market (CAGBC, 2016). The high influence of 'doing the right thing' has strong implications for the best approaches to marketing green products and services effectively to Canadian practitioners. However, the importance of client demand shows the degree to which business factors drive the market. When interviewed, sustainability leaders in Canadian commercial real estate ascribed a high level of importance to the role of clients and tenants in encouraging their green investments and they showed a broad awareness of the importance of sustainability in Canada (CAGBC, 2016). Notably, these leaders cited the importance of institutional clients whose sustainability commitments are helping to drive the market in Canada, partly through adoption of rating tools.

The capacity of green buildings to promote greater health and wellbeing for Canadian occupants has influenced the growth in this market, and 60% of survey respondents stated this was the top social reason for their current investments in green (CAGBC, 2016). The hypothesis is that if the value of the potential benefits of health and wellbeing can be captured more effectively in the return associated with green buildings, this can help to generate a new wave of green building investments (CAGBC, 2016). It follows that if the same conditions and drivers exist in other countries, similar trends will prevail.

Among respondents using rating systems, the highest percentage (73%) reported better-performing buildings were the main benefit, exceeding the second most popular benefit, marketing and competitive advantage, which scored 54%. This suggests the decision to use a rating system is driven more by the rigour required in the approach to green, than by the promotion of the building as green, which is often associated with the use of such systems. However, that 54% of respondents considered marketing and competitive advantage a benefit to the use of a building rating system demonstrates that having third-party verification can improve marketability and appeal, impacting the feasibility and desirability of making projects green. Forty-nine per cent of respondents felt the way rating systems provide a common industry standard was important. When considered along with the high percentage that found marketing/competitive advantage an important benefit, this indicates that respondents valued the capacity that rating systems have to quell concerns about the reliability of green claims. Meeting mandates or achieving government incentives were not perceived to be significant benefits of rating systems, suggesting that private industry rather than government is more important in Canada for driving the value associated with obtaining a green building rating (CABGC, 2016). However, the challenges for greater uptake of rating tools include concerns and misconceptions about the higher capital costs involved, current low energy costs, and gaining market share in smaller urban settlements outside of the major capitals. Such concerns were confirmed in the analysis of LEED rating tool adoption in US commercial offices by Wilkinson *et al.* (2015). Here Yudelson and Myer's (2013) claim that LEED, as the 'most influential rating tool in the world with over 20,000 projects and 900 million square metres of LEED rated space and 20 years in the market' has good market acceptance were investigated. Wilkinson *et al.* (2015) showed a total US market of about 32 billion square metres with, at best, 3% being LEED certified, mostly in the lower Bronze and Silver categories. These rating levels require little more than government regulation compliance. Only 6% of certificates are issued in the top Platinum category. So, a mere 6% of the meagre 3% coverage (0.18% or 1 in 550) means that LEED has had limited impact on US cities. That 0.18% figure is therefore criticised for not living up to its promises (Van der Heijden, 2015). This is despite counter-claims that LEED results in higher rental and capital values, thus incentivising investors (Eichholtz *et al.*, 2013).

Others are developing rating tools that move beyond 'reducing resource use', and instead push the boundaries of 'restorative' actions (JLL *et al.*, 2015). Examples of these include the Living Building Challenge (LBC) and One Planet Living, where 'net positive' energy generation or 'zero carbon' status is required as a minimum. Achieving Living Building Certification requires a substantial investment in design team effort and enhanced building features and systems, and currently the mainstream market perceives these tools to appeal only to those wanting to demonstrate leading-edge exemplar sustainability performance (JLL *et al.*, 2015). Other new rating systems are starting to focus solely on health and wellbeing of building occupants. Examples include the WELL Building Standard, developed by the International Well Building Institute (WBI, 2016). In this tool, nourishment, fitness and mental health and wellbeing are covered, along with other more traditional sustainability areas such as air, water and light. Specific initiatives include inclusion of biophilic elements (i.e. nature's patterns) in lighting, space layout and interior design. The biophilia hypothesis posits that humans possess an innate tendency to seek connections with nature and other forms of life (Wilson, 1984) and therefore building design which replicates nature is said to be 'biophilic'. Overall the WELL Building Standard tool is not considered relevant to the adaptive reuse market yet and is not covered further in this chapter. However, the LBC and One Planet Living tools are.

8.3   Leading Rating Tools and Conversion Adaptation

This section provides an overview of rating tools in the key markets of the UK, USA, Canada, Europe and Australia. A brief description is provided, along with the land-use types typically covered by the tools. The following tools are reviewed;

- One Planet
- Living Building Challenge
- BREEAM
- Green Star/NABERS
- LEED.

Finally, there is a review of the AdaptSTAR tool, which has been specifically developed for sustainable adaptive reuse projects (Conejos *et al.*, 2012), although it has not yet had take-up in the commercial sector.

Table 8.1   Ten One Planet principles.

One planet principle	Headline goals and targets
Health and happiness	Foster a strong sense of community
	Foster a healthy community
Equity and local economy	Ensure a diversity of housing type and tenure
	Encourage residents to engage in fair trade and local economy programmes
Culture and community	Create a culture of sustainability
	Create a culturally vibrant community
Land use and wildlife	Create two new habitats
	Contribute to an increase in biodiversity
Sustainable water	Reduce potable water use by 75%
	Reduce flooding risk – 100% stormwater treated on site
Local and sustainable food	Access to food growing space (100% of dwellings)
	Edible landscaping (30% of landscape trees)
	Encourage sustainable and healthy purchasing habits
Sustainable materials	Reduced embodied energy of construction
	Sustainable materials in operation
Sustainable transport	Enable a sustainable transport carbon footprint
	Reduced private car ownership
Zero waste	Maximise construction waste recycling (95%)
	Reduction in household waste in operation (30%)
	Recycling rate of household waste (70%)
Zero carbon	Maximise energy efficiency (34% reduction)
	Renewable energy generation (100% renewable energy)

Source: Bioregional (2015).

8.3.1   One Planet Living

One Planet Living is a global initiative developed by WWF and Bioregional, using the concept of the ecological footprint to calculate the impact of human activities (UNEP, 2008). The ecological footprint concept posits that, if every human on the planet lived and consumed like the average American citizen, five planets would be required to sustain us; and for Canadians 4.5 planets (Bioregional, 2015). It follows that, using this analogy it is necessary to reduce our environmental impact by up to 80% if humans are going to live within the planet's natural means (UNEP, 2008). This philosophy is behind the One Planet Living tool. There are ten principles to structure thinking and inform action (see Table 8.1 above). The principles stemmed from empirical work in the UK BedZED residential development in South London during the early 2000s, but the focus is very much on new build, residential stock and social sustainability. The initiative was established in 2003.

These ten principles set the One Planet approach apart from others in terms of the level of the targets: zero carbon and zero waste, for example, are very ambitious compared to the standards set in other tools. Furthermore, commitment to social goals of culture and community, health and happiness are also quite different in scope and degree from other established tools, such as LEED and Green Star. Where an adaptive reuse project involves change of use from non-residential to residential, this tool/framework may have some principles worth applying. For example, the One Planet proposal for the WVG project in Perth, Western Australia recognises the preservation of an existing Sullivan Hall as a community facility in the new development under the 'Culture and Community Principle'. However, it does not offer a bespoke framework or tool for the analysis and evaluation of optimal sustainable adaptive reuse or conversion at the building scale.

8.3.2   Living Building Challenge

The Living Building Challenge (LBC) is a relatively new building certification programme, advocacy tool and philosophy. It calls for the creation of building projects at all scales that operate 'as cleanly, beautifully and efficiently as nature's architecture' (LBFI, 2016). The overriding concept is regenerative design; that is design that has a positive, as opposed to a negative, impact on the environment (LBFI, 2016). It was established in 2006, in North America, and it has expanded to other countries, for example Australia.

Amongst nearly 300 LBC projects globally, representing almost 100,000 m², there are few fully certified 'living buildings', so LBC-rated projects cover a minute proportion of the total building stock. For projects to be certified under the LBC, they must achieve ambitious performance requirements over a minimum 12-month period of continuous occupation. This requirement makes the LBC quite different from some other more established tools, such as Green Star, which separate design and construction from performance (see Section 8.3.4).

The LBC comprises seven performance categories called 'petals':

- place
- water
- energy
- health and happiness
- materials
- equity
- beauty.

The petals are subdivided into twenty 'imperatives', each focused on a specific sphere of influence. For example, place is about 'restoring a healthy inter-relationship with nature' and has four imperatives: limits to growth, urban agriculture, habitat exchange and human-powered living. All the petals and imperatives are shown in Table 8.2 below.

Where the LBC exists in a country, there is a steward. For example, the steward of the Living Building Challenge Program in Australia is the Living Future Institute of Australia (LFIA). The International Living Future Institute is a hub for programs. The LFIA was established in 2012 and in 2014 the Living Future Challenge was established as a framework for re-thinking the

Table 8.2 Petals and imperatives for the LBC.

Petal	Imperatives
Place Restoring a healthy interrelationship with nature	1. Limits to growth 2. Urban agriculture 3. Habitat exchange 4. Human powered living.
Water Creating developments that operate within the water balance of a given place and climate	5. Net positive water
Energy Relying only on current solar income	6. Net positive energy
Health and happiness Creating environments that optimise physical and psychological health and wellbeing	7. Civilised environment 8. Healthy interior environment 9. Biophilic environment
Materials Endorsing products that are for all species through time	10. Red list 11. Embodied carbon footprint 12. Responsible industry 13. Living economy sourcing 14. Net positive waste
Equity Supporting a just equitable world	15. Human scale and humane places 16. Universal access to nature and place 17. Equitable investment 18. Just organisations
Beauty Creating design that uplifts the human spirit	19. Beauty and spirit 20. Inspiration and education

Source: Author.

way humankind designs its systems, products, buildings and communities. Predicated on the Living Building Challenge, and using nature as the metric for success, the Living Future Challenge branches into all aspects of society as described below:

- Living Building Challenge (claimed as the built environment's most rigorous and ambitious performance standard)
- Living Community Challenge (applying living building concepts to entire communities or cities)
- Living Product Challenge (challenging designers and manufacturers to create net positive products)
- Net Zero Energy Building Certification (certifying successful energy conservation in both new and existing buildings)
- Just (the social justice label for organisations)
- Declare (the materials nutrition label)
- Reveal (the energy efficiency label for buildings).

One advantage is that the Living Building Challenge can apply to any building project, including (LBFI, 2016):

- new or existing buildings
- single-family residences
- multi-family (market rate or affordable) housing
- institutional (government, educational, research or religious) buildings
- commercial premises (offices, hospitality, retail)
- museums, galleries and botanical gardens
- medical and laboratory buildings.

The challenge in the corporate and commercial sector is the competition from more established and recognised tools. The LBC has three categories:

- renovation
- landscape or infrastructure
- building.

Renovation is for projects that are not part of a complete building reconstruction. For example, projects include single-floor tenancy improvements, residential kitchen renovations or historic rehabilitations of a portion of a building, which may or may not feature adaptive reuse. Projects comprising more than 75% of an existing building and alter the envelope or heating, ventilation, air-conditioning (HVAC) systems are not classed as renovations but as building projects. Landscape or infrastructure (non-conditioned developments) covers any project that does not include a physical structure as part of its primary programme, and therefore open-air, parklike structures, restrooms, and amphitheatres fall into this category. Projects can include roads, bridges, sports facilities or trails. Finally, the building category is for any project that encompasses the construction or substantial adaptation of a roofed and walled structure for permanent use. Projects that occupy more than 75% of a building and alter either the envelope or major systems are considered building projects. See summary matrix in Table 8.3.

In the same way as the One Planet Living concept, the LBC is an ambitious holistic framework, which is gaining traction is some markets, although currently not the corporate sector where BREEAM, Green Star and LEED dominate. However, it does not specifically target adaptive reuse, nor does it explicitly identify resilience as an attribute to measure.

8.3.3   BREEAM

This tool led the way in rating buildings for sustainability, with its inception in the UK in 1990. BREEAM comprises a number of rating tools for different land-use types, such as offices, student accommodation, retail, care homes and residences. Public buildings, such as schools and healthcare buildings, are also covered. Specific criteria exist for heritage buildings, taking into account the constraints imposed by legislation. There are tools covering new build and also refurbishment (Balson et al., 2014; Global BRE, 2016). It is the refurbishment tool that is the focus in this chapter. There is a suite

Table 8.3   Living Building Challenge 3.1: summary matrix.

	Building	Renovation	Landscape and Infrastructure	20 imperatives of the Living Building Challenge: Follow down the column associated with each category to see which imperatives apply.
Place				01 Limits to growth
	scale jumping		scale jumping	02 Urban agriculture
			scale jumping	03 Habitat exchange
				04 Human powered living
Water			scale jumping	05 Net positive water
Energy			scale jumping	06 Net positive energy
Health and happiness				07 Civilised environment
				08 Healthy interior environment
				09 Biophilic environment
Materials				10 Red list
			scale jumping	11 Embodied carbon footprint
				12 Responsible industry
				13 Living economy sourcing
				14 Net positive waste
Equity				15 Human scale and human places
				16 Universal access to nature and place
			scale jumping	17 Equitable investment
				18 Just organisations
Beauty				19 Beauty and spirit
				20 Inspiration and education

KEY

Solutions beyond project footprint are permissible

Imperative not applicable

of tools covering fit-out of commercial buildings, domestic or residential building refurbishments, and heritage-building refurbishments, with attributes and sustainability metrics suited to these different land-use types.

BREEAM is used in many countries, and specific variations are available to suit different climates and countries. As with other tools, where specific issues are addressed, credits are awarded. Depending on the number of issues covered and the extent of the measures adopted, a score is calculated and a certificate indicating the level of sustainability is issued. The highest score is 'BREEAM Outstanding', followed by 'Excellent', 'Very Good', 'Good' and 'Pass' (Global BRE, 2016). A licensed assessor undertakes the evaluation and certification. Issues covered included changes to the structure and envelope, the building services and the interior design of the building. The perceived benefits of refurbishment to investors, owners, landlords and occupiers are social, environmental and economic and are:

- retaining and improving and future proofing existing built assets instead of demolition and rebuild
- increasing asset value by attracting buyers/users looking for improved standards and conditions that enhance occupiers' wellbeing, productivity and satisfaction
- improving overall building performance and reducing operational costs
- allowing owners and occupiers to demonstrate corporate social responsibility (CSR) and sustainable business leadership
- providing certification and assurance from third-party licensed assessors that the building's environmental performance standard has been met.

The technical standard comprises four parts: fabric and structure, core services, local services and interior design. Clients can seek certification against these parts depending on the scope of the project. So a listed or heritage building might not be able to change or alter the external envelope or fabric of the building, and may therefore seek certification under the remaining parts only. Independent, trained and licensed BREEAM refurbishment and fit out assessors undertake the assessments, and a rating is awarded after the inspection from 'Pass' to 'Outstanding'. The BREEAM Refurbishment and the Sustainable Refurbishment of Heritage Buildings tool was updated in 2014 (BRE, 2016) and focuses on issues affecting refurbishment and refurbishment of heritage stock. So, unlike Green Star or LEED, BREEAM has specific adaptation or refurbishment tools, but change of use or conversion adaptation are not dealt with explicitly.

8.3.4   Green Star

Green Star is a voluntary rating tool developed by the Green Building Council of Australia (GBCA). It was launched in 2003. By August 2015, there were 325 registered Green Star projects and 983 certified projects in Australia (JLL et al., 2015). However, this is a minute proportion of the total building stock. The GBCA is a member-based organisation, and has been applied in New Zealand and Africa. According to GBCA (2013), Green Star certified buildings produce 62% fewer greenhouse gas emissions than average Australian buildings and use 51% less potable water compared to minimum industry requirements. If Green Star is adopted early in design and an effective team appointed, it is stated there may be 'no additional construction costs compared to a typical building'; industry research concluded that 4-star Green Star projects can be delivered at 'no premium on business-as-usual construction budgets' (JLL et al., 2016). However, 5- and 6-star ratings come at a small cost premium, typically 3–5% and 8 + % respectively, although this may be recouped in higher rental returns, lower vacancies and higher capital values: a 6% income return and just under 4% capital return on their investment for green building owners (JJL *et al.*, 2015. Newell *et al.*, 2011). The following Green Star rating tools are available for building projects:

- *Design & As Built* certifies the design and construction of any building or major refurbishment.
- *Interiors* assesses the sustainability attributes of interior fit-outs.
- *Communities* assesses the sustainability attributes of community-level projects, such as precincts.
- *Performance* assesses the sustainability performance of existing buildings.

Green Star ratings are outlined below:

- 4 Star Green Star (score 45–59): 'Best practice' in environmentally sustainable design and/or construction.
- 5 Star Green Star (score 60–74): 'Australian excellence' in environmentally sustainable design and/or construction.
- 6 Star Green Star (score 75–100): 'World leadership' in environmentally sustainable design and/or construction.

Green Star is a whole-of-building rating, using nine categories to measure the building's overall rating:

- management
- indoor environment quality
- energy
- transport
- water
- materials
- land use and ecology
- emissions and innovation.

Each category is assessed, a percentage score is calculated, and Green Star environmental weighting factors are then applied. Owners cannot publicly claim or promote a Green Star rating or use the logo for the design, project or building unless the GBCA has validated the project's achievement through a formal assessment. Green Star rating can be assessed either at the design stage or at the end of the construction. Refurbishment and adaptation are covered in 'Design and As Built v1'. Resilience now features as an innovation point within the tool, which greatly helps to raises awareness amongst the professions of these issues.

8.3.5   NABERS

Two Australian rating systems measure on-going commercial building performance: the National Australian Built Environment Rating Scheme (NABERS) and Green Star Performance. NABERS is well established and was adopted recently in New Zealand. NABERS compares actual operational performance of existing buildings and tenancies relative to similar buildings within a particular state or territory. The tool covers either energy or water. The ratings are based on the previous 12 months of measured performance data, and use parameters such as hours of use and building area. NABERS is scaled from 0 to 6 stars, with half-star increments, where the higher the star rating, the greater the level of environmental performance delivered. When achieved year-on-year, this shows the building or tenancy is well maintained.

Energy is the most popular NABERS application. In Australia, the Property Council of Australia has compiled a quality matrix for office buildings, where rankings are awarded from the highest level of quality, 'Premium', through 'A', 'B', 'C' and finally 'D' grades. With NABERS ratings, 4.5 stars is a typical minimum requirement for new high 'A' grade construction and 5 star is typical for 'Premium', the highest commercial office grade. The Australian Government Commercial Building Disclosure (CBD) programme mandates disclosure of the NABERS energy ratings for commercial office spaces of $2000\,m^2$ or more (Warren and Huston, 2011). Disclosure before sale or leasing assists buyers and tenants to make informed decisions regarding energy efficiency and greenhouse gas emissions. NABERS water ratings are gaining traction in the office market. According to JLL *et al.* (2016), it is possible that the success of the CBD programme in the office market may mean its scope will be extended to other building types, for example data centres and shopping centres.

Green Star Performance assesses operational performance across nine categories, and shows a building's environmental performance year on year using third party certification. Green Star Performance recognises NABERS, so the tools are complementary. Similar to NABERS and Green Star Performance, the LEED Building Operations and Maintenance rating tool endeavours to reduce resource use of existing buildings. thereby demonstrating the issue is important in other rating tools. NABERS ratings can support a Green Star performance rating. However, a performance rating includes assessment of other key aspects of sustainability such as management systems, materials and land use, and not just the energy and water criteria covered in NABERS. The Green Star Performance tool has moved from the pilot version into version 1 (v1).

The NABERS and Green Star tools both measure a building's environmental performance. They are important because in providing a measure of building performance, they are an effective way to promote building retrofits. NABERS rates a building on the basis of its measured operational impacts on the environment, and provides a simple indication of how well these environmental impacts are being managed compared with similar buildings. NABERS uses a star rating system, where:

- 5 stars is 'Excellent' – best building performance
- 4 stars is 'Very good' – strong performance
- 2.5 stars is 'Market average performance'
- 0–2 stars means 'Underperforming'.

NABERS uses a structured methodology to make the assessment. A set of rules is applied, a spreadsheet is used for recording the data and an electronic tool calculates the assessment based on the data collected. The building is defined by its primary use, net lettable area, hours of occupancy and level and quality of building services. Both the number of computers and number of occupants is factored into the calculations. The building's performance is measured on data across a 12-month period and the building has to be occupied during this time. The energy/water use of the whole building, the tenancy or the base building (the landlord area not covered in tenanted areas) will be used in the calculations. The percentage of green power sourced also has a bearing on performance results.

Assessments may take between 10 and 50 hours, depending on building size. The cost of the assessment varies depending on the size and quality of the documentation provided. As the process becomes more routine (annual), the cost of conducting the assessment is reduced, as the documentation required is updated. In a retrofit of space over 2000 m², it is mandatory to conduct a NABERS rating:

- before the retrofit begins, so there is a benchmark against which to measure its success; twelve months of energy/water data prior to retrofit is needed
- one year after the retrofit is complete; 12 months of energy/water data is again required.

In order to maintain the NABERS rating, owners are required to conduct an assessment every 12 months and to make this information publicly available.

In 2016 the Australian Sustainable Built Environment Council (ASBEC) outlined a national 'Plan Towards 2050 Net Zero Emissions Buildings', targeting 100 Mt of greenhouse gas (GHG) savings and A\$9 billion in savings through existing building retrofits (ASBEC, 2016). This is an encouraging development, because ASBEC sees building retrofits as the second highest opportunity for GHG reductions, after distributed energy. Retrofits are estimated to deliver up to 300 Mt GHG savings, whereas appliances and equipment deliver 71 Mt and new builds 47 Mt to 2050 (ASBEC, 2016). There is no tool specific to adaptive reuse of buildings in Australia.

8.3.6   LEED

Leadership in Energy and Environmental Design (LEED), developed in 1994, is a globally applied, voluntary rating tool, developed by the United States Green Building Council (USGBC). It covers offices, shopping centres, hotels and data centres. The latest version is LEED v4. There are four rating systems:

- Building design and construction.
- Interior design and construction.
- Neighbourhood development.
- Maintenance and operations.

In 2014, the USGBC stated that the market needed time to prepare because some new concepts in LEEDv4 were hard to comprehend and document, for example, documentation linked with 'product transparency', which involves submission of environmental product declarations, health product declarations and materials ingredient reporting. The attributes included in the tool are typical of those adopted in rating tools and include energy and water conservation and use of renewables (tri-generation, PV, solar, geothermal and so on), black water recycling, green features such as green roofs and walls, waste management and aspects of indoor environments such as air quality, temperature and air changes. As of 2015 (JLL *et al.*, 2015), there were 76,482 projects registered or certified with the USGBC globally, with 38 registered and 18 certified in Australia. However, as Wilkinson *et al.* (2015) found, this US figure actually represents only 0.18% of the total US commercial stock, and so claims of major market penetration must be treated with caution. As with the Australian Green Star tool, there is no tool specifically dealing with adaptive reuse projects at the building level and no separate treatment of resilience issues at the building scale.

According to Poveda and Lipsett (2011) popular tools such as BREEAM, LEED and Green Star use similar approaches in their credit weighting. One Planet and the Living Building Challenge attempt to break this mould somewhat, adopting a different and broader paradigm or notion of sustainability, but their current market penetration is even lower than the market leaders. Some tools, such as LEED and Green Star, incorporate adaptive reuse/refurbishment options within the main tool, whereas BREEAM and the Living Building Challenge have a separate tool for refurbishment. There is a significant debate in the academic community about the relative weighting of sustainability criteria and the degree of importance of social, economic and environmental aspects (Baird, 2009). In addition, issues vary locally in terms of extent and importance. A further criticism of the design-only tools is that operational energy levels are not monitored and often result in higher levels of consumption than predicted (Baird, 2009).

8.3.7   Adaptive Reuse: AdaptSTAR

One model that has been developed for sustainable conversion adaptation or adaptive reuse is AdaptSTAR (Conejos *et al.*, 2012, 2014). Based on a review of the literature and existing rating tools, criteria are weighted under seven categories: physical (long life), economic (location), political, (context) legal (quality standard), social (sense of place), functional (loose fit) and technological (low energy). These criteria were validated (Conejos *et al.*, 2012): within each category, different aspects are weighted, as indicated in Figure 8.1; the criteria and weightings were determined by an expert group of 15 practitioners. The result is an AdaptSTAR rating. This model is proposed as a holistic design tool for future buildings, ensuring that greater levels of adaptive reuse are achieved.

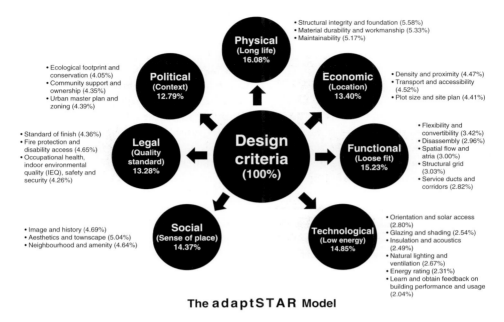

The adaptSTAR Model

Figure 8.1   The AdaptSTAR model. Source: Conejos *et al.* (2012).

Interestingly the degree of importance attached to the seven categories has the following rank order:

1. physical (long life) 16.08%
2. functional (loose fit) 15.23%
3. technological (low energy) 14.85%
4. social (sense of place) 14.37%
5. economic (location), 13.40%
6. legal (quality standard), 13.28%
7. political (context) 12.79%.

The categories are fairly evenly spread in terms of significance, but it is the physical, functional and technoloigcal factors that are perceived as most important to sustainable adaptive reuse. In the AdaptSTAR model (Conejos *et al.*, 2014), physical and functional criteria are building-scale issues relating to physical and structural sustainability; technological and legal criteria are also building scale issues, but relate to environmental sustainability. Economic sustainability at the urban and buidling scale are encompassed in the economic criteria. Social, environmental and political sustainability issues at the urban scale are covered by the social and political criteria (Conejos *et al.*, 2014).

An assessment process gives an AdaptStar score and then a rating:

■   5 stars (AdaptSTAR score 85–100)
■   4 stars (AdaptSTAR score 70–84)

- 3 star (55–69)
- 2 star (40–54)
- 1 star (25–39).

Buildings scoring below 25 are unranked. The AdaptSTAR model takes the form of a checklist of design considerations that, if implemented, should lead to higher potential for adaptive reuse at a later period. An advantage of the tool is that it can apply to single buildings and also precincts and districts (Conejos *et al.*, 2014).

Conejos *et al.* (2016) acknowledged that resilience and the capacity of buildings – including, in their study, heritage buildings – for adaptive reuse play a vital role in mitigating climate change. Although the social, economic and environmental benefits are recognised, they perceive in Australia a tension between adaptive reuse of heritage stock and conformance with legislation on energy efficiency and access for people with disabilities (Conejos *et al.*, 2016). They conclude that a green adaptive reuse protocol is needed in respect of heritage buildings to overcome the barriers. They call on the government to take a leadership role in this respect.

8.4   Resilience Challenges

As shown in Chapter 1, resilience challenges can be social, economic, technological or environmental in nature and are classed as acute or chronic (100 RC, 2016). Acute challenges occur rapidly, often with little warning, and cause excessive damage; recovery can take from days to years (Meerow *et al.*, 2016). An example is weather related events such as storms, cyclones and blizzards. Some of these acute resilience issues are climate change related, for example, heatwaves where areas and cities face temperature increases. The second classification, chronic, describes challenges that are on-going, long-term, and deep-seated (100 RC, 2016). Examples here include chronic energy shortages, poverty, poor health infrastructure and endemic crime and violence (Meerow *et al.*, 2016). Chronic resilience issues have multiple causes and are complex problems.

The Rockefeller Foundation for Resilient Cities (100 RC, 2016) identified 49 resilience issues:

- ageing infrastructure
- blizzard
- chronic energy shortage
- coastal flooding
- commodity price fluctuations
- cyber attack
- declining or aging population
- depletion of natural resources
- disease outbreak
- drought
- earthquake

- economic inequality
- economic shifts
- endemic crime and violence
- epidemic of drug and alcohol abuse
- food shortage
- hazardous materials accident
- heat wave
- high unemployment
- hurricane, typhoon, cyclone
- inequality
- infrastructure failure
- insufficient educational infrastructure
- intractable homelessness
- invasive species
- lack of affordable housing
- lack of social cohesion
- landslide
- overpopulation
- over taxed/under developed/unreliable transportation system
- political instability
- pollution or environmental degradation
- poor air quality/pollution
- poor health infrastructure
- poor transportation system
- pronounced poverty
- rainfall flooding
- rapid growth
- refugees
- resource scarcity
- riot or civil unrest
- rising sea level and coastal erosion
- social inequity
- terrorism
- tropical storms
- tsunami
- volcanic activity
- water management issues
- wildfires.

It is clear that some of the issues are environment focussed, whereas others are technological, social, economic or regulatory/governance issues. As such, some are directly related to buildings. For example, the design of a resilient building would allow for continued use during rainfall flooding: locating building services on the first floor and above rather than in a basement would mean they would be unaffected. Similar provisions could cover resilience to rising sea levels and tsunamis at the building level in the short term. Furthermore, basement and ground floor construction would ensure water was able to flush through the building easily rather than ponding.

For wildfires, building design could adopt best practices, ensuring that there was little flammable material to ignite the building easily. Where heatwaves are a resilience issue, then buildings which provide passive design and effective shading would be said to be resilient, especially compared to lightweight glazed facades.

Clearly not all resilience issues can be dealt with directly at the building scale. An example is social inequity. Social inequity could be addressed in part and indirectly, however, by tenants or owners donating a portion of business profit to charities supporting people affected by inequality. Terrorism, another resilience issue might be addressed in the design and lighting and digital surveillance of a building, avoiding poorly lit areas where terrorists might remain undetected. Although terrorism is a social, political and governance issue, some measures are possible at the building level. Moreover, designers and other built environment stakeholders, do not currently have a means of identifying resilience issues that relate to an area or city and therefore to a building. It might be possible to develop a framework for stakeholders to formally assess which resilience issues affect their area. They could thereafter consider which of those issues might be addressed at the building level. The next stage would be to determine how effective the proposed measures would be at mitigating the resilience issue(s). Ultimately, the resilience issues could or should be added to existing rating tools such as One Planet and LBC, Green Star, LEED and BREEAM. It could be said that some tools include resilience issues implicitly, and Green Star does have an explicit resilience innovation credit, but overall explicit mention and credit for resilience issues – be they environmental, social or economic – is currently limited. If appropriate resilience issues are added to some of the existing tools, the provision of a framework would ensure that where sustainable rating tools are adopted, stakeholders would actively discuss, and hopefully address them, at building level. Consequently, the building level measures would contribute to resilience at precinct and city scale level.

Rotterdam is one of the 100 Resilient Cities in the Rockefeller Foundation study and has a figure illustrating resilience scales (see Figure 8.2) (100 RC, 2016). Seven scales exist from the building to the global level. This figure shows clearly how resilience at the building level ultimately contributes to global resilience. By not explicitly addressing resilience issues in our building rating tools, where they are known at city level, we are failing to actively contribute to ameliorating resilience in our communities. This lack of awareness and gap in understanding needs to be addressed.

For example, Rotterdam has flooding as a resilience issue. It follows that buildings that adopt flood-resilient design, such as locating building services above basement and ground level and using permeable designs that allow water to flow through the building relatively easily, will recover from a flood much more quickly and at a much lower cost. This is resilience at building level; resilient buildings as a whole will enable precincts and cities to recover from acute shocks, such as flooding. Currently these issues are not part of the sustainability rating tools, so it makes sense to augment them with a resilience section to allow designers, owners or tenants to acknowledge and demonstrate resilience.

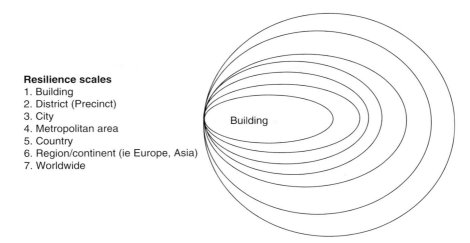

Resilience scales
1. Building
2. District (Precinct)
3. City
4. Metropolitan area
5. Country
6. Region/continent (ie Europe, Asia)
7. Worldwide

Building

Figure 8.2   Resilience scales (source Rotterdam Resilience Strategy, 2016).

Another resilience issue from the Rockefeller list is ageing infrastructure. Here, buildings that adopt on site energy production, use less energy or have on-site rainwater retention and black water treatment will lower demand on the existing infrastructure, thereby extending its useful life. Metrics need to be determined for the resilience issues. In this way, we will be able to quantify the resilience of the building stock to acute and chronic issues.

8.5   Conclusions

This chapter has explored the nature and extent of existing sustainable building rating tools and the degree to which they either account for refurbishment separately or within the main tools. BREEAM, LEED and Green Star share many similarities and have been in the market since the early 1990s. These tools have also been adopted by the commercial and corporate sector, although the percentage of buildings achieving the highest levels of sustainability is low. This is possibly an indication that uptake in the corporate sector is mostly of a minimal level to demonstrate some level of corporate social responsibility, but not a wholehearted belief in the need for sustainability.

Two other tools, One Planet and the Living Building Challenge, are relative newcomers, having been launched in the mid-2000s. Their market share is minimal compared to the mainstream tools above and they have not yet received a reasonable take-up from the corporate sector. Possibly this is because these tools are quite different both in scope and degree. Social issues such as happiness and culture are embraced, as well as environmental issues. As such, these tools offer a fundamentally different approach to sustainability and adopt a different paradigm. Some social and environmental resilience issues are covered in these tools although not explicitly so.

Finally Adapt Star was reviewed. This tool has seven weighted categories covering all attributes considered in adaptation. If the checklist were adopted in design, greater adaptive reuse potential is likely to result (Conejos *et al.*, 2012, 2014). However, this tool has not yet been taken up at all in industry and whilst the tool has merit it has made no impact as yet. BREEAM also has a specific refurbishment tool, which is used in the market and so does have an impact, although again the breadth of measures and levels of attainment fall short of other tools.

Therefore, the tools offer a framework to follow and, depending on whether the intent is to convert an existing building in the most sustainable way or to increase capital and rental value and meet CSR standards, there is some choice available. It seems there is some way to go before we are truly practising sustainable adaptive reuse with tools that measure broadly and meaningfully.

This chapter also explored the issues of resilience identified by the Rockefeller Foundation for the 100 Resilient Cities. Twenty two of the 49 issues are either social, governance, political and or economic issues, outside of physical building metrics. However, the majority of issues, 27, can be addressed in some way in the design and construction and operation of a building. This idea is explored further in Chapter 9. Some examples of how resilience issues can manifest at building level were discussed and the resilience scale figure from the City of Rotterdam strategic plan shows how buildings affect and contribute to resilience at the precinct/district scale, then the city, metropolitan, country, and regional scales, and ultimately at the global or worldwide scale. As of now, bar the Green Star tool, we do not address resilience in our sustainable building rating tools for adaptive reuse or conversion or for new build or building performance. This gap needs to be addressed; we need to raise awareness, at all levels and within the property and construction industry and professions, of resilience issues and how they can play a part in delivering a more resilient built environment.

References

100 RC (2016) 100 Resilient Cities. Retrieved on 24 August 2016 from Http://Www.100resilientcities.Org/Cities#/-_/.

ASBEC (2016) *Low carbon, high performance. how buildings can make a major contribution to Australias emissions and productivity goals*. Summary report May 2016. Retrieved on October 6th 2016 from www.asbec.com.au.

Baird, G., (2009) Incorporating user performance criteria into building sustainability rating tools (BSRTs) for buildings in operation. *Sustainability*, 1(4): 1069–1086.

Balson, K., Summerson, G. and Thorne, A. (2014) Sustainable refurbishment of heritage buildings – How BREEAM helps to deliver. Briefing Paper, BREEAM. Retrieved on 17th December 2016 from http://www.breeam.com/filelibrary/Brochures/Heritage-Sustainable-Refurbishment-v2.pdf.

Bioregional. (2015) WGV by LandCorp – One Planet action plan. http://www. bioregional.com/wp-content/uploads/2015/11/WGV_OPAPSummary_201115.pdf [26 November 2016].

Brounen, D., Kok, N. and Quigley, J.M., (2012) Residential energy use and conservation: Economics and demographics. *European Economic Review*, 56(5): 931–945.

CAGBC (2016) *Canada green building trends: benefits driving the new and retrofit market*. Canada Green Building Council.

Conejos, S., Langston, C. and Smith, J. (2012) AdaptSTAR model: A climate-friendly strategy to promote built environment sustainability', *Habitat International*, 37: 95–103.

Conejos, S., Yung, E.H.K. and Chan, E.H.W., (2014) Evaluation of urban sustainability and adaptive reuse of heritage buildings: a case study on conservation in Hong Kong's CBD. *Journal of Design Research*, 12(4): 260–280.

Conejos, S., Langston, C., Chan, E.H.W. and Chew, M.Y.L. (2016) Governance of heritage buildings: Australian regulatory barriers to adaptive reuse. *Building Research & Information*, 44(5–6): 507–519.

Eichholtz, P., Kok, N. and Quigley, J.M. (2013) The economics of green building. *Review of Economics and Statistics*, 95(1): 50–63.

Fuerst, F. and McAllister, P. (2011) Green noise or green value? Measuring the effects of environmental certification on office values. *Real Estate Economics*, 39(1): 45–69.

GBCA (2013) *The value of Green Star: a decade of environmental benefits research key findings*. https://www.gbca.org.au/uploads/194/34754/The_Value_of_Green_Star_A_Decade_of_Environmental_Benefits.pdf [27 November 2016].

Global BRE (2016) BREEAM International New Construction 2016. Technical Manual SD233, (1.0).

Hurst, N. and Wilkinson, S. (2015) Housing and energy efficiency: What do real estate agent advertisements tell us? In: *RICS COBRA Conference UTS Sydney July 8–10th 2015*.

JLL, WSP and Parsons Brinckerhoff. (2015) An overview of the rating tool landscape in Australia. Discussion paper. http://www.jll.com.au/australia/en-au/Research/AU-EnvironmentCert-v9.pdf [27 November 2016].

LBFI (2016) Living Building Challenge 3.1 A visionary path to a regenerative future. Living Building Future Institute. https://living-future.org/sites/default/files/16-0504%20LBC%203_1_v03-web.pdf [27 November 2016].

Meerow, S., Newell, J.P. and Stults, M. (2016) Defining urban resilience: A review. *Landscape and Urban Planning*, 147: 38–49.

Newell, G., McFarlane, J. and Kok, N. (2011) *Building better returns–A study of the financial performance of green office buildings in Australia*. University of Western Sydney, Sydney.

Poveda, C.A. and Lipsett, M.G. (2011) A review of sustainability assessment and sustainability/environmental rating systems and credit weighting tools. *Journal of Sustainable Development*, 4(6): 36.

UNEP (2008) Green building rating systems: going beyond the labels. http://www.unep.org/sbci/pdfs/Paris-JLL_briefing.pdf [27 November 2016].

Van der Heijden, J. (2015) On the potential of voluntary environmental programmes for the built environment: a critical analysis of LEED. *Journal of Housing in the Built Environment*, 30(4): 553–567.

Warren, C.M. and Huston, S. (2011) Promoting energy efficiency in public sector commercial buildings in Australia. In: *RICS Construction and Property Conference*, p. 143.

WBI (2016) *We believe that people's health and wellness should be at the center of design*. Well Building Institute.

Wilkinson, S., Van Der Heijden, J.J. and Sayce, S. (2015) Tackling sustainability in the built environment: mandatory or voluntary approaches. The smoking gun? In: *RICS COBRA Conference UTS Sydney July 8–10th 2015*.

Wilson, E.O. (1984) *Biophilia*. Harvard University Press.

Yudelson, J. and Meyer, U. (2013) *The World's Greenest Buildings*. Routledge.

Conclusions on Building Resilience through Change of Use Adaptation: A Manifesto for the Future

Sara Wilkinson
University of Technology, Sydney

9.1 Introduction

This chapter collates the issues raised in and the findings of the preceding chapters and the Australian, UK, Canadian, US and Dutch case studies. The issues related to change of use adaptation in the different countries at regional and local and individual building levels are compared and contrasted. The qualities of resilient systems in the context of sustainable change of use are reviewed. Resilient systems are said to embody the following seven qualities: reflectiveness, resourcefulness, robustness, redundancy, flexibility, inclusiveness and integration (100RC, 2016). Within this chapter, the model from Chapter 1 (Figure 1.2) is revisited to demonstrate how policymakers, practitioners, investors, building owners and occupants can derive the optimum benefits from various sustainable change of use adaptation options in the context of resilience. In Table 9.1, the Resilient Cities challenges are expanded and classified in respect of issue types, and in this way the relationship of the issues to buildings, precincts and cities is made clear. Finally, this chapter sets out a manifesto for future directions and a series of checklists to identify and clarify issues in respect of sustainable change of use adaptation and resilience.

9.2 Overview of Resilience Issues, Sustainability and Change of Use Adaptation

Chapter 1 set the scene and highlighted that many stakeholders around the world are actively taking up resilience as an issue to be addressed. Our collective understanding of resilience and how to increase it in the built

Building Urban Resilience through Change of Use, First Edition.
Edited by Sara J. Wilkinson and Hilde Remøy.
© 2018 John Wiley & Sons Ltd. Published 2018 by John Wiley & Sons Ltd.

Table 9.1   Resilience challenges faced by cities and issue classification.

Resilience challenge faced	Type of issue
	■ social
	■ economic
	■ governance
	■ political
	■ technological
	■ building (design, construction or operation)
Ageing infrastructure	Building (design, construction or operation) – on site energy generation/renewables and water retention
Blizzard	Building design of structure and fabric
Chronic energy shortage	Building design, construction and operation
Coastal flooding	Building design – permeable
Commodity price fluctuations	Economic
Cyber attack	Technological – IT/services
Declining or aging population	Multi-generational design/flexible and adaptable
Depletion of natural resources	Building design/construction operation re-use, recycle materials, flexible adaptable
Disease outbreak	Building design – sanitation and healthy measures
Drought	Building design/construction operation – water economy
Earthquake	Building design – flexible joints, movement and safe shelter within in design
Economic inequality	Social/economic/governance
Economic shifts	Economic
Endemic crime and violence	Social/economic/governance
Epidemic of drug and alcohol abuse	Social/economic/governance
Food shortage	On site food production – rooftops
Hazardous materials accident	Environmental
Heat wave	Building design, construction and operation – fabric and envelope
High unemployment	Social/economic/governance
Hurricane, typhoon, cyclone	Building design for high winds
Inequality	Social/economic/governance
Infrastructure failure	Social/physical
Insufficient educational infrastructure	Social/economic/governance
Intractable homelessness	Social/economic/governance
Invasive species	Building design – green infrastructure/habitat
Lack of affordable housing	Social/economic/governance
Lack of social cohesion	Social/economic/governance
Landslide	Physical
Overpopulation	Social/economic/governance
Overtaxed/underdeveloped/ unreliable transportation system	Social/economic/governance
Political instability	Social/economic/governance
Pollution or environmental degradation	Building design and performance – minimise pollution and bio-remediate
Poor air quality/pollution	Building design and performance – green infrastructure
Poor health infrastructure	Social/economic/governance

Table 9.1   (Cont'd)

Poor transportation system	Building design/performance – use bicycles and car share
Pronounced poverty	Social/economic/governance
Rainfall flooding	Building design – permeable designs, site services above flood levels
Rapid growth	Social/economic/governance
Refugees	Social/economic/governance
Resource scarcity	Building design, construction/performance – reuse and recycle
Riot or civil unrest	Social/economic/governance
Rising sea level and coastal erosion	Social/economic/governance
Social inequity	Social/economic/governance
Terrorism	Social/economic/governance – also secure by design
Tropical storms	Building design, construction
Tsunami	Building design – permeable design
Volcanic activity	Building design – planning
Water management issues	Building design, construction and performance – water economy
Wildfires	Building design, construction

Source: Adapted from 100 RC, 2016.

environment is growing. At the city scale, policies and guidelines are being produced and experiences shared through the 100 Resilient Cities program and the UN. Our built environment has a pivotal role to play in delivering resilience, from the individual building to the masterplan and city scales. There are opportunities with existing buildings to retain heritage and a sense of place, whilst enhancing resilience for existing and future generations. There is great potential to learn from different approaches taken in cities globally and to communicate experiences in the developed and developing world, where resilience issues are often shared. Resilience, we have learned, is complex and messy. We need to be cognisant of whose resilience agenda is prevailing. We should embrace the positive aspects of resilience and be aware that we can make change for the better. Adaptive reuse, or change of use adaptation, is part of a transitional change to a new state of equilibrium within resilience and we need to acknowledge this. When we propose change of use, we must be cognisant that some retention of flexibility is useful to cope with the unexpected and to factor this into our decision-making to some extent. Finally, there are the different scales and timescales in which resilience can be delivered. With individual buildings, some degree of resilience and sustainability can be delivered in the short term, but at the precinct or masterplan and city scales, the change may take many years.

Laura Wynne and Chris Reidy concluded that while resilience can to some extent be achieved at the scale of individual buildings and precincts, the real potential of the sharing paradigm can be realised only at the city scale. The city is a shared public realm, an urban commons; one that can be designed and adapted collaboratively, not only to facilitate a sharing paradigm, but also to deliver greater resilience. To reach this goal demands a transformation in existing infrastructure and the social, cultural and political engagement of citizens in shaping the city. Urban public spaces can support crucial social infrastructure in which democratic deliberation can flourish. Some cities are adapting urban spaces to support social, cultural and political sharing: Seoul's 2012 'Sharing City' project aims to connect people to one another and encourage sharing services, to recover a sense of trust and community, to reduce waste and over-consumption, and activate the local economy. All these developments, they argue, build resilience and enhance sustainability. Grants for libraries, community gardens and tool libraries in apartment buildings, encouragement for startup companies to share, pursuit of intergenerational cohousing, car sharing, car park sharing, and public wifi are all examples of what is being provided there. Government leadership is crucial, but the focus is on public–private partnerships weaving sharing into the urban fabric. Encouragingly, the international Sharing Cities Network is growing and has over 50 members. A Shareable Sharing Cities Toolkit provides resources for establishing sharing initiatives, from tool libraries to cooperatives. To date, few cities are embedding sharing opportunities into the urban fabric and more should be encouraged. Adaptive reuse developments provide an opportunity to experiment with support for sharing and to create sharing nodes or hubs around which sharing cities can crystallise. We can start at the building scale and filter up to the precinct and the city scales.

In Chapter 3, Erwin Heurkens, Hilde Remøy and Fred Hobma also focused on the city scale, but from a governance perspective, looking at how planning policy instruments can deliver resilient urban redevelopment. They investigated the ability of public and private actors to respond to changes in property market demand through adaptive reuse of existing offices. Using Rotterdam as an example, they show how stakeholders there used policy instruments in a co-operative manner, with multi-level governance efforts, to address their resilience issues. Confirming similar approaches promoted by Wynne and Reidy in respect of the sharing paradigm, they concluded that planners, in their efforts to redevelop urban areas with resilience, should understand economic and property markets and deploy planning instruments so that private stakeholders make decisions in favour of office conversions. Office conversions can contribute to increasing societal and economic resilience, giving space to new groups and ensuring economic viability of the city. The Rotterdam case study showed that making urban areas more resilient in terms of providing affordable housing for students and new city centre apartments for communities through the conversion of obsolete offices needed a mix of hard and soft planning policy instruments. These instruments have to be aligned with market needs at city and local development level, and to combine policy formation with policy implemen-tation measures. Overall, this implies that cities and their stakeholders have to find their own mix of planning policy instruments to cope with their resilience challenges, and this variability reinforces the characteristics of complexity advocated by Meerow *et al.* (2016). Further research might focus on the relationship between public planning policies and private market decisions, because meeting built environment resilience challenges necessitates collective efforts. These challenges can be met, in part, by deploying planning policy instruments.

Hannah Baker and Alice Moncaster focussed on the location and site scales in Chapter 4, highlighting decision-making criteria previously identified at an individual building level about whether to demolish or adapt. These include technical and other factors such as heritage value, planning polices and economics. As they explored how decisions can differ in the context of a large-scale masterplan regeneration site, they noted that stakeholders weight criteria differently and have different priorities. Three UK case studies showed that decision-making factors were national and local policy, place-making and its link to economic viability, technical aspects, and phasing and market changes. The factors are not mutually exclusive, and the case studies revealed that multiple factors combine to make the decision context dependent, again reiterating Meerow *et al.*'s (2016) study on resilience. On masterplan sites, transport networks and compromises of demolishing one building to enable investment in another, came into play in decision making. Retention of historic buildings can add character and contribute to place-making, and while the retention of an individual building may not be economic, within a larger scheme other values may be weighted higher as the building could contribute to the character and identity of the area, while its cost could be offset by the rest of the development. In their case studies, historic buildings were landmark features within the masterplan and were combined with new build. The case studies gave examples of intangible values, such as the retention of a canal network that was seen as a reflection of an area's industrial past. With masterplan sites the phasing of demolition or adaptation of different buildings is important. On large developments, construction occurs over long periods, with projects having increased vulnerability to any local and/or global economic changes. The benefit of redeveloping existing buildings first is the creation of a community hub and identity, but in other circumstances new build can create necessary cash flows for the following phases of the development. Decision-making around adaptation and demolition on larger sites is more complex; there are often more influencing factors. When making these decisions, which can have significant impacts on an urban area, it is vital that all stakeholder perspectives are recognised and that the balance between influencing factors is considered appropriately.

Craig Langston concentrated on the building in the urban scale and decision-making with respect to resilient and sustainable urban renewal. He concluded that it is important to ensure that money spent on renewal of existing buildings is allocated wisely to deliver maximum social, political and environmental benefits. His decision-making model considered the optimal selection of urban renewal projects, to quantify the benefits so that projects that provide the highest collective utility and national benefit are pursued. In the future, revitalising existing neighbourhoods is likely to be a key focus for built environment stakeholders. The redesign of cities and the strengthening of communities to be resilient and sustainable are vital steps in ensuring increasing value for money and quality of life respectively. His model is predicated on the belief that urban planning decisions follow a sequence from the feasible to the useable, to the achievable, and finally to the sustainable. The model changes the focus from individual and unique project evaluation to understanding the underlying behaviour of stakeholders and their interactions. The proposed urban renewal decision-making model is complex and bespoke, again embodying acknowledged qualities of resilience (Meerow et al., 2016). Langston noted the nexus between urban renewal, system dynamics and multi-criteria decision analysis and suggested that the combination of the three domains has not been attempted previously. There is no quantitative decision-making model for urban renewal evaluation that includes an objective measurement of project success. The combination of a 4P conceptual framework and GIS-supported integrative decision-making that optimises and balances core criteria in a transparent and objective manner over time is unique. This 'big picture' approach to the evaluation of urban renewal projects is advocated over past bias towards economic feasibility and techniques such as life-cycle costing (LCC), which give a practical, yet limited view of what represents good design within narrow system boundaries. In the case of building conversion, use of LCC can help to identify the lowest cost of a proposal over a given time horizon, but not necessarily the best value to the owner or indeed to society more generally. As such, LCC is unlikely to expose wider social and political objectives of urban renewal projects, and assesses sustainability only in terms of its cost implications rather than the more important issues of climate change, ecological footprint and resilience.

Gordon Holden concluded that while the concept and definition of urban resilience remains a work in progress it is generally accepted that it may be understood as a measure of a city's capacity to adapt, survive and even thrive under stress. Adaptive reuse through the construction of apartments on top of existing buildings engages mainly with the big-picture resilience concepts of sustainable growth and wellbeing of citizens, several subtopics of which he explored. Building-top apartments are contributing to urban resilience and sustainability in numerous ways, under the principles discussed and illustrated in the case studies, none of which independently would be seen as outstanding or a 'silver-bullet' solution. There are however many transferable lessons, not the least being the sharing of opportunities and constraints across national and city government leaders, public servants, financiers and entrepreneurs, professionals, developers, and the community as a whole. With such a combination in creative interaction, urban resilience must surely be strengthened.

In Chapter 7, Rob Geraedts, Theo van der Voordt and Hilde Remøy explained a conversion potential assessment tool at the building scale. Their Conversion Meter has been developed to assess the potential of vacant office buildings for conversion to housing, but follow-up studies have shown the underlying principles and criteria are relevant to other change-of-use adaptations such as churches, healthcare facilities, banks, retail buildings and so on, albeit with minor amendments. The newly developed Conversion Potential Assessment Tool was created for use in a Dutch context, although it may be applicable in other countries. Further testing of the new Conversion Potential Assessment Tool in existing Dutch cases is needed to provide a better insight into the impact of national and local legislation, as well as the economic and cultural context. Further testing of the financial feasibility scan and the financial ratios components is also recommended to increase the validity of the tool and reliability of cost data. Potential improvements could be to digitise the tool and to explore the need for extra modules looking at particular issues such as sustainability. Finally, the criteria could be linked to tools for adaptable buildings to make future conversions functionally and technically simpler and less expensive. They assert that, in an ever-changing real-estate market, it will be more straightforward to convert buildings that are designed with adaptive reuse in mind.

Chapter 8 explored the nature of extent of existing sustainable building rating tools and the degree to which they either account for refurbishment separately, or, include it in the main tools. The main tools reviewed were BREEAM, LEED and Green Star, which share many similarities. These rating tools have been in the market since the early 1990s and have been adopted by the corporate sector, although the percentage of buildings achieving the highest levels of sustainability is low. Possibly, this is an indication that uptake in the corporate sector is mostly at a minimal level to demonstrate some level of CSR, but that there is not a wholehearted belief in the need for sustainability per se. BREEAM has a specific refurbishment tool, which is used in the market and so does have impact, although again the breadth of measures and levels of attainment fall short of other tools. The One Planet and the Living Building Challenge tools are relative newcomers, launched in the mid-2000s, and their market share is minimal compared to the mainstream tools. They have not yet been taken up in the corporate sector, perhaps tellingly. These tools are different in scope and degree, for example including social issues such as happiness and culture. These tools offer a fundamentally different approach to sustainability and adopt a different paradigm. Whilst the tools provide a framework to follow, and depending on whether the intent is to convert an existing building in the most sustainable way or to increase capital and rental value and meet CSR standards, there is some choice available. There is some way to go before we are practicing sustainable adaptive reuse with tools that measure broadly and meaningfully. The resilience issues identified by the Rockefeller Foundation for the 100 Resilient Cities comprise 22 social, governance, political and/or economic issues and 27 building related issues. The building-related resilience issues demonstrate how buildings affect and contribute to resilience at the precinct/district scale, then the city, metropolitan, country, regional and ultimately at the global or worldwide scales. We must start to acknowledge and address resilience explicitly in more of our sustainable building rating tools for change of use, and for new build or building performance too. This gap in knowledge needs attending to. We need to amend our rating tools and, importantly, to raise awareness at all levels for all stakeholders in the property and construction professions of resilience issues and how they can play a part in delivering a more resilient built environment.

9.3   Qualities of Resilient Systems in the Context of Conversion Adaptation

Resilient systems embody the following seven qualities: reflectiveness, resourcefulness, robustness, redundancy, flexibility, inclusiveness and integration (100RC, 2016). Clearly each is interpreted differently in different locations and cities. However, the qualities are universal and apply wherever buildings are sited, and some indicative examples are given below to show how the different qualities might be applied.

9.3.1   Reflectiveness and Resourcefulness

Reflectiveness and resourcefulness are about the 'ability to learn from the past and act in times of crisis'. In the context of buildings, this translates into the individual experiential learning and formal education of the design team and project stakeholders as well as design information from local sources in respect of local resilience issues. This would manifest in respect of measures provided in the conversion adaptation, possibly correcting previous design defects and also considering future or likely possible scenarios in respect of changing climate. For example, in Sydney the predictions are for increased likelihood of heatwaves, so building envelopes that provide shade or the possibility of easy retrofit with shading devices are a way of preparing for the future. Where increased frequency and level of flooding is an issue, conversion adaptations that allow for permeable ground and below-ground-floor design allows a faster and cheaper return to operation after a flood. Furthermore, siting services above the first floor also ensures a fast return to operation and full functionality.

9.3.2   Resourcefulness

Resourcefulness applies to people and institutions and reflects the ability to use other resources at times of crisis to meet the needs of the community (individual citizens and institutions). For example, where earthquakes might interrupt a city's water supply, having on-site supply via wells and/or storage for the inevitable disruption to supply, is a way of being resourceful.

9.3.3   Robustness, Redundancy and Flexibility

These qualities help to deliver systems and assets that are able to withstand shocks and stresses as well as enabling the use of alternative strategies to deliver rapid recovery. Robust design, for example, is design that is well conceived, built and managed and includes provision to ensure its failure is predictable, safe and not disproportionate to the cause. An example is infrastructure that does not fail catastrophically when design thresholds are exceeded. Safety factors are important considerations. Redundancy refers to spare capacity purposively created to accommodate disruption due to extreme pressures, surges in demand or an external event. Redundancy includes diversity, where there are numerous ways to achieve a given need. For example, energy systems that incorporate redundancy provide multiple delivery pathways that can accommodate surges in demand or disruption to supply networks. Flexibility is the willingness and ability to adopt alternate strategies in response to changing circumstances and sudden crises. Systems can be more flexible through introducing new technologies or knowledge, including recognition of traditional practices. An example might be the redeployment of public buses for emergency evacuation in a city.

9.3.4   Inclusive and Integrated Practices

Inclusive and integrated practices are processes of good governance and effective leadership that ensure investments and actions are appropriate, address the needs of the most vulnerable, and collectively create a resilient city for all citizens. Inclusive processes emphasise the need for broad consultation to create a shared ownership and joint vision of city resilience. For example, early warnings that reach everyone at risk will enable people to protect themselves and minimise loss of life and property. Integrated processes bring together systems and institutions and can catalyse additional benefits, as resources are shared and people work together to achieve greater ends. An example is where cities establish integrated plans to cope with multidisciplinary issues such as climate change, disaster risk reduction or emergency response coordination. The sharing paradigm advocated in Chapter 2 is an example of added resilience through inclusivity and integration.

Clearly, some interventions are possible at the building level to enable delivery of the seven qualities above. These qualities need to become part of the lexicon of design for conversion adaptation so that the design team and all stakeholders are cognisant of the steps that can be taken to mitigate risk and build resilience in their city. In each of the chapters, the authors have repeatedly touched on these qualities, both directly and indirectly, with reference to sustainable change of use adaptations at the building, precinct and city scales.

9.4   Resilience and Sustainable Conversion Adaptation

In Chapter 1 we reviewed the breadth and scope of chronic and acute resilience issues as identified by the Rockefeller foundation in the 100 Resilient Cities. We showed that resilience issues are not currently included explicitly in sustainability rating tools, which may or may not be used in adaptive reuse projects. Clearly, a first step is to commence a dialogue with all stakeholders involved in the process to identify the nature and type of issues affecting an area or city, and then those which may be dealt with at the building level.

Some issues need to be addressed at a number of levels or scales, from national and local government down to the individual level. Examples include rising sea levels and flooding. Clearly a societal response would be to develop or improve flood defences, which might include sea walls, provision of flood-plains and the like. At the building level, design solutions might include locating services at first floor level and above, so that when and if flooding does occur the building is able to return to operation quickly. Another design solution might be to ensure ground and basement levels are fairly permeable, allowing flood water to pass through the building without excessive damage to the building structure. Again, such an approach ensures the building is able to return to an operational state in a short space of time. There are examples in Brisbane, Australia, where commercial office buildings adopting such design solutions were operational within 1 week of a flood in 2014, whereas neighbouring office buildings without these attributes were out of action for 6 months (Bhattacharya Mis *et al.*, 2016. Lamond *et al.*, 2017). The total economic, social and environmental costs to insurers, businesses, the local economy and people are considerably higher when measures are not adopted.

In some cases, measures will be covered by regulations that set minimum standards that must be adopted. However, stakeholders are urged to review whether the mandatory minimum standard is the level required for a long-term sustainable and resilient solution.

A series of questions or checklists have been developed as a means of identifying which resilience issue(s) are faced in any location (see Appendix 9A). For those cities in the 100RC program this will be fairly straightforward, whereas for other cities it may be a case of using one's knowledge of local conditions to identify which issues are likely to apply. The second checklist then addresses whether the issue(s) faced are acute or chronic; this will deepen understanding of the nature of the issue(s) faced in any location. The third checklist asks respondents to select the relevant issues faced and clarifies whether the issue is social, economic, environmental, governance, regulatory/legal, and/or technical. Again, the purpose of the checklists is to provide a simple way of identifying which issues are relevant and the nature and extent of those issues. The fourth checklist asks whether the resilience issue is building related and if there is change-of-use potential. Finally, the fifth provides a summary table to map the resilience issues related to the building. An example is provided for Sydney to show how the table might be populated. This is a simple series of steps that will allow a discussion of relevant issues to be undertaken by built environment stakeholders involved in decision-making for change-of-use adaptation.

9.5 The Manifesto for Sustainable and Resilient Conversion Adaptation

This book has explored the issues humanity faces with regards to resilience within cities and urban settlements. Clearly, many existing buildings within our cities have the potential for adaptation to deal with some of the resilience issues faced. Unless these issues are currently legislated for in some form – for example energy efficiency in the building regulations might be said to contribute to resilience in respect of resource scarcity – they are not likely to be addressed in the individual built form. This is a lost opportunity and reflects the lack of widespread debate about resilience currently. This needs to change and will do so, particularly if we give stakeholders a means of understanding what these issues are and how they relate to the built form. Table 9.1 shows the 49 resilience issues identified by the Rockefeller Foundation for Resilient Cities (2016) and then identifies the type of issue: social, economic, environmental, governance, political or technological in nature. Clearly some issues may have multiple dimensions. At the building level, some issues are related to design whereas others relate to construction and others to the operational or in-use phase. For each resilience challenge, there are suggestions as to the stage of the building lifecycle the issue relates to and, where relevant which aspects should be focussed on.

In Figure 1.2, the resilience scales in the Rotterdam Resilience Strategy clearly show how buildings are the smallest resilience scale within the system. However, it is argued that they are the heart of the solution, for adaptation and adoption of resilience attributes within buildings undoubtedly contributes to resilience at the district and city scale and so on. Clearly, existing local sustainability tools need amending to incorporate the local building-related resilience issues. For example, in Australia, the Green Star rating tool for refurbishment could include resilience issues identified for buildings in the two cities of Melbourne and Sydney, which are part of the 100 Resilient Cities program. As awareness of resilience issues extends and grows, other cities will add their issues to the tools for inclusion and assessment. A start, albeit it modest, has been made in Australia to address issues of Adaptation and Resilience in 2014 when, in 2014, the opportunity to earn one Innovation point was made possible in three Green Star rating tools. The three Green Star rating tools are; Design and As-Built (Legacy rating tools), Interiors and Performance. It is clear in many markets (Fuerst *et al.*, 2015. Newell *et al.*, 2014. Robinson and McAllister, 2015) that acknowledgement of the measures stakeholders, such as owners of commercial office buildings, take in respect of sustainability has a positive effect on economic and environmental image and performance. It is envisaged that similar positive outcomes will ensue for adoption of resilience issues.

9.6 Moving Forward

A manifesto for future directions in respect of resilience and sustainable change-of-use adaptation is presented below, the themes taken from each of the preceding chapters.

1. Built environment professionals and stakeholders need to develop understanding and cognisance of resilience, its attributes and how it impacts at the building, precinct and city scales.
2. A sharing paradigm at the city scale fosters resilience and sustainability by reducing demand for materials, supporting local economies and fostering social engagement.

3. The sharing paradigm can operate at the building scale and we should explore opportunities to incorporate it wherever possible.
4. To handle resilience issues at the city level, it is necessary to use hard and soft planning policy instruments in a co-operative manner through multi-level governance efforts.
5. Public planners, in their efforts to redevelop urban areas in a resilient manner, should understand real estate markets so that private stakeholders can make decisions in favour of sustainable and resilient change of use adaptations.
6. Revitalisation of neighbourhoods is likely to be the main source of activity for built environment stakeholders in future. The redesign of cities and strengthening of communities to be economically and politically resilient, and to be socially and environmentally sustainable, is vital to ensuring value for money and quality of life.
7. Building top-up apartments contributes to urban resilience and sustainability in numerous social, economic and environmental ways.
8. There are many transferable lessons with top-up adaptive reuse that we need to apply, such as the sharing of opportunities and constraints across national and city government leaders, public servants, financiers and entrepreneurs, professionals, developers and the community.
9. With adaptation and demolition at masterplan or precinct level, we need to be cognisant of the different interpretation of decision-making factors.
10. There is potential to adopt a new tool; the Conversion Potential Assessment Tool, to aid decision-making potential of vacant office buildings and other land-use types.
11. We need to examine the potential to incorporate resilience issues into existing building sustainability tools.

9.7 Conclusions

Adaptive reuse or change of use adaptation clearly has an important part to play in delivering resilience in cities. The opportunity exists to retain familiar landmarks and links with the past, and to deliver contemporary facilities that meet user and investor needs. Given the low rates of addition of new stock of buildings, adaptation and change of use offer more opportunities to integrate resilience into the stock. This book has examined the pressing acute and chronic resilience issues that affect our cities now and in the future. It has shown that currently there is a gap in terms of linking resilience issues to the building level, and this needs addressing so that opportunities to deliver resilience are not missed.

Whilst there are some emerging examples of tools and approaches that link resilience at building, precinct and city scale to sustainability and change of use adaptations, further work is needed to mature the tools and embed practices. Currently, where resilience is delivered in conversion adaptation at the building level, it is likely that this is fortuitous rather than intended, and this needs to change. There is evidence in the chapters that existing approaches do embody the seven resilience qualities of reflectiveness, resourcefulness, robustness, redundancy, flexibility, inclusiveness and integration to some extent. However, it is necessary to raise awareness and understanding throughout all built environment stakeholders and to set out clear frameworks and decision-making tools to enable them to make informed decisions on behalf of existing and future generations.

References

Bhattacharya Mis, N., Lamond, J., Proverbs, D., *et al.* (2016) An international understanding of Building Surveyors in the context of commercial properties at risk of flooding. In: *RICS COBRA Toronto, Canada*, September. George Brown College, Toronto.

Fuerst, F., McAllister, P., Nanda, A. and Wyatt, P. (2015) Does energy efficiency matter to home-buyers? An investigation of EPC ratings and transaction prices in England. *Energy Economics*, 48: 145–156.

GBCA. (2014). *Adaptation & resilience. Innovation challenge summary*. https://www.gbca.org.au/uploads/78/34894/Adaptation_and_Resilience_FINAL_JUNE2014.pdf [29 March 2017].

Lamond, J.E., Bhattacharya Mis, N., Chan, F., *et al.* (2017) *Flood risk mitigation and commercial property advice: an international comparison*. RICS Research Trust Report March 2017. http://www.rics.org/Global/Flood_Risk_Commercial_Property_Research_March_17.pdf

Meerow, S., Newell, J.P. and Stults, M., (2016) Defining and resilience: a review. *Landscapes and Urban Planning*, 147: 38–49.

Newell, G., MacFarlane, J. and Walker, R., (2014). Assessing energy rating premiums in the performance of green office buildings in Australia. *Journal of Property Investment & Finance*, 32(4): 352–370.

Robinson, S. and McAllister, P., (2015). Heterogeneous price premiums in sustainable real estate? An investigation of the relation between value and price premiums. *Journal of Sustainable Real Estate*, 7(1): 1–20.

100RC (2016) 100 resilient cities. http://Www.100resilientcities.Org/Cities#/-_/ [24 August 2016].

Appendix 9.A   Checklists for Building Resilient Cities though Sustainable Change of Use

Q1   What are the resilience challenges faced in this city/town or region? *(tick all which are appropriate).*

Challenge	Tick all which apply
Aging infrastructure	
Coastal flooding	
Chronic food and water shortages	
Disease outbreaks	
Drought	
Earthquake	
Economic shifts	
Economic inequality	
Endemic crime and violence	
Hazardous materials accident	
Heat wave	
High unemployment	
Hurricane, typhoon, cyclone	
Infrastructure failure	
Lack of affordable housing	
Overtaxed/under developed/unreliable transportation system	
Pollution or environmental degradation	
Pronounced poverty	
Rainfall flooding	
Rapid growth	
Refugees	
Rising sea level and coastal erosion	
Social inequity	
Terrorism	
Tropical storms	
Wildfires	

Q2   Are the issues acute or chronic or both? *Please tick all challenges which apply.*

Challenge	Acute	Chronic
Aging infrastructure		x
Coastal flooding		
Chronic food and water shortages	x	
Disease outbreaks	x	
Drought		
Earthquake	x	
Economic shifts		
Economic inequality		x
Endemic crime and violence		x
Hazardous materials accident	x	
Heat wave	x	
High unemployment		x
Hurricane, typhoon, cyclone	x	
Infrastructure failure		x
Lack of affordable housing		x
Overtaxed/underdeveloped/unreliable transportation system		x
Pollution or environmental degradation	x	x
Pronounced poverty		x
Rainfall flooding	x	
Rapid growth		x
Refugees	x	x
Rising sea level and coastal erosion	x	
Social inequity		x
Terrorism	x	
Tropical storms	x	
Wildfires	x	

Challenge	Social	Economic	Environmental	Governance	Regulatory and legal	Technical
Aging infrastructure				x		
Coastal flooding	x	x	x			
Chronic food and water shortages	x	x				
Disease outbreaks	x			x		
Drought			x	x		
Earthquake	x	x	x	x		
Economic shifts		x		x		
Economic inequality	x	x		x		
Endemic crime and violence	x			x		
Hazardous materials accident	x	x	x	x		
Heat wave	x	x	x			
High unemployment	x	x		x		
Hurricane, typhoon, cyclone	x	x	x			
Infrastructure failure	x	x	x	x	x	
Lack of affordable housing	x	x		x		
Overtaxed/under developed/ unreliable transportation system		x		x	x	
Pollution or environmental degradation		x	x	x		
Pronounced poverty	x	x				
Rainfall flooding	x	x	x	x		
Rapid growth	x	x	x	x		
Refugees	x	x		x		
Rising sea level and coastal erosion	x	x	x	x		
Social inequity	x			x		
Terrorism	x			x		
Tropical storms	x	x	x			
Wildfires	x	x	x			

Q4 Is this a building-related issue and is there change of use potential? *Please tick all challenges which apply.*

Challenge	Building related (Y/N/DK)	Change of use potential (Y/N/DK)
Aging infrastructure		
Coastal flooding		
Chronic food and water shortages		
Disease outbreaks		
Drought		
Earthquake		
Economic shifts		
Economic inequality		
Endemic crime and violence		
Hazardous materials accident		
Heat wave		
High unemployment		
Hurricane, typhoon, cyclone		
Infrastructure failure		
Lack of affordable housing		
Overtaxed/under developed/unreliable transportation system		
Pollution or environmental degradation		
Pronounced poverty		
Rainfall flooding		
Rapid growth		
Refugees		
Rising sea level and coastal erosion		
Social inequity		
Terrorism		
Tropical storms		
Wildfires		

Q5 Map of resilience issues related to the building. Summary table for [insert name of building], Sydney, Australia.

Challenge	Chronic/ acute	Nature of issue: <ul><li>social</li><li>economic</li><li>environmental</li><li>governance</li><li>regulatory</li><li>technical</li></ul>	Building-related issue and solution (Y/N/DK)	Change of use solution possible (Y/N/DK)	Notes
Ageing infrastructure	Chronic	Economic, governance	Y indirectly	Y	Increase independence from grid and infrastructure as much as possible in water, energy and waste
Heatwave	Acute	Social, economic and environmental	Y	Y	Include shading devices to envelope and energy efficient design to protect against excessive heat

Index

Building Urban Resilience through Change of Use, First Edition.
Edited by Sara J. Wilkinson and Hilde Remøy.
© 2018 John Wiley & Sons Ltd. Published 2018 by John Wiley & Sons Ltd.